UNCONSCIOUS
PHANTASY

Unconscious Phantasy is one of a series of low-cost books under the title PSYCHOANALYTIC **ideas** which brings together the best of Public Lectures and other writings given by analysts of the British Psycho-Analytical Society on important psychoanalytic subjects.

The books can be ordered from:
Karnac Books
www.karnacbooks.com
Tel. +(0)20 8969 4454
Fax: +(0)20 8969 5585
E-mail: shop@karnacbooks.com

Other titles in the Psychoanalytic Ideas Series:

Shame and Jealousy: The Hidden Turmoils
Phil Mollon

Dreaming and Thinking
Rosine J. Perelberg (editor)

Spilt Milk: Perinatal Loss and Breakdown
Joan Raphael-Leff (editor)

Psychosis (Madness)
Paul Williams (editor)

Adolescence
Inge Wise (editor)

UNCONSCIOUS PHANTASY

Edited by
Riccardo Steiner

Series Editors
Inge Wise and *Paul Williams*

KARNAC

LONDON   NEW YORK

Published in 2003 by
H. Karnac (Books) Ltd.
6 Pembroke Buildings, London NW10 6RE

A subsidiary of Other Press LLC, New York

British Library Cataloguing in Publication Data

A C.I.P. for this book is available from the British Library

   ISBN 1 85575 987 X

Edited, designed, and produced by The Studio Publishing Services Ltd,
Exeter EX4 8JN

Printed in Great Britain

10 9 8 7 6 5 4 3 2 1

www.karnacbooks.com

CONTENTS

ACKNOWLEDGEMENTS

I wish to thank Inge Wise and Prof. Paul Williams, Series Editors, for their editorial help, and Rosalind Oliver for her careful reading and copy editing of the manuscript.

I wish also to thank all the authors, the Sigmund Freud Copyright and the International Journal of Psychoanalysis for having allowed me to publish their papers, or amended version of their papers, in this anthology.

Chapter 1 "Formulations on the two principles of mental functioning", by S. Freud, *S.E.*, *12*. © 1958 A. W. Freud *et al.*; translation and editorial matter © 1958 Institute of Psycho-Analysis and the Estate of Angela Richards. Reproduced by arrangement with Paterson Marsh, London.

Chapter 2 "Phantasy and its transformations", first published in *The International Journal of Psychoanalysis*, 1994, Vol. 75, 387–394.

Chapter 4 "Fantasy and the origins of sexuality", first published in *The International Journal of Psychoanalysis*, 1968, Vol. 49, 1–18.

Chapter 5 "The nature and function of phantasy", first published in *Developments in Psychoanalysis*, edited by M. Klein, P. Heimann, S. Isaacs and J. Riviere, 1952 by Hogarth Press & The Institute of Psycho-Analysis.

Chapter 6 "Phantasy and reality", first published in *The International Journal of Psychoanalysis*, 1994, Vol. 75, 395–401.

Chapter 7 "Imagination, play and art", by Hanna Segal. In *Dream, Phantasy and Art* by Hanna Segal, published by Routledge in 1991. Reprinted with permission by Routledge.

Riccardo Steiner, PhD, Editor

Introduction

Riccardo Steiner

T here is no doubt that "phantasy", or "unconscious phantasy", as it started to be used in the English translation of Freud's work in the late 1920s and 1930s to differentiate it from "fantasy",[1] is one of the most important theoretical and clinical concepts of psychoanalysis. The collection of papers gathered together in this book, starting with the fundamental paper by Freud, "Formulations on the two principles of mental functioning" (1911), bears ample witness to that.

I thought it would be worthwhile to start this Introduction by mentioning the problems related to the English translation of the original German term used by Freud, "die Phantasie", and the related verb, "phantasieren". Indeed, Freud used the same pair of German words to refer to conscious fantasies and pre-conscious fantasies—the once conscious and then changed into unconscious "phantasies"—and to phantasies which, according to him, as we will see, have always been unconscious.

This has created several misunderstandings. For instance, not all the authors included in this collection (see, for example, J. Laplanche, J.-B. Pontalis (1968) and J. Sandler & A.-M. Sandler, 1994) agree with the solution adopted by the English translators, and in particular by James Strachey—a fact which does not help to clarify the problems related to the meaning of this concept.

As was the case with many other concepts and terms which Freud used originally in German, "die Phantasie" and "phanta-sieren" were borrowed by him from other non-analytic or pre-analytic disciplines; and when he introduced them into psycho-analysis he was maintaining, in some ways, the complex semantic history of these terms.

It is impossible here, for obvious reasons, to trace a detailed history of the cultural vicissitudes that preceded the discovery of psychoanalysis or continued to develop independently from psychoanalysis itself. Yet I think it is appropriate to remind the reader that the term "phantasia" and the verb "phantasthein", as we find them in ancient Greek, were already used by Plato to indicate a purely mental activity that did not have any relationship with external reality. The term was also used by Aristotle and other later ancient Greek philosophers with slightly different meanings. It was then borrowed by the Romans, and in ancient Latin appears as "fantasia". Subsequently, it circulated all over Europe during the medieval, Renaissance, and Romantic periods, translated in various ways, and again assuming slightly different meanings across the various European languages (Burdy, 1927; Starobinski, 1970; Engell, 1981; Lepschy, 1986). It is interesting that in some of the Romance languages, as for example in Italian, the term "fantasia" has been retained, owing to a close relationship between these and Latin.[2]

In French and English things are not so simple. The term which seems to correspond most closely to the ancient Greek and Latin "phantasia", "fantasia" or the German "Phantasie" is the French "fantaisie", which nevertheless has connotations of whimsy, eccentricity, and even triviality, although it also denotes a creative activity and the contents of this activity. "Fantasme" is commonly used in French psychoanalysis, but has overtones of a more philosophical kind than the "Phantasie" used by Freud (Laplanche & Pontalis, 1973, p. 314). In French there is also the term "l'imagination". We have already noted the English terms used to translate the German "Phantasie" used by Freud. One should nevertheless bear in mind that in both French and English "imagination" seems to be related to creativity in a deeper and more profound sense.[3] This is important to emphasize because, for instance, Melanie Klein and her followers, as we shall see, will link even the mature imagination to primitive unconscious phantasies.

In German the term "die Phantasie", borrowed originally from the French "fantaisie" (Grimm & Grimm, 1889), began from the sixteenth-century onwards, and especially in the seventeenth, to assume more and more the meaning of "free", and at times "unknown", activity of the mind. The contents of this activity were defined as "Phantasie", too. However, the same term was also used to define the contents of the dreams or delusions of mentally ill or sick people. This was true also of the verb "phantasieren". A quick glance at the Grimms' *Deutsches Wörterbuch*, from which I have just quoted—a text, incidentally, that was very popular in Freud's youth and among people of his background—will confirm this. Here the reader can also find a number of very interesting quotations taken from many of the German writers Freud read as an adolescent and young man before he discovered psychoanalysis, such as Goethe, Schiller, Hoffman, Tieck, Lessing, Fontaine, and Heine. Many of them, like Freud, used "die Phantasie" and the verb "phantasieren" to refer to creativity, but also to what happens in dreams, madness or when one falls in love.

In the same *Deutsches Wörterbuch* one can find some very interesting quotations taken from the late eighteenth-century German philosopher Kant, who had a great influence on many of the psychiatrists and philosophers whom Freud read and admired, and by whom he was inspired—notably, W. Griesinger and T. Lipps.[4]

I have tried to remind the reader briefly of some of the historical vicissitudes of the concepts of fantasy and phantasy and of their cultural context in some of the European languages. Those vicissitudes have to be considered if one wants to understand some of the characteristics of Freud's use of these terms and concepts and the way they have been developed and used by his followers even today. Let us now try to understand how Freud came to his own views and conclusions.

*   *   *

"... A universal event in early childhood ..."
Freud, Letter to Fliess, 15 October 1897, in Masson, 1985, p. 272

In order to give the reader an idea of the complexity of the issues involved and of some of the factors which led Freud to come to the conclusions he came to and of the time scale he chose, I think it is worthwhile briefly to try to track down the path—which at times inevitably will appear a rather confusing one—that led Freud to write his 1911 paper "Formulations on the two principles of mental functioning". This will also help us get a better understanding of the points of common ground and points of difference between Freud and those who tried to develop his views later on. One could claim, as Laplanche and Pontalis rightly do (1968), this collection p. 109, that more or less implicit references to the existence of unconscious phantasies or fantasies in Freud's work could be traced back to the origins of psychoanalysis itself, to the case of Anna O. (Freud, 1895) and her "private theatre" (*op. cit.*, p. 22). The term emerges, or is implicit, in many of the cases of the *Studies on Hysteria* (Breuer & Freud, 1895), linked to the earliest aetiological theory of the neuroses, which was based on the belief of an actual traumatic seduction, exercised by an adult over the patient when she or he was a child, and never properly overcome. The events of the traumatic seduction were supposedly forgotten, or as Freud started to say, "repressed", in such a way that following the concurrence of later traumatic events in the patient's life, a symptom emerged.

Very often in these early cases described by Freud there is an overlapping between unconscious memories or reminiscences and the notion of unconscious phantasy. But what should really be explored is the correspondence between Freud and Fliess, in particular the letters that immediately precede those that concern Freud's revolutionary discovery: the role in the aetiology of mental disturbance played, not so much by actual trauma derived from the seduction by an adult during the patient's childhood (and during that of Freud himself), but by unconscious sexual phantasies already present in the child (see, for example, the letters to Fliess of 7 March, 16 March, 6 April, and 22 June 1897, Masson, 1985).[5]

Of course the notion of "unconscious", of unconscious repression, of defence, and likewise the notion of infantile sexuality, and that of the splitting of the ego—which can often remind one of Janet's and other authors' "double personality" present in those letters (Steiner, 2000a), as in Freud's papers of those same years—were still at times very confused and even rather primitive. Freud's clinical practice was very rudimentary, too. Yet in this context, of particular importance is the letter of 21 September 1897, in which Freud announced to Fliess that he had to abandon the theory of the traumatic origin of the neuroses. Indeed, it is in this letter that Freud, after having told Fliess, "I no longer believe in my *neurotica* [theory of the neuroses]" (Masson, 1985, p. 264), mentioned the importance of "unconscious fantasy", as Jeffrey Masson translated from the original German "Phantasie" in this case. And what Freud says is worth quoting:

> ... There are no indications of reality in the unconscious, so that one cannot distinguish between truth and fiction that has been cathected with affect. (*Accordingly there would remain the solution that the sexual fantasy invariably seizes upon the theme of the parents*). [Freud, Letter to Fliess, 21 September 1897, in Masson, 1985, pp. 264–265; my emphasis]

And in the same letter, as in many other papers and letters of these years, Freud mentions something else which I think should also be quoted: the notion of "Nachträglichkeit",[6] translated in English as "deferred action". This notion will remain at the core of Freud's thinking, and without it, it is impossible to understand what he meant by "unconscious phantasy" (or fantasy), or, later on, many of the divergences between the so-called classical psychoanalysts and Melanie Klein and her school. For instance:

> It seems once again arguable that only later experiences give the impetus to fantasies, which [then] hark back to childhood, and with this the factor of a hereditary disposition regains a sphere of influence from which I had made it my task to dislocate it—in the interest of illuminating neurosis. [*op. cit.*, p. 265]

(Freud has in mind here his theory of the actual infantile sexual traumata which led to a sort of sociological explanation of the neurosis, with an insistence on the role played by the environment—fathers, uncles, nannies, and the like.)

The "fiction which has been cathected with affect", therefore— and notice the observation that the sexual "fantasy" seizes upon the theme of the parents, which already hints at what will follow in a few days—described in the letter of 3 October, and then in the famous letter of 15 October 1897, will, together with the notion of "Nachträglichkeit", from now on characterize some of the core aspects of Freud's notion of unconscious phantasy.

However, briefly to complete what I wish to recall, let us now consider what Freud wrote to Fliess on 15 October 1897. Freud told his friend that he was convinced now of the existence of what he called a "universal event related to early childhood", present in the unconscious of the adult (Masson, 1985, p. 272). This event was characterized by the child having been in love with his own mother and jealous of his father (as far, at least, as the male child was concerned). Of course Freud was speaking about himself, too (and for the moment ignoring the vicissitudes of the girl!) It was in this letter that Freud mentioned Sophocles' *Oedipus Rex*, Shakespeare's *Hamlet* and Grillparzer's *Die Ahnfrau*—to prove the universality of this "event", but also, implicitly, to prove the universality of the terrible phantasies of guilt and retaliation, or punishment for these feelings and wishes, stressing the persistence in time and the transcultural character of this "event". He also linked, for the first time, in a very clear way what unconsciously motivates symptoms of mental disturbance to the unconscious motivations of creativity and to the content of a number of masterpieces of European literature (Steiner, 1994).[7] With hindsight, obviously, I do not think one would be too far from the truth in putting unconscious phantasy, or fantasy, together with that universal event, as Freud himself will do in 1918b in the case of the Wolf Man (*S.E.*, *17*, p. 201); for this letter of 1897 constitutes the first explicit description of what later on Freud will call Oedipal wishes, the Oedipus complex, and the castration complex, and the phantasies and the anxieties he will explore connected with these.[8]

In his previous letter to Fliess of 3 October 1897 Freud had mentioned that the "awakening of his libido towards *matrem*", as he called her in Latin—in other words, his libidinal wishes and phantasies towards his own mother—was brought back to him as unconscious memory through his self-analysis and his dreams. Unconscious phantasies, or fantasies, events, unconscious memories, dream contents, all seemed to flow through, or be kept in some kind of creative suspension in, Freud's mind during those revolutionary months of 1897, overlapping and gradually leading him to try to make sense of his new intuitions. But I would insist, in particular, on Freud's convictions that these "events" were universal: because Freud will come back to this belief that what he was discovering and describing had a universal value, even as far as the "primal phantasies" are concerned.

There is something else that I think should be emphasized. In the letter of 15 October 1897 Freud is extremely vague when he tries to establish a precise chronological date as far as the appearance of those universal events in the life of the child are concerned (although he stresses that there is a difference between normal childhood and "children who have been made hysterical", as far as the chronological time of the appearance of those "events" are concerned (in the latter case he postulated that those events had been experienced earlier than in normal childhood). In his previous letter, dated 3 October, when he spoke about himself and his memories concerning his "libido towards *matrem*", he mentioned that he was between the age of two and two-and-a-half years old (Masson, 1985, p. 268).

It is, to my mind, important that the reader should consider Freud's views concerning the chronology of those "events", or as we could call them, those "phantasies"—a problem to which I shall have to come back, more than once, later on. If one studies carefully other letters of these months, such as the one of 6 April 1897, or the important paper on screen memories of 1899—which will play such an important part in Freud's thinking even many years later (Steiner, 2000a)—the problem will be self-evident: for besides being vague, Freud was enormously cautious when it came down to pointing out in any precise way the year or the months in which these events and phantasies are to be considered to start to appear in the infant, or in which the infant may be thought to be able to make sense of all this. It is interesting that in the letter of 6 April 1897, which still belongs to his earliest aetiological explanation of hysteria and other disturbances—and which he will give up a few months later—Freud claims that the hysterical fantasies of his patients go back to things that children overhear at an early age and understand only subsequently. The age, Freud added, at which they take in information of this kind is, "strangely enough, from six to seven months onwards" (Masson, 1985, p. 234)!

As I have tried to demonstrate elsewhere (Steiner, 2000b), Freud and his immediate followers never went further back than this date in their hypotheses in respect of the existence of, albeit rudimentary, unconscious and conscious life in the infant.[9]

*   *   *

> "The phantasies possess *psychical* as contrasted with *material*
> reality, and we gradually learn to understand that *in the*
> *world of the neuroses it is psychical reality which is the decisive*
> *kind"*
>
> Freud, 1916–1917, Introductory Lecture 23, *S.E.*, *16*, p. 368

There is no doubt, therefore, that one could claim there is some sort of line of continuity between what I have just roughly recalled here and what Freud wrote later on in order to clarify his views concerning unconscious phantasies or fantasies. I have particularly in mind the very well-known Lecture 23, "The paths to the formation of symptoms", of the *Introductory Lectures on Psycho-analysis* (1916–1917), in which he explicitly stresses and summarizes the role played by unconscious phantasies in our mental life in general, and not only in the formation of symptoms (p. 372). Nevertheless, confining ourselves to what Freud called the neuroses, just think of what he said when he wrote the following:

> It remains a fact that the patient has created these phantasies for himself, and this fact is of scarcely less importance for his neurosis than if he had really experienced what the phantasies contain. The phantasies pose *psychical* as contrasted with *material* reality, and we gradually learn to understand that *in the world of the neuroses it is psychical reality which is the decisive kind*. [1916–1917, p. 368]

Yet the line of continuity I have mentioned is a rather complex and uneven one. Indeed, if we look, for instance, at *The Interpretation of Dreams* (1900), which Freud was writing at more or less the same time, and in which he was communicating with Fliess through the letters I have quoted, and try to follow Freud's development chronologically, we will find that Freud very rarely referred to unconscious phantasies (see, for example, *S.E.*, *5*, pp. 491–492). Furthermore, as I have already alluded, he uses, even here, the same German term, "Phantasie", to define *both* dream thoughts (*op. cit.*, p. 491) *and* day dreams—the latter, according to him, being something analogous or akin to dream thoughts in waking life. Furthermore, these phantasies or day dreams "are the immediate forerunners of hysterical symptoms. ... Hysterical symptoms are not attached to actual memories, but to phantasies erected on the basis of memories" (*ibid.*).

Let us consider something more from the same pages, because they will give us the feeling of Freud's creative striving to make sense of something that was extremely complicated for him to define:

> The frequent occurrence of conscious day-time phantasies [notice the change in the expression: ed.] brings these structures to our knowledge; but just as there are phantasies of this kind which are conscious, so, too, there are unconscious ones in great numbers, which have to remain unconscious on account of their content and of their origin from repressed material. Closer investigation of the character of these day-time phantasies shows us how right it is that these formations should bear the same name as we give to the products of our thought during the night—the name, that is, of "dreams". [1900, pp. 491–492]

In another passage from *The Interpretation of Dreams* we find Freud speaking of unconscious phantasies as *unconscious scenes*, and linking them more strictly to the unconscious as such. As Laplanche and Pontalis have pointed out:

> The phantasies in question are those which are bound to unconscious wishes and which are the starting-point of the metapsychological process of dream formation: the first portion of the "journey" which ends with the dream, was a progressive one, leading from the unconscious scenes or phantasies to the pre-conscious. [1973, p. 316]

Thinking about these statements, but also about *The Interpretation of Dreams* in general, and about Freud's later work, one has to remember that Freud will always give enormous importance to the notion of the *unconscious wish*, linked first to the drive of self-preservation and to the libidinal drives, and later on to the life and death drives, to the extent that one could perhaps say that the unconscious wish, through which the drives manifest themselves psychologically speaking, is the *conditio sine quo non* even of the unconscious phantasy.[10]

Freud went back to the notion of fantasy and unconscious phantasy even before writing his paper of 1911, and even before what he wrote at the end of Lecture 23 of the *Introductory Lectures on Psychoanalysis* of 1916–1917. I am thinking in particular of his 1908 paper "Creative writers and day dreaming" (Freud, 1908b, p. 151f.).

If we had the chance to examine, under the comprehensive terminological umbrella of "Phantasie" and "phantasieren", all those papers, together also with what I have quoted above from *The Interpretation of Dreams*, we could claim that there seem to emerge several lines of thinking about phantasies and fantasies during those years. On the one hand the "phantasies" seem to be related to day dreams, which can be conscious or pre-conscious, as I have already noted. Some of these day dreams can become unconscious through repression (Freud, 1908a, p. 161), but as is already apparent from *The Interpretation of Dreams*, and as Freud elsewhere claims, a second line of thought, too, seems to emerge: "Unconscious phantasies can be unconscious all along and have been formed in the unconscious" (*ibid*.). This he will also claim in his 1911 paper, as we shall see.

Accordingly I quite agree with Laplanche and Pontalis (1973) when they say that it seems to be possible for us:

> to distinguish—although Freud himself never did so explicitly— between several levels at which phantasy is dealt with in Freud's work: conscious, subliminal and unconscious (β). Freud's principal concern, however, seems to have been less with establishing such a differentiation than with emphasising the links between these different aspects. [1973, p. 316]

Inevitably, Freud's thinking was tentative and at times faced by difficulties. Indeed, at this particular time it was not clear what he meant by, "phantasies [which] have been formed in the unconscious" and were "unconscious all along". We shall have to wait until the introduction of the notion of primal phantasies a few years later to find a possible answer to what he meant. What needs to be clearly kept in mind is that, following the nineteenth-century German philosopher T. Lipps, as he did (Steiner, 1987, 1999), Freud believed that besides being the unconscious, "[the] true psychical reality, in its innermost reality 'the unconscious', ... is unknown to us as the reality of the external world and is as incompletely presented by the data of consciousness as is the external world by the communications of our sense-organs". Freud stated this in Chapter 6 of *The Interpretation of Dreams*, and he was never to change this conviction during the whole of his life (Steiner, 1987, 2000a).[11]

Even unconscious phantasies, therefore (see Solms, 1997, this collection pp. 106–107), are, by definition, only known incompletely and inferred through their derivation from the unconscious itself. This area will, however, constitute one of the major points of disagreement between Freud's more orthodox followers and Melanie Klein and her school, as we shall see—particularly in conjunction with Freud's theoretical convictions from these years I have just mentioned.

During the first decade of the twentieth-century Freud was still trying to systematize his first theoretical model of the mind, born out of the "affect trauma" (Sandler *et al.*, 1997) model of the mind from the years preceding 1897. He had already hinted at this model in several letters to Fliess, and especially in Chapter 7 of *The Interpretation of Dreams* (1900, pp. 509–621). This model, defined as the topographical one (Sandler *et al.*, 1997), was based on hypotheses concerning the self-preservative and libidinal drives and on the notions of the descriptive and the dynamic unconscious —the laws governing the dynamic unconscious based on the primary process and on thing-presentations, and the laws governing the pre-conscious and consciousness based on the secondary process and on word-representations. This was also of great importance as far as the differentiations between unconscious phantasies, day dreams, and the like, were concerned, owing to the fact that Freud was implying the presence and the action of different systems of defences, based on the censorship between the unconscious and the pre-conscious, and the censorship between pre-conscious and consciousness, which affected the way fantasies and phantasies (to use Freud's schema of differentiation) according to its English translation were represented and perceived. (The reader may wish to consider, in this regard, "A note on the unconscious in psychoanalysis", Freud, 1912; and then what Freud says, only a few years later, in his metapsychological papers "Repression", 1915a, and "The unconscious", 1915b.)

And yet it would be difficult to understand some of the reasons which lie behind Freud's wish to write his 1911 paper "Formulations on the two principles of mental functioning", without taking into account his increased clinical experience, which led him to consider more and more the meaning and importance of the transference, where many of these unconscious phantasies could be observed *in vivo*. Just think, for instance, of the case of "Dora", as it is known (1905b), but also of some aspects of Freud's research in the work *Delusions and Dreams in Jensen's "Gradiva"* (1907).

*   *   *

"... A closer connection arises, on the one hand, between the sexual instinct and phantasy and, on the other hand, between the ego-instincts and the activities of consciousness"

"Formulations on the two principles of mental functioning",
Freud, 1911, p. 222; this collection, p. 70

After all that I have noted and tried to remind the reader of, let us now look in more detail at some of the issues contained in Freud's paper of 1911. Examining some of the statements he makes in this paper *in context* will help us further understand the complexity of his thinking, and some, at least, of the reasons why he came to certain conclusions. These reasons are of fundamental importance if we want to clarify, for instance, the issues concerning why unconscious phantasies play such a part in the thinking and clinical practice of Klein's and her followers, in contrast to other schools of psychoanalysis.

Strachey, in his Editorial note (*S.E., 12*, pp. 215–216) defined the "Formulations on the two principles of mental functioning" (1911) as one of the classics of psychoanalysis, despite its condensed nature—the paper being not easy to assimilate even today. What I think particularly important and interesting is the distinction Freud introduces between what he calls the two regulating principles of our mental apparatus: the pleasure principle (which Freud defines as such for the first time in this paper) and the reality principle.

Both principles follow a sort of developmental path as far as the maturation of our mental apparatus is concerned. This is another point that has to be stressed, and I shall come back to comment on it. The abandonment of the pleasure principle, which according to Freud dominates the life of the baby and the infant for several months, based as it is on the hallucinatory fulfilment of the baby's needs, occurs as a consequence, on the one hand, of disappointment, frustration, and the failure of the arrival of the expected satisfaction, and, on the other, of the necessity to grow up, and to face reality. This leads to the search for a more realistic, although only partial, satisfaction of internal needs, based on the possibility of taking into consideration the existence of the external reality in all its aspects. It is on this particular point that Freud writes some of the most important passages of the paper. Just think of what he says about the characteristics of the pleasure principle—the "quasi" total sufficiency of the baby,[12] who hallucinates his own satisfaction of his needs and seems to be content for a while. And then think of what he adds, at a certain point, in consideration of the role played by the reality principle: the gradual heightening of consciousness, and the gradual emergence of attention, memory, judgement, and, in particular, of the function of thinking which controls motor discharge and action.

In the course of this developmental process, Freud claims, the sexual instincts and the self-preservation instincts, or ego-instincts, as he called them at that time, follow a different destiny. The sexual instincts, finding their original satisfaction in auto-erotic activities— that is, in the subject's body (another extremely important point, to which I shall come back):

> ... Do not find themselves in the situation of frustration which was what necessitated the institution of the reality principle; and when, *later on* [my emphasis: ed.], the process of finding an object begins, it is soon interrupted by the long period of latency, which delays sexual development until puberty. These two factors—auto-eroti-cism and the latency period—have as their result that the sexual instinct is held up in its psychical development and remains far longer under the dominance of the pleasure principle, from which in many people it is never able to withdraw.
>
> *In consequence of these conditions, a closer connection arises, on the one hand, between the sexual instinct and phantasy and, on the other hand, between the ego-instincts and the activities of consciousness.* [Freud, 1911, p. 222; this collection, p. 70; my emphasis]

Therefore, according to Freud, because the auto-erotic sexual satisfactions do not have to match reality and can remain imaginary for a long time in relation to the real satisfaction which can derive from a "real" sexual object, phantasy and phantasizing about sexuality remain quite an important aspect of the psychic life of a normal human being (let us forget for the moment that of the neurotic, too). Phantasy and phantasizing, Freud stresses, begin already in children's play, and later on "continue[s] as *day-dreaming*" (*ibid.*).

Freud comes back to the specific character of the "unconscious (repressed) processes", as he calls them, at one moment implying, I think, phantasies, and at the end of the paper clarifying further their importance:

> ... They equate reality of thought with external reality, and wishes with their fulfilment—with the events—just as happens automatically under the dominance of the ancient pleasure principle. Hence also the difficulty of distinguishing unconscious phantasies from memories which have become unconscious. But one must never allow oneself to be misled into applying the standards of reality to repressed psychical structures, and on that account, perhaps, into undervaluing the importance of phantasies in the formation of symptoms on the ground that they are not actualities ... [Freud, 1911, p. 225; this collection, p. 72]

As the reader can see, it is possible to find in this paper echoes of Freud's thinking which go back to the late 1890s. Just think, for instance, of the problem related to the difficulty of distinguishing at times between unconscious memories and phantasies, besides of course the theoretical framework represented by sexual phantasies, repressed day dreams, and the like. But one can already find anticipations of what Freud will write in his 23 *Introductory Lectures on Psychoanalysis* of 1916–1917, particularly when he stresses the importance of psychic reality. Together with very important statements concerning the role played by unconscious phantasies in the case of religion, science and education, it is possible also to find here, in a very condensed and clear form, what he wrote in his paper of 1908 (Freud, 1908b) concerning the role of unconscious phantasies in the realm of the arts. Particularly interesting are his observations concerning the role played by artists and their creations in our life, in so far as we all recognize in their work our own attempts to deal with our dissatisfaction, which their works of art help us to overcome.

One further thing is clear, however: from what Freud says in this paper, one comes to the conclusion that unconscious phantasies are mainly the result of repression and regression, and that, for him, they start to become significant once the reality principle and the role of the ego-instincts have been firmly established. One has, therefore, to agree with Strachey on the importance of this paper;

and indeed, in spite of the fact that later on Freud will introduce his so-called "structural model" (Sandler *et al.*, 1997) of the psychic apparatus—just think of *The Ego and the Id* (1923), with all the complications related to the unconscious origins of the ego and superego—he will not fundamentally change his views concerning the genesis of unconscious phantasies and day dreams from this point on.[13]

The 1911 paper, incidentally will constitute one of the main points of reference during the Freud–Klein Controversies of 1941–1945 (see King & Steiner, 1991), when both Anna Freud and her colleagues, and Susan Isaacs, Paula Heimann, Melanie Klein and others, will try to use it to support or criticize their different viewpoints. To my mind, some of the basic ideas contained in this paper are, as I shall try to show later on, still at the core of Joseph and Anne-Marie Sandler's paper on unconscious phantasies (Sandler & Sandler, 1994) and Laplanche and Pontalis's paper of 1968, both included in this collection. Even Hanna Segal in her 1994 paper, also included in this collection, will still refer to Freud's 1911 paper, accepting some of his views while also differentiating herself from him.

It is true that in the 1911 paper Freud does not explicitly mention the role played by the pre-conscious in shaping some aspects of the unconscious phantasies, nor does he refer explicitly to a notion like "Nachträglichkeit"; but from what I have already mentioned it is obvious that one could not make sense of Freud's statements in this paper, particularly those related to the symptoms in the case of the neuroses, but also those related to religion, art etc., without considering these factors.

However, there is something else that I think should be added. I called attention to the fact that Freud uses a developmental model to describe how unconscious phantasies manifest themselves in our mind at a certain point in time, and to the fact that he insists on the notion of auto-eroticism to establish the moment in time in which the first traces of sexual phantasies start to appear. All this, according to Freud, owing also to the slowness with which the sexual instinct gives up its auto-erotic sources and owing to the late appearance of a proper sexual object, explains why unconscious phantasies as such do emerge at a certain moment in time and in some way function as a sort of substitute—a compensation, and at times a very pathological one—for a more realistic way of finding satisfaction.

To understand all this, but also to clarify further these extremely important theoretical implications of Freud's 1911 paper, one must link this paper to all the work and thinking Freud had done during those years in relation to the characteristics and the existence of child sexuality. The developmental model derived from Hughling Jackson and other Darwinian sources (Steiner, 2000a) is part of Freud's general background, and he applied it to understanding child sexuality too. But what he said about auto-eroticism, in relation to unconscious sexual phantasies, has to be directly related to the *Three Essays on The Theory of Sexuality* (1905a); and the reader must bear in mind also the famous clinical history, "Analysis of a phobia in a five-year-old boy" (1909) and the paper "On sexual theories of children" (Freud, 1908c), as far as the relationship between infantile play and phantasies is concerned. Moreover, only a few years separate Freud's 1911 paper from another landmark in his theoretical and clinical thinking: "On narcissism: an introduction", published in 1914.

Despite what he wrote to Fliess, but kept rather private, Freud came to the conclusion of the importance of child sexual phantasies rather late in the development of his thinking, which is also reflected in the chronology of his work.[14] Therefore, there is a strict relationship between all these elements, which needs to be considered if one wants to understand the complexity of the 1911 paper. Furthermore, as I have already noted in referring to the Freud–Fliess correspondence, Freud was very cautious about establishing a precise chronology for the appearance of these sexual phantasies. This is also reflected in the *Three Essays on The Theory of Sexuality*[15] and in the differentiation Freud makes between a sort of original oral stage, where the sexual instinct does find its satisfaction under the predominance of the self-preservative instinct and the satisfaction of the needs related to hunger and sucking of mother's breast, and hallucinatory wish fulfilment, and a phase of auto-eroticism where the sexual instinct detaches itself from hunger, becomes objectless and uses hallucinatory wish fulfilment solutions, and therefore becomes auto-erotic (the child getting his erotic satisfactions only through the his body). All this seems constantly to emphasize the slow, painful thinking of the baby and infant's mind, sensations, perceptions, emotions, and also of his phantasies relating to external reality.[16]

The views expressed in Freud's paper "On narcissism" (1914) will further confirm all this, to the point that the expression "primary narcissism" would become synonymous with the classical psychoanalytic views concerning child development, although (and as I shall try to show in more detail later on) during the Scientific Meetings of the Freud–Klein Controversies (1943–1944; see King & Steiner, 1991) Melanie Klein and her followers made use of several contradictory statements contained in Freud's work[17] to support their own views concerning narcissism, which they considered secondary, and concerning the existence of an inner phantasy life in the baby from the beginning of life; this was in opposition to the views of Anna Freud and her co-workers, who continued to defend the notion of an objectless primary narcissism phase, thought by them to last for several months.

To further complicate the issues concerning unconscious phantasies and Freud's views about them, something else needs to be mentioned—without, again, risking accusing Freud of inconsistency. The same term, "die Phantasie", was used by Freud more or less during the years between the end of the nineteenth-century and the beginning of the twentieth-century, but in particular during the first two decades of the twentieth-century, to try gradually to define the nature of a specific type of unconscious phantasy to which I have already called the reader's attention, This was the body of phantasy which seems to be present in the unconscious, ontogenetically speaking, from the beginning of life, and which is of such a type that it never emerges into consciousness other than through its derivatives, and "nachträglich"—by deferred action. By the fact that they are there "from the beginning" these phantasies guarantee that sexuality in the human being, to quote Laplanche and Pontalis (1973),

> ... Is not a ready-made mechanism but is established during the course of the individual's history, changing in both its mechanics and its aims, it cannot be understood solely in terms of a biological evolution; on the other hand, however, the facts show that infantile sexuality is not a retroactive illusion.
>
> In our view ... the idea of primal phantasies ... serves in a way as a counterweight to the notion of deferred action. ... Sexuality cannot

therefore be explained solely in terms of the endogenous maturation of the instinct—it has to be seen as being constituted at the core of intersubjective structures which predate its emergence in the individual. [Laplanche & Pontalis, 1973, p. 421]

I would add here that phantasies of this kind can nevertheless be understood only via deferred action, too, as I said—as far as the individual history of the individual is concerned.

These phantasies, which Freud calls in German "*Urphantasien*" (translated by Strachey as "primal phantasies") in Lecture 23 of his *Introductory Lectures on Psychoanalysis* (1916–1917, p. 371), and in the clinical case of the so-called "Wolf Man", written in 1914 but published with some addenda in 1918 (1918b, pp. 119–120), are, according to him, transmitted to us "phylogenetically". In other words, strictly speaking they *do not belong to us and to our personal history as such*. We are "acted by them": they belong to the prehistory of the human race in the sense that what today in our unconscious presents itself as phantasies had in our prehistoric past been "actual facts", the memory of which is still now transmitted to us through time.

One could note at this point, perhaps, that what Freud threw out of the door (for instance, the theory of the actual traumatic seduction that took place in the childhood of his patients, and even in that of his own) seems to come back in through the window—as if, owing to his realistic orientation, Freud could never give up the idea of finding some sort of "event" in the outside reality to link with or anchor to his revolutionary views concerning the role played by unconscious phantasies in our life. A mythical prehistoric past with its actual events became the foundations of the psychic "reality" of our unconscious phantasy life! A body of primal phantasy seems to constitute the core of the unconscious. It is not clear, logically speaking, how this has been repressed in the unconscious. But as Laplanche and Pontalis observe in their *Language of Psychoanalysis* (1973), primal phantasies seem to be related in one way or another to what Freud also during those years started to call "primary repression" (see "Repression", 1915a, p. 148; and "The unconscious", 1915b, p. 181):

Although Freud himself never connected primal phantasies ("*Urphantasies*") with the hypotheses of primal repression, it is impossible not to notice that they fulfil almost identical functions relative to the ultimate origins of the unconscious. [Laplanche & Pontalis, 1973, p. 476]

Another important question concerning the notion of primal phantasies is that of their relationship to what Freud called conscious fantasies—day dreams, symptoms, jokes, parapraxes or cultural productions like the arts. Freud emphasizes that primal phantasies seem to orient towards them or to attract to the unconscious inner psychic vicissitudes: "the possibility of the neuroses [bears witness] to the existence of those earlier, instinct-like, preliminary stages", as he defines the primal phantasies at the end of the case of the Wolf Man (1918b, p. 120).

But what is the content of these primal phantasies? Their number is very restricted, and they are related to the so-called "primal scene" (the sexual intercourse between the parents), "seduction [by an adult]", "castration", "and others"—as Freud says without specifying further in "A case of paranoia running counter the psychoanalytic theory of the disease" (1915c, p. 269), where he first mentions their existence.

It is nevertheless important to stress that even from an ontogenetic point of view—by which I mean from the point of view of the personal history of the patients—Freud never denied the contribution of actual traumatic events to the awakening and to the pathological outcomes related to the primal phantasies in the child and then in the adult. These actual events could be confused observations, made by the child, of such scenes as the coitus of the parents or the copulation of animals, which are then unconsciously related to the primal phantasies. Sometimes these events could even have been experienced by the child, as in the case of seduction.[18] As he had already stated before, in Lecture 13 of his *Introductory Lectures on Psychoanalysis* (1916–1917), he claimed:

> You must not suppose, however, that sexual abuse of a child by its nearest male relatives belongs entirely to the realm of phantasy. Most analysts will have treated cases in which such events were real and could be unimpeachably established. [p. 370]

Moreover, one should look also at what Freud stated in the case of the Wolf Man (1918b, pp. 120–121).

Yet what also matters is that in applying his phylogenetic views to the notion of primal phantasies, Freud had the chance to come back to his convictions that what he had discovered was of universal value. Phylogenesis and the universal nature of these primal phantasies could explain why we find the same kind of phantasies even in individuals who in their analysis do not show that they had in one way or another witnessed or been part of the primal scene. " . . . Real occurrences in the primaeval times of the human family", have now become "phantasies" in children, who "in their phantasies are simply filling in the gaps in individual truth with prehistoric truth": these are the expressions Freud uses to explain all this (1916–1917, p. 371). And this all seems to have been "repressed" in the service of human evolution, deposited in the unconscious, like a sort of living negative of a film that can be constantly brought to life and developed over and over again.

It is impossible here to go into precise detail to try to understand how Freud came to these conclusions. One should consider, for instance, what he had noted concerning the existence of sexual theories in children (Freud, 1908c), or what he observed in the case of "Little Hans" (1909), or wrote in *Totem and Taboo* (1912–1913). But for what matters more, particularly in relation to the issue of universality, one should go back again to those revolutionary months of 1897 which marked the discovery of the role played by unconscious phantasies as such in our unconscious life. I am thinking, in particular, of the letter dated 2 May 1897 (Masson, 1985, p. 240 and 242n.), where Freud mentions for the first time the existence of *Urszenen* ("primal scenes"), a term he will also use later on in the case of the Wolf Man (1918b, p. 39), to define what he at that time still believed were actual sexual events present in the experience of every child but which very often are elaborated in fantasies "manufactured by means of things that are *heard* and utilised *subsequently*, and thus combine things experienced and heard, past events *(from the history of parents and ancestors)*" [my emphasis: ed.], and things that have been seen by oneself (Masson, 1985, p. 240).

But besides the universality, and therefore the constant presence in our unconscious, of the Oedipus complex, which Freud—not by chance, clearly—included among "those precipitates from the history of human civilisation", as he comments in the case of the

Wolf Man (1918b, p. 119), when he recapitulates the issues related to phylogenesis and primal phantasies, one should go back again to *The Interpretation of Dreams* (1900) to find some all too often forgotten statements concerning these issues—in particular where Freud mentions the power of unconscious wishes.[19]

As far as the importance that the phylogenetic hypotheses plays in Freud's thinking, there is enough evidence today (see Jones, 1957; Gay, 1988; Ritvo, 1990; and, especially, Grubrich-Simitis, 1987, 1993; and further, the second volume of correspondence between Freud and Sandór Ferenczi, ed. Falzeder & Brabant, 1996) to show that Freud was enormously stimulated by Lamarck's theories, particularly during the first years of the first world war. Together with Ferenczi he had planned to write a work on the possible links between Lamarck and psychoanalysis. His views concerning primal phantasies, therefore, cannot be understood and properly evaluated without considering all this. It is impossible to discuss here, as one should, Freud's interest in Lamarck and his theory of the inheritance of acquired characteristics, or indeed mention his interest in Haeckel, and his longstanding interest in Darwin, too (see Ritvo, 1990). We may note, nevertheless, that in spite of all the criticisms raised against Lamarck, Freud was to remain loyal to the former's views until the end of his career (see, for instance, what he says concerning the phylogenetic importance of primal phantasies in his *Outline of Psycho-Analysis*, 1940, pp. 132–133, 167, 188–189). All this had an undoubted influence on the way unconscious phantasies would be reinterpreted, or further developed, by Freud's followers, as we shall see. I am thinking particularly of Melanie Klein's views concerning phylogenesis.

One should not forget some of Freud's other statements concerning the complex problem of primal phantasies, because even as far as primal phantasies are concerned, it is possible to find many analogies and resonances of his views in the work of those who would try to develop his thinking, as in the case of Klein, again, and of that of some of her pupils—in particular, Roger Money-Kyrle and Wilfred Bion.

Towards the end of the Wolf Man's case Freud made some of the most important theoretical statements concerning the status of primal phantasies, and ones which one tends to forget, or which seemed to have been forgotten later on, as I shall try to show in some cases. I am thinking especially of what Freud says at one moment when he tries to define primal phantasies, speaking of them as "phylogenetically inherited schemata, *which like the categories of philosophy* [my emphasis: ed.]—and it is highly probable that Freud had Kant in mind] are concerned with the business of 'placing' the impressions derived from sexual experiences". In mentioning here the Oedipus complex as an example, he concludes: "I am inclined to take the view that they are precipitates from the history of human civilisation" (1918b, p. 119). I have in mind also what he claims some lines further on, where he further refines his views and insists on, "some sort of hardly definable knowledge, something, as it were, preparatory to an understanding"—something analogous, he says, to the "far-reaching *instinctive* knowledge of animals", such as would constitute "the nucleus of the unconscious, a primitive kind of mental activity" (Freud, 1918b, p. 120).[20]

Yet even in the case of the primal phantasies Freud was very cautious in establishing a chronological order as far as their appearance is concerned, and in particular, as far as the capacity of the baby and the infant to make sense of them is concerned. Is it not curious—thinking of what will happen later on in the dispute between Anna Freud, her followers and the Kleinians (see the Scientific Meetings, 1943–1944, of the Freud–Klein Controversies, 1941–1945; King & Steiner, 1991; Steiner, 2000b), but also of more recent viewpoints like those of Laplanche and Pontalis (1968), or even of those of the Sandlers (1994)—that Freud should speak of "the dark period of the first year of childhood", when he deals with the possibility of establishing exactly when the Wolf Man had witnessed his parents' *post tergum* (anal) intercourse? And is it not even more significant, thinking of what I have earlier called attention to, that when Freud tries to establish a proper date, even in the case of the Wolf Man, he says that "the child's age at the date of the observation [of his parents' coitus: ed.] was established as being about one and a half years" (Freud, 1918b, p. 36), and that in a note, as if fleetingly he was reminded of what he had written to Fliess on 6 April 1892 (see p. 7 above), he puts: "*The age of six months came under consideration as a far less probable, and indeed scarcely tenable, alternative*" (Freud, 1918b, p. 36; my emphasis).

Phantasy life, at any rate, seems always to make its appearance rather later in Freud's baby's and infant's unconscious way of functioning.

There is a final issue that I think should be mentioned, because it is strictly related to many of Freud's views concerning unconscious phantasies, which, one should not forget, can be constructed without the patient's having a proper memory of them, or can, according to Freud, confidently be retraced in dreams, which he refers to as a particular form of remembering (1918b, p. 51). I have in mind what he says about unconscious symbolism. More or less at the time at which he put down in writing his views related to primal phantasies, in the famous lecture, "Symbolism in Dreams", which is part of his *Introductory Lectures On Psychoanalysis* (1916–1917, pp. 149–169), Freud emphasized the importance of *unconscious symbolism*, which he thought to be universal and, what matters more, acquired phylogenetically, too (*ibid.*, p. 199). To my mind, therefore, there is a sort of overlapping of themes between primal phantasies and unconscious symbolism both as far as their phylogenetic origins and their universality are concerned. Indeed, during the first decade of the twentieth-century, because also of the work of his pupils (in particular Rank, but also Stekel, not to mention Jung), Freud became more and more interested in the unconscious symbolism of dreams.

He had mentioned the existence of unconscious symbolism *en passant* already in the first edition of *The Interpretation of Dreams* (1900; see Steiner, 1975)—an unconscious symbolism which he found present in the symptoms of his patients but also in every other manifestation of our psychic activities, such as parapraxes, jokes, the arts—to the point, indeed, that in 1914 he added a special chapter on unconscious symbolism to *The Interpretation of Dreams* (1900, p. 350f.). Significantly enough, besides being thought of as phylogenetically transmitted like primary phantasies, the number of symbols present in the unconscious is rather limited: the human body as a whole, the parents, the children, brothers and sisters, symbols of birth, of death, of nakedness, and, as in the case of primal phantasies, Freud adds, "something else besides" (Lecture 10, 1916–1917, p. 153). Moreover, Freud insists that it is in the field of sexuality—of the representations of genitals, of sexual intercourse, and so forth—that we find so much use of symbolism, owing to the importance that sexual life has for us.

The link between primal phantasies and unconscious symbolism needs to be kept in mind also, I think, because it would be difficult to imagine how to interpret primal phantasies, and the disguised, defensive way they manifest themselves in dreams and other symptoms, without making use of unconscious symbolism. Indeed, many of these symbols are an intrinsic part of the primal phantasies. But having said that, I have to stop here as far as Freud is concerned.

*   *   *

"Thus it follows that unconscious transference phantasies exist in the present unconscious, not in the past unconscious"

"Phantasy and its transformations: a contemporary Freudian view", Sandler & Sandler, 1994, p. 391; this collection, p. 82

What I have tried to remind the reader of, as far as Freud is concerned, can perhaps help towards an understanding of the way his work has been developed and taken further by those who consider themselves among his more orthodox and faithful followers. To help the reader understand these developments, I have chosen to include in the present collection what are, nevertheless, two quite different papers, that of Joseph and Anne-Marie Sandler (1994) and that of Mark Solms (1997), though in the case of the former one has to emphasize that, as in many other of their contributions during the last 25 years, the Sandlers have tried to develop the views of Freud and Anna Freud in their own way, even where the issues we are dealing with here are concerned.

The Sandlers' 1994 paper is significant in that it was written for a particular occasion—the 50th anniversary of the Controversial Discussions between Anna Freud and Melanie Klein; and it can be considered as a very important point of reference for those who have been held to be some of the most eminent figures in the field of post-Freudian psychoanalysis (not only in England), as far as their views of Kleinian and neo-Kleinian thinking on unconscious phantasy are concerned. The Sandlers' paper needs, of course, to be put into context, and in order to understand some of its underlying motives, one should go back to the leading role played already in the 1950s by Joseph Sandler as director of research at what were then called the Hampstead Clinics. This work led to the creation of the Hampstead Index of Classical Psychoanalytic Concepts, which was the outcome of a study of the development of such concepts and their change over time. One should also bear in mind the Sandlers' longstanding interest in linking their way of thinking to aspects of genetic academic psychology, like that of Piaget and, more recently, the research work of Daniel Stern and others. The 1994 paper reflects the Sandlers' historical approach to the notion of phantasy and unconscious phantasy, in addition to containing significant critical links to and comments on the American school of ego psychology, as it is known, of Hartmann, Kris, and Lowenstein, among others.[21]

However, overall, one should have in mind when considering this paper, as I have already hinted, all the work done at a theoretical and clinical level by its authors to develop their own notion of object relationship—having worked as they did for so many years inside the British Psychoanalytic Society. They were critically stimulated by the presence of the two other schools of the Society, the Kleinians and the Independent School of object relations, which they themselves acknowledge at the beginning of their paper. To be noted in this last respect are the Sandlers' views on the importance of transference phantasies, anxieties, and resistances existing in the relationship between patient and analyst from the outset of the analysis, and their understanding of what they call projection and externalization in the transference.

Therefore, although expressed in their own language, their emphasis on the importance of transference phantasies etc. from the outset of analysis constitutes a creative cross-fertilizing influence coming from the Kleinians and from the Independent group of analysts (see also Sandler & Sandler, 1998). All this of course involves a particular way of considering the input and the role played both theoretically and clinically by the notion of unconscious phantasy (as the Sandlers have decided to spell it, in English, in this paper).[22] Yet what also needs to be stressed is the strong and particular line of continuity between their own way of considering unconscious phantasies and many aspects of Freud's views.

Take, for instance, the core concept of the 1994 paper—the differentiation between what they call the past and the present unconscious—which is introduced in this paper by reference to theoretical and clinical material from their work in the 1980s and early 1990s, with the focus on an attempt to define what they mean by this pair of concepts (see also Sandler & Sandler, 1984, 1987).

The differentiation between past and present unconscious as presented in the Sandlers' 1994 paper, which, one must not forget, is mainly focused on the use its authors make of the notion of unconscious phantasy in their clinical work, derives from the importance they give to Freud's first psychoanalytic model of the functioning of the psychic apparatus, based on the topographical model (Sandler *et al.*, 1997). The Sandlers insist on their view that this model has never been superseded by the structural one, which according to them has created confusion and is even responsible for the ambiguity of the concept of phantasy as used by the Kleinians; this, they claim, is due to the way Freud began to consider the unconscious and the role played by the id, the unconscious ego and the unconscious superego in the structural model.

It is interesting to notice the importance the Sandlers give to the pre-conscious and to the second censorship between the pre-conscious and the conscious, introduced by Freud during the first decade of the twentieth-century, starting with *The Interpretation of Dreams* (1900) and then elaborated in particular in his paper "The unconscious" (1915b). Incidentally, if one looks at the Freud–Klein Controversies (1941–1945; see King & Steiner, 1991), one can easily see how Anna Freud and her followers were insisting on the importance of the topographical model, and of the pre-conscious, too, in maintaining their objections to the views of Klein, Isaacs, Heimann, and others concerning the possibility of having access to primitive unconscious phantasies. Needless to say, Anna Freud and her followers insisted very strongly on the inferred, and only derivative, "nachträglich" way one could understand primitive phantasies, particularly as far as the analysis of children was concerned. Here it is also possible to see the links between the Sandlers' views and some of the views of Anna Freud, although, as already mentioned, the Sandlers developed their own views in a more independent way, particularly during the 1980s and 1990s.

Nevertheless, in their 1994 paper the Sandlers do not explicitly mention primal phantasies as such, and they avoid entirely the complex debate concerning the validity of Freud's phylogenetic Lamarckian hypotheses. What they constantly stress is the bi-partition between the past and present unconscious. *The past unconscious is not experiential and contains the most remote phantasies related to our childhood*; whereas, like Freud, they establish a strict relationship between the pre-conscious and the present unconscious. The phantasies of the past unconscious can only be *reconstructed* and are based mostly on the analyst's theories of mental functioning and of child development.

The Sandlers thus insist far more on the role played by unconscious phantasies present in the present unconscious, because, according to them, these are much more accessible to the analytic work in the here-and-now. Without excluding the possibility that these phantasies can be linked and related to the phantasies of the past unconscious, the Sandlers claim that the unconscious phantasies of the present unconscious are "different in structure" and "more closely linked with representations of present-day persons, and [are] subject to a higher level of unconscious secondary-process functioning" (1994, p. 390; this collection, p. 82). I do not think I am far from the truth in claiming that the Sandlers could strongly link the phantasies of the present unconscious to what Freud called the pre-conscious roots of the day dream. What matters, however, are their conclusions (which, not by chance, are written in italics) in their paper: *"Thus it follows that unconscious transference phantasies exist in the present unconscious not in the past unconscious" (ibid.).* The derivative, highly "nachträglich" and entirely hypothetical character of the unconscious phantasies of the past unconscious could not have been more clearly emphasized and described.

Another extremely important aspect of this paper of the Sandlers is their insistence on the gyroscopic, stabilizing function of the unconscious phantasies of the present unconscious: together with the second censorship between the pre-conscious and the conscious, these play a very important part in the development of the child, preventing the direct emergence into consciousness of unconscious phantasies. Referring to one of Joseph Sandler's most important theoretical and clinical concepts, the authors conclude their paper by emphasizing "the ... central point that what is organised into the form of unconscious phantasy ... serves the function of creating and maintaining a feeling of self-preservation ... [and of] safety and well-being in the face of disruptive urges of various kinds" (*op. cit.*, p. 392; this collection, p. 86). This is something again that can remind one of the compensatory, but necessary, role played by unconscious phantasies, as they are described by Freud, as an attempt to escape from too harsh a reality.

*   *   *

"The closest possible approximations of 'the real state of affairs' (Freud, 1940 [1938], *S.E.*, *23*, p. 196)"

Solms, 1997, this collection, p. 100

A rather different point of view is expressed by Mark Solms in his paper of 1997, written for a public lecture on "Unconscious Phantasy" organized by the British Institute of Psychoanalysis in London.

With his pioneering studies in the neuropsychology of dreams, and with the theoretical and clinical material presented by himself and his wife in their book (Kaplan & Solms, 2000), Solms is trying, with extremely interesting results, to link psychoanalysis to contemporary research in the neurosciences. Freud's attempts in the same direction, which he had to abandon after 1895, when he wrote the "Project for a scientific psychology", seem to come to a fruition of a more realistic kind today with Solms's work. In this 1997 paper, where Solms makes some very interesting links between the neurosciences and psychoanalysis, and insists on the fact that both disciplines study the same subject—namely the human mind—from different but convergent angles, he is trying to show the validity of Freud's thinking as far as unconscious phantasies are concerned. He does not prefer one model of Freud's description of the psychic apparatus to another, as the Sandlers do.

Through a crystal-clear illustration of the role played by our perceptual apparatus as far as perceptions of outside and inside worlds are concerned, and the meaning given to "reality" in these areas, and with attention given to the limitations of this apparatus, Solms firmly emphasizes the importance and validity of what I would call the inevitable philosophical implications of the models of the psychic apparatus as understood by Freud. It should be noted, too, that Freud never altered his views throughout his whole scientific life—a fact which also explains the particular nature and the particular "reality" of unconscious phantasies. Especially significant is the differentiation which Solms, following Freud, makes between the ways we make sense of the outside world through scientific instruments, and the inevitably derivative and much more hypothetical characteristics of our knowledge of internal reality and of unconscious phantasies—unconscious because the unconscious can never be reached as such and can never be really known.

Here is not the place to discuss whether the so-called objectivity one can achieve in studying external reality and the experience of what we call external reality are in actuality completely objective— though it can be true that, for example, study of the tissues of the brain can be subjected to public scrutiny, using identical instruments of analysis and by means of repeated and repeatable observations and experiments, and this fact undoubtedly gives to these observations and results a much more reliable degree of objectivity and certainty compared with the attempt to try to describe, or measure, unconscious feelings and phantasies. What matters here is the fact that Solms, accepting Freud's views, *insists on the specificity of internal psychic reality* as understood by psychoanalysis, which cannot be investigated with the same instruments we use to understand external reality. It can be investigated only via a specific phenomenological language—that of the subjective experience of the patient, and also of the analyst.

Even if Solms does not touch specifically on Freud's cultural background—in particular the deep influence on Freud of the neo-Kantian philosophy of T. Lipps, who in effect (see Steiner, 1987, 1999; and see also above, pp. 3 & 10) inspired Freud's views on the unconscious until the end of his scientific career—Solms is able to remind the reader of those fundamental issues without which psychoanalysis would be practically unthinkable, whatever the partisans of empirical psychoanalysis might wish to claim today. Like the Sandlers, Solms makes no mention in his paper of primal phantasies, and all the problems related to Freud's phylogenetic views about them. These phantasies, one has to acknowledge, were already described by Freud using to a certain extent the subjective language of his patients and his own personal, inner experience. Yet I think one needs to emphasize what Solms says about the difficulties classical psychoanalysis ran into because it made or took for "too real" the metapsychological language Freud used in its attempts to provide as objective as possible a description of the psychic apparatus. Solms is quite critical of this naïve "concretiza-tion". He compares all this to the attempt made by Melanie Klein and some of her followers to describe Freud's metapsychological language in terms of subjective experiences and unconscious phantasies: one has only to think of such terms as "ego" and "superego", or the concepts of defence, repression, and the like. In this, Solms acknowledges the positive achievements of the Kleinian School. It is quite significant, therefore, that Solms, who at times has been criticized for being a sort of fundamentalist in his defence of Freud's thinking, appears in reality in this paper quite open to developments in psychoanalysis which tried to carry forward Freud's thinking, with results that even in the field of unconscious phantasies can be quite different from Freud's original thinking. And yet, at the end of this paper Solms stresses the danger inherent in the Kleinian point of view, which can be used in an excessively "realistic" way, too. Even Klein's way of looking at unconscious phantasies is inevitably a derivative one, based on inferences— because the unconscious *per se* can never be reached or actually definitively known. Rather, Kleinians, according to Solms, should never forget that their way of conceiving and describing uncon-scious phantasies is only the most appropriate analogy, the closest possible approximations of "the real state of affairs", to re-iterate Solms's use of Freud's expression, and not, in any unequivocal way, reality itself. That would lead even Kleinian psychoanalysis to become a dogmatic, prescriptive doctrine.

*   *   *

"... Far from deriving fantasy [sic] from the drives, he [Freud] preferred to make them dependent on earlier fantasy structures"

"Fantasy and the origins of sexuality", Laplanche & Pontalis, 1968, this collection, p. 131

Laplanche and Pontalis's paper "Fantasy and the origins of sexuality" was originally published in France in 1964; it was translated and published in English in 1968. Laplanche, in particular, has since come back to many of the issues touched on in this paper, and we owe to Perron (2001) a very recent and interesting *mise à point* of the way French psychoanalysts consider the problem of unconscious phantasies. Yet the paper I have decided to include in this collection remains fundamental if one wants to understand the way different psychoanalytical cultures and their representatives, with their at times very important non-psychoanalytical backgrounds, too, have tried to understand and develop Freud's views. In the case of the French, one has to consider their particular relationship to Freud's text based on the glorious French tradition of *"l'explication de texte"*, and their attempt to remain loyal to Freud's views without becoming simplified echoes of them. One has, therefore, also to consider the often purely theoretical character of the French approach to psychoanalysis, which does not refer to clinical cases and vignettes, and its constant implicit, if not explicit, references to other human sciences, such as linguistics, anthropology, and philosophy, which deeply influence French psychoanalysis. This is particularly so in view of the fact that in the years in which Laplanche and Pontalis were writing this paper French psychoanalysis was under the influence of Lacan and his "return to Freud". Even today French psychoanalysis could not be conceived without referring to Lacan, who, besides having a direct influence on Laplanche and Pontalis, has been of paramount importance even for André Green and others, noted for their criticism and disagreement with him. Hence the particular quality of this paper, which English-speaking readers can find at times quite difficult to understand.

To get a clearer understanding of the issues dealt with in this paper one should also consider what the two authors wrote in *The Language of Psychoanalysis* (1973) concerning "phantasy or fantasy and primal phantasies". What I think should be stressed first is that Laplanche and Pontalis have tried to give us one of the most intelligent, complex and detailed "readings" of Freud's at times tortuous developments, which from 1895 onwards led him to the gradual discovery of the role played by what in their paper they call "fantasies, infantile sexuality, primal phantasies". At times, one has to say, their reading of Freud can be considered rather idiosyncratic[23] owing also to their critical attitude towards, for instance, the way Klein and Isaacs developed their views on unconscious phantasy, relying as they did on an "instinct-based" interpretation of quotations from Freud—and as Hanna Segal, too, will do. Laplanche and Pontalis do not agree with this interpretation, which, according to them is too reductive and biological, as I shall try to show later on.

It is interesting to see how Laplanche and Pontalis have emphasized the importance of Freud's early seduction theory, and the resonance this theory retained in Freud's further developments of his views on unconscious phantasies and primal phantasies, or, as the two French authors would prefer to spell the word, "fantasies". Rightly so, I think, Laplanche and Pontalis are able to show us how Freud was constantly preoccupied with the need to find in one way or another "something" that would provide a place from which to start. The primitive traumatic event on which Freud had based his earliest aetiological theory of the neuroses was then, later on, simply transposed into a mythological explanation of their origins—the phylogenetic transmission and inheritance of actual events that took place in the prehistory of the development of the human species—when he introduced his discovery of the primal phantasies. Laplanche and Pontalis make a great deal of this. They like very much the idea that the primal phantasies, which were already anticipated by the notion of *"Urszenen"*, and which Freud mentions at the time when he still believed in the seduction theory,[24] refer to a sort of *pre-subjective unconscious*, structured according to the laws of composition of these *"Urphantasien"* ("primal phantasies"). This, then, according to the two French authors, is to be understood as a fundamental concept of Freud's, which of course could bring to mind what Lévi-Strauss and Lacan, each working on the structuralist views of the linguist Roland Jakobson, and before Jakobson, of De Saussure, had put forward during the 1950s and 1960s in anthropology and psychoanalysis—influencing in this way developments across the whole field of the human sciences in France, and not only in France (see Safuan, 1968; Roudinesco, 1994).

I think that Laplanche's and Pontalis's insistence on the fundamental importance of primal phantasies as structures that act independently of our personal subjectivity, and which are activated in our ontogenetic history to a certain extent by the more-or-less seductive and unconscious relationship of the "Other" (the adult), is of fundamental importance in understanding many aspects of French psychoanalysis, even as far as such authors as André Green, Joyce McDougall, and Janine Chasseguet-Smirgel—who do not necessarily share all of Laplanche and Pontalis's further theoretical and clinical developments and views—are concerned.

Indeed, their insistence on the fact that we are "acted" on by a more archaic, impersonal and, by definition mythical and inaccessible past; their need to underemphasize the role played by the subjective intentionality of the subject, which, ontogenetically speaking, is not there at the beginning, particularly not as an active intentionality, but is created through the interaction with an adult, the mother; and their view of the mother as someone who in turn cannot be thought of without an understanding of the role played simultaneously by a present or absent father, in her more-or-less seductive interaction with the baby, are all themes which in one way or another are characteristic of French psychoanalysis today— although Laplanche (1999) will, in particular, further elaborate the notion of the primal phantasy of seduction, and the role played by the sexuality of the mother, and the adult in general, in the experience of the baby and child.

Another very interesting and important aspect of the 1968 paper, which, as I repeat, is a purely theoretical paper, is the insistence of its two authors on considering still very much valid now what Freud claimed in the *Three Essays on Sexuality* concerning the auto-eroticism of the baby and the role this plays in the process of phantasizing. It is in the auto-erotic baby that Laplanche and Pontalis see the beginning both of fantasy or of fantasizing (as they spell the terms), and that of human sexuality as such, which thus is seen to be not so much related to the instincts as to the emergence of fantasy (phantasy), which, in turn, is of course related to the primal phantasies, as Freud himself claimed in his paper on the Wolf Man (1918b):

> When Freud asked himself whether there was anything in man comparable to the "instinct in animals" (Freud, 1915 [1915b], p. 195) he found the equivalent not in the drives (Triebe) but in primal phantasies (Freud, 1918b, p. 120 note.). It is a valuable clue since it demonstrates indirectly his unwillingness to explain fantasy on biological grounds: far from deriving fantasy from the drives, he preferred to make them dependent on earlier fantasy structures. [1968, p. 14; this collection, p. 131]

The insistence on fantasy and sexuality also leads Laplanche and Pontalis to emphasize the difference between needs and their satisfaction and "desire", as the French translate "Wünscherfül-lung"—a differentiation particularly underlined by Lacan. Needless to stress here, I think, is the importance Laplanche and Pontalis give to the concept of "Nachträglichkeit" (translated in French as "après coup"). As I have already suggested, Laplanche and Pontalis are quite critical of Klein and Isaacs, and, implicitly, of the develop-ments made by the Kleinians in relation to unconscious phantasies, which followed. For instance, the authors do not accept the bi-partition between fantasy and phantasy introduced by Freud's English translators and accepted by Isaacs. They find the Kleinian approach, which links unconscious phantasies to the instincts, using some of Freud's statements in his paper "The unconscious" (1915b) or the *New Introductory Lectures on Psychoanalysis* (1933), overly biological and restrictive. Yet Laplanche and Pontalis have some very interesting observations to make on Klein's attempts to describe primitive unconscious phantasies, which appear to be structured on the basis of opposites: good/bad, inner/outer, and so on. According to them, this seems to imply a way of thinking on Klein's part that is based on some sort of intuitive structuralistic model of communication similar to the structure of verbal language.

What matters more, however, is, I think, Laplanche and Pontalis's disagreement with the intentional role that both Klein and Isaacs attribute to the primitive experiences and attitude of the baby, motivated and fuelled by what they mean by unconscious phantasies. "So long as there is some idea of a subject, even if playing a passive, role", Laplanche and Pontalis ask at one point (1968, p. 14; this collection, p. 131)—going beyond even Klein's and Isaacs' notion of an active role of the subject—"are we sure to reach the structure of deepest fantasy?" Here they are referring at the same time to Klein's and Isaacs' most radical interpretation of Freud's phylogenetic transmitted primal phantasies.

These last criticisms in Laplanche and Pontalis's paper (1968) can paradoxically help the reader to grasp some of the most original aspects of the work of Klein and Isaacs (1948) and of Hanna Segal (1991, 1994) concerning unconscious phantasies. Indeed, the whole Kleinian approach to the understanding of how our psychic apparatus and our inner world work is based on the role played by unconscious phantasy.

*   *   *

"Analytic work has shown that babies of a few months certainly indulge in phantasy-building. I believe that this is the most primitive mental activity and that phantasies are in the mind of the infant almost from birth"

"Weaning", Klein, 1936, p. 290

Owing to its relevance, I thought it would be worthwhile briefly to clarify for the reader how Melanie Klein herself came to her views concerning the role played by unconscious phantasies in our inner life. There is no doubt that from the beginning of her work, but particularly in the late 1920s, Klein emphasized the active role played by the ego of the infant from the beginning of its psychic life; and this role cannot be understood without implying the presence of unconscious phantasies which permeate the nonetheless rudimentary psychic life of the infant. This is due to the fact that Klein, inspired by Freud and Hug-Hellmuth, and encouraged by Ferenczi,[25] started analysing very small children using her play technique, putting into words the primitive phantasies that she observed in their play. Through her own observations and those of her colleagues, particularly when she emigrated to England in the second half of the1920s (after being analysed in Budapest by Ferenczi and in Berlin by Karl Abraham) Klein came to the conclusion that what Freud called primary narcissism was in reality a form of secondary narcissism at times used as a defence, and that, therefore, *an object relation, however rudimentary, did exist in the baby from birth*. In this complex relationship with the outside world, based on a rudimentary inner world of objects, very primitive unconscious phantasies, linked to part-object relations—these being also seen to be the psychic manifestation of the life and death drives—played a fundamental role through processes of projection and introjection.

Besides motor actions, therefore, *psychic actions*—intensively emotionally charged with love and hate, with anxieties and mental pain, with guilt towards damaged external but also internal objects, and with the urge to repair them—seemed to dominate the psychic experience of infants from the beginning of their lives. Freud's caution, as far as the existence of a psychic life in the infant in the early months was concerned, which I have mentioned more than once, was therefore overcome by Klein, with her strong conviction of the existence of an inner world in the baby and infant. This of course led to deep disagreements between herself and Freud, and between herself and Anna Freud, who, during these years, had also started to be interested in the field of child psychoanalysis (see Steiner, 2000b).

To quote from Klein's 1936 paper "Weaning", in which she very clearly condenses her previous work and at the same time elaborates on a clinical basis Freud's notions of the life and death drives:

> The baby reacts to unpleasant stimuli, and to the frustration of his pleasure, with feelings of hatred and aggression. These feelings of hatred are directed towards the same objects as are the pleasurable ones, namely, the breasts of the mother.
>
> Analytic work has shown that babies of a few months of age certainly indulge in phantasy-building. I believe that this is the most primitive mental activity and that phantasies are in the mind of the infant almost from birth. It would seem that every stimulus the child receives is immediately responded to by phantasies, the unpleasant stimuli, including mere frustration, by phantasies of an aggressive kind, the gratifying stimuli by those focusing on pleasure. [Klein, 1936, p. 290]

To really understand all this one should, of course, go into further detail about the way Klein came to her revolutionary conclusions and revision of Freud's and his followers' views concerning the first months of the life of the baby. One should certainly study the importance Klein gave to the primitive processes of defence—notably splitting of the object and of the self—which precede repression as such, and the fundamental role in her thinking during these years, and indeed throughout her career, of Freud's notion of the death drive, which for her manifests itself clinically in terrible persecutory anxieties which the baby needs to project outside to survive, from the beginning of its life. It was this that led Klein to postulate during the 1930s what she called the "paranoid position" in the baby, and to pre-date the emergence of the superego, and the Oedipus complex, of which she described a very primitive form, based on the combined figures of the parents. It led also to the gradual emergence in her work of what could perhaps be considered her major achievement during these years:

the discovery of what she called the depressive position and its fundamental theoretical and clinical importance in the baby's development. These new views made it possible to have a better understanding of psychotic disturbance in children and in adults and led to better treatment approaches. Here I must refer the reader to Segal's classical work, *Introduction to the Work of Melanie Klein* (1962), and also, though with some caution, to Phyllis Grosskurth's *Melanie Klein: Her World and her Work* (1986), and now to Julie Kristéva's, *Le Génie Féminine: Mélanie Klein* (2000).

There is no single paper of Klein's devoted exclusively to her views concerning unconscious phantasies. Yet her ideas can be reconstructed in the light of what she had already written in the early 1920s in her first seminal papers (1921, 1923a,b, 1925, 1926) concerning the analysis of small children and child and adult patients. Through some extremely moving and expressive vignettes of their phantasies Klein was able, much more vividly than was Freud, to show us the importance of the internal world of her very young patients, dominated in the here-and-now by the richness of their phantasies that were imbued at times with extreme anxieties and destructiveness and at others with enormous libidinal excitement, lust, and love for their external and internal objects. Particularly important are her observations made studying the play and the phantasies of her very young patients concerning the mother's body, the genitals of the parents, the parental intercourse, and the like.

It is Klein herself who helps us to understand something fundamental about her views of unconscious phantasies. For instance, in her 1937 work, *Love, Guilt and Reparation*, in which she is even more explicit than in the paper "Weaning", she insists: "primitive ... phantasy-building" is "a mental activity which I take to be the most primitive one", and which "more colloquially", she says, could be called "imaginative thinking" (Klein, 1937, p. 308). This link is then restated in her description of primitive phantasying (*sic*) as "the earliest form of *the capacity which later develops into the more elaborate workings of the imagination*" (*ibid.*; my emphasis).

Such a statement in itself clarifies the link made by the Kleinians later on between unconscious phantasy and imagination (two concepts which, nevertheless, should not be confused), and to which Hanna Segal, as we shall see, has applied some of her most interesting observations (see further p. 51 below).

It is obvious, therefore, if we look at what I quoted, that during those years Klein already had a rather different view from that of Freud concerning the unconscious roots of day dreams and fantasies. For her, they were all related to the deep unconscious in a much more straightforward way. And what matters more, perhaps, is her insistence not only on the content of the phantasies as such, which she describes and re-describes in all her papers, but also on the primitive unconscious activity of phantasizing as such, without which more sophisticated, adult forms of imagination could not be conceived. One need only think of her papers on children who had difficulties in learning (Klein, 1923a, 1931). Phantasizing, with all its omnipotent distortions at the beginning, but also with its potential creativity, is thus for Klein a fundamental part of the process of thinking, not only in the baby but also in the adult: thinking cannot be conceived of without phantasizing.

As for the *content* of unconscious phantasies, Klein insists on their omnipotent and extremely concrete and realistic quality for the baby; this is due also to their pre-verbal character and to the prevalence, though not absolute dominance, of the primary process at this stage of the baby's development. According to Klein, the baby really believes it has got hold of the mother's breast or the father's penis; it really does believe that, when, in frustration, it attacks the mother's breast or body, their contents, or the parental intercourse, it has actually destroyed its external or internal objects, and, in consequence of its paranoid anxiety, that it will be subjected to an enormous retaliatory punishment.

Particularly important besides external objects, for Klein, are the *internal* ones, strictly related to unconscious phantasies through projection and introjection. Thus, when the baby is frustrated, its *internalized objects*—and not only the external ones—become persecutory objects. Hunger becomes equated with a bad object, whereas having been properly fed becomes equated with a good internal object, and so on, due to the power of the process of phantasizing (Klein, 1935, 1936, 1937).

Yet what also needs to be stressed is something else that can help to clarify both the presence of unconscious phantasies and their pre-conscious presence in the baby. From the time of her earliest paper, under the influence of Freud, but also of Ferenczi (1924),[26] Klein constantly insisted on the fact that the phantasies present in her patients and evident in their play—or, more hypothetically, present in babies in general—have a phylogenetic origin. For instance:

> In their play children represent symbolically phantasies, wishes and experiences. Here they are employing the same language, the same archaic phylogenetically acquired mode of expression as we are familiar with from dreams. [Klein, 1926, p. 134]

Here Klein seems to insist on the phylogenetic inherited symbolism which children use to express their unconscious phantasies and wishes, just as adults use it in their dreams. However, one should also read what she stated in a paper written a little earlier, in 1927, "Criminal tendencies in normal children". In this paper, and in the course of an elaboration of Freud's views concerning sexual theories found in children, Klein addresses the subject of unconscious phantasies and, emphasizing how important it is for the psychoanalyst to maintain an attitude entirely free from ethical and moral criticism, comments:

> The sexual theories are the basis of a variety of most sadistic and primitive fixations. We know from Freud that there is some unconscious knowledge which the child obtains, apparently in a phylogenetic way. To this belongs the knowledge about parental intercourse, birth of children, etc.; but it is of a rather vague and confused nature. According to the oral- and anal-sadistic stage which he is going through himself, intercourse comes to mean to the child a performance in which eating, cooking, exchange of faeces and sadistic acts of every kind (beating, cutting, and so on) play a principal part. I wish to emphasise *how important the connection between these phantasies and sexuality is bound to become in later life*. [Klein, 1927, pp. 175–176]

Klein then goes on to describe in more detail all those phantasies first related to the mother's breasts and body, and subsequently to the father and the parental intercourse itself, again stressing how important all these phantasies are even for the child's later life when he has become an adult: these phantasies are, she says, "the foundation of all the attractive and socially important creative tendencies" (*op. cit.*, p. 176).

Yet consider now what Klein wrote in 1944 in her paper "The emotional life and ego-development of the infant with special reference to the depressive position". Read by her at the Scientific Meetings during the Controversial Discussions between herself and Anna Freud (King & Steiner, 1991), she states here:

> Freud described unconscious sexual theories of children as a phylogenetic inheritance. The analysis of young children has not only confirmed this discovery, but revealed in many details the significance of these infantile theories in the intellectual and emotional life of children. This interest in the sexuality of the parents is fundamental since it is so closely linked up with the child's own sexuality. It is obviously *still more fundamental* that, when he becomes separated from his mother at birth, the infant who was one with her body feels her to be his first and main object; and thus the phylogenetic inheritance is reinforced through his ontogenetic needs and experiences. One may assume that from the beginning the mother exists as a whole object in the child's mind, but in vague outlines as it were, and that this picture becomes gradually filled in as perception develops. [Klein, 1944, p. 797][27]

Although it is quite clear that the focus of Klein's attention at this later stage of her thinking was mainly on the mother and the breast, and the unconscious phantasies related to the latter as far as the earliest unconscious phantasies of the baby are concerned—never, for all that, forgetting the links of these primitive phantasies with the Oedipus complex—what seems to me to be quite clear is *that more than inventing a new kind of unconscious phantasy, Klein took Freud's phylogenetic hypothesis concerning primal unconscious phantasy and unconscious symbolism extremely seriously and worked on these concepts to the very end of her career.* Locating them in the inner world of the baby, from the beginning of its life, she created an extraordinarily dramatic and articulate phenomenology of the way the baby phantasizes through constant psychical actions and the use of its body: a rich "living theatre", as Solms in his paper rightly describes it, constructed out of the actions of mouth, anus, penis, vagina, and internal organs, and the manipulation of excreta, urine, faeces, and saliva.

To clarify Klein's position even further, one can say that if one studies her work up to the 1940s, it becomes entirely evident that she took Freud's structural model of the psychic apparatus for granted, and that she would keep to this model right to the end of her career. The notion of the pre-conscious, on the other hand, does not appear to have played any great importance in her thinking, although she did not discard it. Having postulated during the late 1920s and 1930s the existence of defensive processes, such as splitting, which precede repression—basing this on statements of Freud's contained in *Inhibitions, Symptoms and Anxieties* (1926) and in later work—she succeeded in giving to her way of describing the unconscious a particular character of immediacy and permeability with the deep unconscious itself. However, although she was of course very aware of the inferred character of her descriptions of the primitive, pre-verbal unconscious phantasies of the baby, based on a part-object relationship, and highly distorted in both their positive and negative aspects, it is true that she never spelled out the notion of "Nachträglichkeit" in any very open way. Indeed, there can be no doubt that at times a naïve reader of her descriptions of her clinical material can have the impression that Klein believed herself to have some sort of near direct contact with the deepest unconscious in the infant, or the infant in the adult.

Whereas Freud considered unconscious phantasies, and even primal phantasies, as only one of the aspects of what he called "die Phantasie" or "phantasieren", creating an extremely complex system of defensive filters which allows conscious fantasies and day dreams to seem at times to have an entirely autonomous structure, Klein adopted a radical stand that had great innovative consequences for the treatment of both small children and severely disturbed adults. For those who accept her theoretical views and clinical psychoanalytic technique, it has also given rise to a very dynamic view of the unconscious and conscious aspects of the development of the "normal" mental apparatus.

If the ego and the superego, which one should not forget play a fundamental role in the most primitive and distorted unconscious phantasies of the baby,[28] have their roots in the unconscious which Freud called the "id" (Freud, 1923), and which can never be conceived as autonomous, this for Klein has bearings even as far as an understanding of unconscious phantasies is concerned. She is convinced that what metaphorically speaking could be called the primitive hotch-potch of our mind is *constantly fuelling* the content and way of functioning, perceiving, imagining, and feeling of the whole of adult psychic life, not merely of that of the infant and child, although in various different ways according to the level of maturation in each particular case. That is, much as she obviously accepted Freud's views concerning primary and secondary repression, she believed that there was a great permeability between the unconscious phantasies of the deep or primitive unconscious and those of normal conscious life, particularly in the case of small children but also in that of adults. One has only to think of the notion of "positions" in her work, and to consider what she says specifically concerning these issues in her 1944 paper (see further below).

*   *   *

> "Phantasy (in the first instance) is the mental corollary, the psychic representative of the instinct. And there is no impulse, no instinctual urge which is not experienced as unconscious phantasy"
>
> "On the nature and functioning of phantasy",
> Isaacs, 1948, p. 83; this collection, p. 161

All of the above said, I think at this point it should not be difficult to understand the views concerning unconscious phantasy contained in Susan Isaacs' paper of 1948. For in effect they constitute a comprehensive reformulation of the major theoretical statements of Klein's approach to unconscious phantasies, reshaped and expressed by Isaacs in a systematic, academic language following from her background and knowledge of academic and developmental psychology. Certainly, Isaacs' paper needs to be put into context, with thought given to the particular time in which it was written, and to the circumstances that brought the author to write it, under the constant guidance of Melanie Klein—so much so, in fact, that it can be considered even today an unchallenged milestone in Klein's and her followers' ways of thinking. Isaacs' paper was read as the first paper that opened the Scientific Discussions of the Freud–Klein Controversies in 1943 (King & Steiner, 1991, pp. 264–319), although the paper presented in this collection is a reduced version of the original (of 1943), and was published in 1948.

Following Klein, Isaacs is convinced that unconscious phantasies are present in every aspect of our psychic life. Freud's hallucinatory oral wish fulfilment, which could be considered a sort of psychic primitive activity, of a hallucinatory kind, on the part of the baby, is also considered by Isaacs and Klein as an unconscious phantasy (see

Klein, 1944; King & Steiner, 1991, p. 753). Further, the existence of a
primitive object relationship, based on the notion of primitive
separation and on a psychic awareness of this separation that starts
at birth, is considered by them to introduce the notion of the
existence of the reality principle from the beginning of life. This, as I
have already suggested, does not allow for Freud's, and in
particular Anna Freud's, conviction of the total predominance of
the pleasure principle during the first months of post-natal life.

Primary and secondary processes do interact from the beginning, and affect unconscious phantasies also. Phantasies, therefore,
are "the primary content of all unconscious mental processes",
according to Isaacs (1948). This statement, which condenses very
clearly the extension Klein gave to the term "unconscious
phantasy", has become one of the key definitions of the whole
Kleinian metapsychology. Typical also is Isaacs' insistence on the
psychic reality of unconscious phantasies, using constant quotations
from Freud and extending them. In this way all the claims of
Melanie Klein concerning the existence of primitive internal objects
become justified. One might think, for instance, of the close links
made by Isaacs and, as we shall see, by Hanna Segal, too, between
unconscious phantasies and "instincts", as they call them, following
Riviere and Strachey's translation of Freud's *Triebe*[29]—something
with which, as I have earlier indicated, Laplanche and Pontalis, for
instance, disagree (see p. 34 above). Isaacs used Freud's statements
in the *New Introductory Lectures* (1933) to support her own
statements. In particular, Isaacs quotes from Lecture 31, "The
dissection of the psychical personality": "We suppose that the it [the
id] is somewhere in direct contact with somatic processes and takes
over from them instinctual needs and gives them mental expression" (Freud, 1933, p. 73).[30] She then adds: "... This 'mental
expression' of instinct *is* unconscious phantasy. Phantasy is (in the
first instance) the mental corollary, the psychic representative, of
instinct. And there is no impulse, no instinctual urge or response
which is not experienced as unconscious phantasy" (Isaacs, 1948,
p. 83; this collection, p. 161). Nevertheless, this does not mean—as is
often said with reference to Kleinian views—that there is a total
equation between the instinctual need and unconscious phantasy.
According to Segal (personal communication), the unconscious
wish is the father of unconscious phantasy, even for Klein.

I think that one of the most important issues dealt with by Isaacs in her paper is the developmental aspect of unconscious phantasies. Klein deliberately used a very concrete and anatomy-linked language to describe, in particular, the baby's phantasies concerning the mother, her breast, her body, its contents, and the parental intercourse. This was due to her attempt to make sense of and describe unconscious phantasies as far as possible in terms of the baby's emotional and physical, besides ideational, experience (see further, in this collection, Segal, 1994; Solms, 1997). Isaacs tried to provide a better way of differentiating these phantasies. She accordingly linked the earliest unconscious phantasies to the internal perceptions of the internal physiological and biological processes of infantile life—to the baby's internal organs, sensations, coenaesthesis, and so forth. What is important is that Isaacs stresses the *non-visual* character of these phantasies, which the baby feels concretely as pleasure or pain—full or empty stomach equated by the baby with good or bad (and persecutory) breasts, that threaten to starve it, and so on. Indeed, the word "phantasy", or "phantom", could at times be misleading because it seems, at least colloquially, to imply something related to the visual perceptual apparatus. Only gradually can the internal objects through which the phantasy manifests itself be visualized and memorized as such, and later on, of course, put into words by the very young child.

Another very important theme of the paper, with which Isaacs deals in a masterly way owing to her academic background, is her use of the notion of genetic continuity. It is this which, according to her, can provide a better explanation of the importance of primitive unconscious phantasies and internal objects, and can clarify what Kleinians mean by regression. In her paper she insists—and if one looks at the minutes of the Freud–Klein Controversies (1941–1945; King & Steiner, 1991, pp. 443–445) one can also read what she stated during several related discussions—on the fact that there is no chance of one ever really being able to reach the deepest and most primitive unconscious directly, because by definition the latter is inferred knowledge, and one has to use adult words to describe it (see Solms, 1997, in this collection). Even Klein's descriptions, therefore, are inferences. Isaacs' clarifications came about as a consequence of the criticisms made in relation to the idea of the existence of primitive unconscious internal objects and of unconscious phantasies underpinning them from the beginning of psychic life, as raised by Anna Freud and her followers, and, importantly, by Edward Glover. Yet there is no doubt that through the notion of genetic continuity, Isaacs thinks herself able to reinforce the evidence that there is a line of continuity between the earliest manifestations of psychic life and its later, adult manifestations (Steiner, 2000c, pp. 13–14).

One of the most controversial aspects of Isaacs' paper is the fact that having given to the term phantasy such extended meaning and importance, she at times describes as phantasy even the defensive processes: projection and introjection, omnipotent denial, splitting, and so on. This provoked great criticism and is still today an important bone of contention (see Haymann, 1994; and see also, in this collection, Sandler & Sandler, 1994; Solms, 1997). There is no doubt that what emerges from Isaacs' paper is that the Kleinian way of conceiving unconscious phantasies led to a view and a technique for interpreting them clinically, which is based on the conviction that there is great permeability between the deep and primitive unconscious and what we call consciousness (Segal, 1998; Steiner, 1998, 2000b,c).

I think at this point something else should be added to clarify the Kleinian views concerning unconscious phantasies. Although Isaacs' paper has remained as a cornerstone, even in and for later Kleinian thinking about these issues, the reader should be reminded of certain further developments and clarifications.

Klein's theory of the paranoid–schizoid position, her views concerning projective and introjective identification, published in 1946, and her emphasis, in 1957, on the importance of primary envy, did not add anything fundamentally new to her views in relation to unconscious phantasies, or indeed to Isaacs' paper, except for the fact that some unconscious primitive phantasies were described in more detail. One might think of the phantasy of fragmentation here, or of that of the projection into the other; or the introjection into oneself of unwanted parts of the self or of those parts of the self that one wants to protect (see Klein, 1946). Or one might think again of the destructive role played by envy and the phantasies it arouses (see Klein, 1957). Yet besides Herbert Rosenfeld's contributions to the phenomenology of unconscious phantasies in psychosis (1965), and his further phenomenology of unconscious phantasies related to certain types of pathological projective identifications (Rosenfeld, 1986), we are indebted to Bion's theory of the enlargement of the concept of repression—with the introduction of the idea of the contact barrier between conscious and unconscious, and the elaboration of the notion of alpha function, and the transformation of the beta elements of the unconscious into alpha elements through the alpha function—for a better understanding of the way in which unconscious phantasies do constantly interact with consciousness. This allows Klein and Isaacs' ideas concerning the function of unconscious phantasies to be better refined and elaborated (Bion, 1962; and see also Segal, 2001, p. 157).

To all this something else should be added. Even Isaacs, following Freud and Klein, spoke of the baby's inborn somatic knowledge of the mother's breasts, the nipple, and so on. Contemporary Kleinians, of course, still accept these views; yet with the passing of time even those issues related to primitive unconscious phantasies have been reformulated in a slightly different way. I think, for instance, one should give recognition to Money-Kyrle, even before Bion's famous theory of preconceptions, for his attempt to discard Freud's more speculative and daring phylogenetic hypothesis concerning primal unconscious phantasies. Although Money-Kyrle, in a paper called "Instinct in the child" (1961), still referred to an evolutionary model of the mental apparatus based on Darwin, he stressed the fact that Freud's Lamarckian and overly speculative hypothesis could be better formulated in terms of a brain "which is an organ for producing phantasies and which has *an innate initial structure* [my emphasis: ed.] at birth which 'produces' innate initial phantasies". The most immediately available and used by the baby is, of course, that of the mother's breast.[31]

In *Learning from Experience* (1962), and in many papers that followed, Bion elaborated the theory of inborn preconceptions, which was also aimed at unseating Freud's Lamarckism. These preconceptions could be compared with Kant's views concerning the so-called empty thoughts in our mind. But what about Freud's ideas of primal phantasies, which could be considered as something analogous to "the categories of philosophy which are concerned with the business of placing the impressions derived from actual experiences", as he says in the final passages of the Wolf Man's case history, which I have already quoted (see pp. 21–22 above)? One always forgets to quote these passages of Freud's work when referring to Bion, and it was obvious that Freud had in mind the

Kantian way of conceiving of mind. More recently Hanna Segal, in an unpublished paper of 1998 written for the celebration of her 80th birthday, has tried to compare unconscious phantasies with inborn meta-linguistic structures—the "universal grammar" of Chomsky—which are biologically grounded, something which, if I can quote myself, I, too, had pointed out, in a slightly different manner in 1975.

All this shows the attempt of the followers of Melanie Klein to make sense of what she observed, keeping in touch with modern developments, even in other fields.

One final observation has, I think, to be made. While unconscious phantasies played a fundamental role in the way Betty Joseph interpreted Klein's views—leading Joseph to her influential views concerning the total transference and transference interpretations in the here-and-now (Joseph, 1989)—something which, in spite of their theoretical and clinical differences, can remind one at times of the Sandlers' notion of the "present unconscious"—one has to say that, with the passing of time and as a consequence of criticisms coming over the course of the years from the other two groups that constitute the British Psychoanalytic Society, the general trend as far as Kleinian technique is concerned has been to lessen the use of so-called "deep interpretations", based on anatomical and physiological references to primitive unconscious phantasies. This, of course, has had its own advantages, but, one should not forget, some risks, too. For there is indeed a danger of transforming the deepest intuitions of Klein and her earliest followers concerning the way unconscious phantasies are experienced by the baby—but also by the adult—into a rather abstract, intellectualized, cognitivistic Kleinian psychoanalytic psychology if one forgets what Klein's albeit at times naïve, anatomically oriented descriptive language was trying to achieve: *to describe and be able to make sense, both emotionally and mentally, of the deepest areas of the unconscious in order to capture the elusive link between the body and its primitive psychic representations.*

*   *   *

"... The difference between day-dream and imagination could be seen as a difference between 'as-if' and 'what-if'"
Dream, Phantasy, Art, Segal, 1991, p. 107; this collection, p. 220

Owing to the importance of Hanna Segal's work, and its links with the most characteristic aspects of Klein's and Isaacs' thinking, as far as the problems related to unconscious phantasy are concerned, I thought it would be appropriate to conclude this collection with two of her papers. One is her 1994 paper, written, like that of the Sandlers, to celebrate the 50th anniversary of the Freud–Klein Controversies, although with the agreement of Dr Segal the paper has been slightly altered and some further clarifications concerning her views related to unconscious phantasy have been added. The second is a chapter of her 1991 book, *Dream, Phantasy, Art*. Although written a few years before the 1994 paper, this chapter is strictly related to it, because it illustrates her theoretical views concerning unconscious phantasies, and applies them to the field of creativity and the arts. The reader can therefore find here a further development and clarification of Klein's statements of the 1930s concerning the strict and unavoidable link between very early and primitive unconscious phantasies and the work and the results of adult imagination. Dr Segal has explicitly asked me to add the 1991 chapter of her book to the 1994 paper. Of course, to really understand these papers, one should, as I have indicated in respect of those of the other authors in this collection, put them into context; in this case, especially, one should link them to the author's complex and longstanding creative career. I am thinking particularly here of Dr Segal' interest in psychosis, which led her to write one of the most influential papers in the whole Kleinian literature, "Notes on symbol formation" (Segal, 1957), that had very important implications even for the Kleinians' views on the development of normal thinking; it has furthermore been used by several scholars outside psychoanalysis, notably by the British philosopher Richard Wollheim—besides, of course, influencing the work of her closest colleagues and friends of the 1950s, 1960s and 1970s, Bion and Rosenfeld. In many aspects of their work, the younger generation of Melanie Klein's followers—Ron Britton, Michael Feldman and John Steiner—besides being influenced by these colleagues of Segal's I have mentioned, and also by Betty Joseph, have referred, and constantly still refer to, Segal's seminal papers, too.

Another very important area of Dr Segal's research work should be mentioned. This is her longstanding interest in the psychoanalytic interpretation of creativity and art (Steiner, 2000b), which led her as early as 1952 to publish "A psychoanalytic contribution to aesthetics", a paper which influenced all her later writing on this subject and which has been considered a landmark in the study of the relationships between psychoanalysis, aesthetics and creativity in general, and not only as far as Kleinian thinking in those areas is concerned (Steiner, 2000b).

Now if we briefly consider Dr Segal's 1994 paper, it will be possible to see how she is able to balance the tradition coming from Klein and Isaacs, amongst others, with new views and developments in Kleinian thinking. Indeed, at times Segal still uses Klein's and Isaacs' references to the anatomical characteristics of the primitive part-objects, both external and internal, when she has to describe the earliest phases of the unconscious phantasies of the baby. Furthermore, the importance given by her to the instincts (see pp. 201–202 this collection), and therefore to the biological roots of the primitive unconscious phantasies, remains of paramount significance for her even in this paper, as well as a constant reference to Freud's paper of 1911 among others, the ideas of which she tries at one point to develop in a very original way. Thus Segal recalls here Klein's and Isaacs's views concerning the importance of the reality principle, which for her coexists together with the pleasure principle in the baby's mind from the beginning of psychic life, and which gives such a particular character to the primitive unconscious phantasies. Further, she shows the way in which unconscious phantasies interfere with the mental and perceptive and emotional apparatus in the case of psychotics, and in less disturbed patients, too. Then, towards the end of her paper, in discussing Wollheim's philosophical views concerning what Wollheim calls acting on desire and on phantasy (false belief), she comes, as far as the Kleinian approach to the process of thinking is concerned, to a very important conclusion. She thinks that, even in normal development, acting on desire is based on unconscious phantasy, contrary to what Wollheim claims. Unconscious phantasy can be considered as a wishful hypothesis that is constantly matched by reality. Whereas acting on what Wollheim calls "phantasy" (false belief) is in reality acting on a delusion that is based on an omnipotent misperception of the external and internal reality very similar to what Freud called "hallucinatory wish fulfilment". This is characterized by a compulsion to act, rather than by a choice to act. Segal then goes back to Freud's 1911 paper (and personally I would also have considered here Freud's paper "On negation", 1925b) and develops further views concerning thinking as an experimental action as opposed to omnipotent hallucinatory phantasy (what Freud called "omnipotent hallucinatory wishes"), in dealing with the necessity of recognizing external reality and the capacity to tolerate gaps in satisfaction and one's own ambivalence towards the desired object, in order to be able to grow and to think and feel properly.

Freud saw the emergence of thinking as an experimental action as a rather late result of maturation and of the baby's giving up of the pleasure principle (Freud, 1911), which, according to him, entirely dominates the early months of life. Segal, following, as I mentioned earlier, Klein's and Isaacs' views concerning the role played by the reality principle, and not only the pleasure principle, in the baby's mind from the beginning of its psychic life after birth, states that:

> ...The original experimental action is already alive in preverbal phantasy. Phantasies can be tested by perception; some by action: crying when hungry, biting in anger, attracting attention and love with a smile, etc. But there is also an experimental testing of the phantasy without an action. [Segal, 1994, p. 400; this collection, p. 209]

Particularly importantly, Segal goes on to add:

> If phantasy is, as I suggest, a set of primitive hypotheses about the nature of the object and the world, one can experiment in phantasy with "What would happen if...?"

> It differs from the delusional phantasy, which creates an "as if world", and it introduces a consideration of a "what if?", a consideration of probabilities of "what would happen if?" [ibid.]

Segal deals with similar problems—in particular the differentiation between an "as if" and a "what if ...?, what would happen if ...?" way of thinking and working creatively—in her 1991 chapter, too. Here she focuses on the problem of how to differentiate between art and true art; children's play and play in general; and day dreams and dreams, taking into consideration the different role played by unconscious phantasies in these expressions and activities of our mind. In this piece the reader can understand

how Segal has made important creative use of and developed the
link made by Klein between primitive unconscious phantasies and
the most sophisticated results of adult imagination (see above, p. 37).
Linking herself again to Freud's 1911 paper, which, as I have
already mentioned briefly (see p. 14 above), deals also with issues
related to artistic creativity that Freud had explored in his 1907 and
1908b papers, Segal expresses her new point of view *vis-à-vis*
Freud's theory of the role played by fantasy (as translated by
Strachey; Freud, 1908b, 1910, 1911) and day dream, and by
unconscious phantasies, in creativity, questioning in particular the
importance given by Freud to day dreams in the creative process. Of
course, to gain a better understanding of Segal's views the reader
should read the other chapters of Segal's book *Dream, Phantasy, Art*
(1991). But even in this chapter Segal is able to clarify her theoretical
views, using her own observations from everyday life—just think of
the moving vignette concerning the meaning of a child's play with
which she begins this 1991 piece, and then of some of her extremely
graphic and vivid clinical vignettes taken from the analysis of her
psychotic, borderline, and neurotic patients, notably from their
dreams and free associations, besides the examples taken from her
interpretations of works of art.

Following Freud, Segal claims that in art unconscious phantasy
has to "lose its egocentric character". But according to her, and this
is what the reader should, I think, bear in mind, this

> losing [of] the egocentric character ... involves a modification of the
> pleasure principle. It necessitates integrating one's perceptions of
> external reality that includes others and the perception of one's own
> relation to them. It also includes perception of the relations between
> them". [1991, p. 104; this collection, p. 217]

In other words, Segal adds,

> "imagination"—which for her is the fundamental component of
> true art—"unlike the typical day-dream, necessitates some aban-
> donment of omnipotence and some facing of the depressive
> position. This makes imagination richer and more complex than a
> wish-fulfilling day-dream". [*ibid.*].

It is obvious that Dr Segal's views concerning day dreams, their
role, and therefore the role of what Freud called "fantasy" in the

creative process, are quite different from those of Freud. For Segal, the day dream, even in its normal manifestations, always has the meaning of something superficial and shallow, and in its pathological manifestations seems to characterize schizoid states of mind and to have a very strong defensive pathological function— although Segal does not rule out that in some cases day dreams can mature, evolve, and become imagination. She thinks, nevertheless, that it is children's play, and play in general, more than the day dream or the dream, that resembles more closely the imagination of art. This is because, according to her, play is more *related to reality* when it is not pathological or not inhibited; and the *relationship to reality*—in other words, from a Kleinian point of view, *the role played by the reality principle*—is in addition to being fundamental to explaining normal thinking, fundamental to explaining creativity and art.

Following Klein's and Isaacs' views on unconscious phantasies, this has been stated and re-stated by Dr Segal, from her 1952 paper on (and see especially the whole of her 1991 book). In particular, the reader should remember the importance Segal gives to the link between artistic creativity and the libidinal reparative wishes and phantasies of the depressive position (Segal, 1952, 1981), where the reality principle plays a fundamental role in the mind of the baby *vis-à-vis* its external and internal objects. Without this link, what I am seeking to explain of what she says in her 1991 chapter would be quite incomprehensible. For instance, Segal claims:

> In normal play various aspects of life and its conflicts can be expressed. Unlike a day-dream, it [play] also takes account of the reality of the materials played with, and is thus a process of learning and mastering reality. Art in that way is closer to play than to a dream or a day-dream. [1991, p. 109; this collection, p. 222]

It is of course impossible here to mention all that Segal discusses and claims in this chapter. Nevertheless, I think that some of its most interesting statements can be taken up, which are those in which she tries to differentiate between true art, based on imagination, and something less genuine, based on day dreams, in referring to various kinds of science fiction. It is here that she uses the notion of the "as if" and the "what if" for the first time:

It occurred to me, when reading science fiction, that the difference between day-dream and imagination could be seen as a difference between "as if" and "what if". [1991, p. 107; this collection, p. 220]

Science fiction, when creating an "as if" world, she sees as pure escapism, as a day dream leads one outside reality into a sort of repetitive wish-fulfilling world. Whereas by the idea of a science fiction allowing for a "what if?" experience Segal means the creation of a possible alternative world, which still takes into consideration the reality of our world, is rooted in reality, and allows for the exploration of new possibilities of new aspects of reality, both external and internal. She writes of not denying the reality of this kind of science fiction based on imagination: by this Segal means a true capacity to relate to unconscious phantasies, which she describes as "moulding the world into a new fantasy world, with its own internal consistency and truth".

Quite rightly, Segal claims at one point that this difference applies not only to different kinds of science fiction but to all that the relationship between imagination and unconscious phantasy means for the Kleinian way of thinking that she represents, and has herself innovated: "It applies to all forms of art". "The difference between fantasy and imagination is the degree of denial of reality", she concludes (this collection, p. 222). The former is based mainly on a need to evade internal and external conflicts and a reality felt to be intolerable. In contrast, a creative work, which promotes a "what if" attitude in the minds of those who try to understand it, leads to new potential experiences and creative challenges within a given tradition. Here again one can see what is perhaps the main theoretical characteristic of the Kleinian approach to unconscious phantasy, understood by Segal, too. It insists on the deepest and primitive nature of unconscious phantasy; but at the same time unconscious phantasy cannot be conceived on the pure basis of the pleasure principle because it is always related, from the beginning, to the reality principle, too, to use the two famous definitions of Freud himself in his 1911 paper.

To conclude: as the reader can see, Freud's seminal paper of 1911 has given rise through time, and through different psychoanalytical schools and cultural traditions, to many, and differing, views and developments. One thing, nevertheless, can, I think, be stated with certainty. Whatever view one takes concerning unconscious phantasy, there is no doubt, to use a statement which we find at the end of Joseph and Anne-Marie Sandler's 1994 paper (this collection, p. 86), that "psychoanalysis cannot do without it".

Notes

1. The reasons why in the English translation of Freud's work the two terms phantasy and fantasy have been differentiated one from the other are clearly explained by James Strachey in his Glossary of Freud's technical terms in Volume 1 of the Standard Edition:

    > The spelling of this word causes a good deal of annoyance. The "ph" is adopted here on the basis of a discussion in the large Oxford Dictionary (under "Fantasy"), which concludes: "In modern use *fantasy* and *phantasy*, in spite of their identity in sound and in ultimate etymology, tend to be apprehended as separate words, the predominant sense of the former being 'caprice, whim, fanciful invention', while that of the latter is 'imagination, visionary notion'". Accordingly the "ph" form is used here for the technical psychological phenomenon. But the "f" form is also used on appropriate occasions. [*S.E.*, *1*, p. xxiv]

    I have used "phantasy" and "phantasizing" as a translation of "Phantasie" and "phantasieren" where Strachey translated them as such, and used "fantasy" always according to his translation. There is, however, a problem related to the Freud–Fliess correspondence. Jeffrey Masson (1985) has translated Freud's German using "fantasy", whereas the older translation and the excerpts of it put by Strachey in the Standard Edition have the German translated mainly as "phantasy". Laplanche and Pontalis in the English-language translation of their 1968 paper use "fantasy". In *The Language of Psychoanalysis* (1978) there is a discussion concerning "phantasy" and "fantasy" under the heading "Phantasy" (pp. 314–318).

    In the 1994 paper published in this collection the Sandlers use the spelling "phantasy"; but in previous papers, like American authors, have used the spelling "fantasy". As the reader can see, it is not an easy task to have to quote Freud in English translation.

2. The term "fantasia" in Italian refers mainly to the creative activity of the mind of the artist. This is due to the influence of the great Italian philosopher G. B. Vico, of the late seventeenth-century, who subsequently had an important influence on both German and French Romantics, and more recently due to the influence of B. Croce. Sometimes it refers also to the pathological aspects of the mind (Lepschy, 1986). Something similar occurred in Spanish and Portuguese.

3. Just think of what Coleridge wrote concerning imagination in his *Biographia Literaria* (1975 [1817] pp. 49–50). But even Coleridge had been influenced very deeply by the German proto-Romantics, especially Novalis and Schelling.

4. In his *Anthropologie in Pragmatisches Hinsicht* ([1798] 1839) Kant states: "Die Einbildungskraft sofern sie auch unwillkürlich Einbildungen hervorbringt, heisst Phantasie" ["The imaginative faculty, even in those cases in which it produces involuntary imaginings, is called phantasy"] (p. 113). Laplanche and Pontalis (1973, p. 314) seem to have ignored Kant's views when they try to differentiate rather more than seems warranted between the philosophical sense of "die Einbildung-skraft" and "Phantasie" as used by Freud in German. Incidentally, Kant stresses that "Phantasie" refers to *involuntary* imagination or imaginings (as Einbildungskraft), seeming to hint at something that is not properly controlled by our consciousness.

5. One has nevertheless not to forget that Freud will never exclude the importance of actual traumatic sexual events which occurred in childhood as far as the aetiology of mental disturbances is concerned, even later on. He will nevertheless insist on the different role played by these events. See also p. 19 of this Introduction.

6. Freud applied this notion even in the cases of his theory based on the actual sexual traumatic event to explain the aetiology of mental disturbances. He first mentioned this notion in "Project for a scientific psychology" (1895).

7. One should not forget the link between hysterical fantasies and poetry made by Freud in his letter to Fliess of 31 May 1897 (Masson, 1985, p. 251).

8. Freud, nevertheless, will mention the castration complex with all its phantasies only in 1909, at the time when he treated "Little Hans", and the year before this, when he described the sexual theories of children (1908c). He mentioned the Oedipus complex as such only in 1910, in a paper entitled "A special type of choice of object made by men".

9. The letter quoted, besides stressing the passive role of the infant, is itself a clear example of "deferred action". Freud will claim something similar in the very important appendix to the letter dated 25 May 1897 (Masson, 1985, p. 247). It is interesting that Strachey, in publishing this appendix in the first volume of the Standard Edition (p. 252), retains the "ph" spelling of the original German, whereas Masson (1985) uses "f" (p. 247).

10. André Green (1999) has, in a masterly way, pointed out, nevertheless, all the problems related to drives, including their possibility of manifesting themselves, in the structural model of the mental apparatus elaborated later on by Freud, which will complicate the problems

related to the conditions of representation of the drives as far as the id is concerned.

11. Freud already referred to the impossibility of reaching the unconscious as such in a letter to Fliess of 21 September 1897, where he announced to Fliess that he had to abandon his first aetiological model of the mind and the neuroses based on the infantile actual trauma. He said in this letter: "... The unconscious never overcomes the resistance of the conscious" (Masson, 1985, p. 265).

12. Readers will find in the famous note (n. 8) to this 1911 paper (p. 74 below) Freud's statement concerning the baby's system of self-sufficiency, together, nevertheless, with the very important addendum, "provided one includes with it the care he receives from his mother", which is of course an extremely complicated issue. Freud thinks that the baby does not differentiate between himself and the mother who cares for him in the first months of his life.

13. Indeed in his 1924 paper, "The loss of reality in neurosis and psychosis", although he uses a structural model of the psychic apparatus and differentiates between the use that the neurotic makes and the use that the psychotic makes of the world of phantasy, Freud uses more or less the same words: "a world of phantasy ... a domain which became separated from the external world at the time of the introduction of the reality principle ... a kind of 'reservation' kept free from the demands of the exigencies of life" (p. 187).

14. To enter here into a discussion of the reasons why Freud decided to publish his views concerning child sexuality and sexual phantasies some years later than that which he had already written to Fliess would be too complicated here. As even Strachey and Ernest Jones recognized later on (Steiner, 2000b), Freud became persuaded only gradually of the role played by sexuality, and phantasies related to it, in children. There are many contradictory statements concerning his views in the papers he published during the early years of his work as a psychoanalyst [see, for instance, "The aetiology of hysteria" (1896), "Sexuality in the aetiology of the neuroses" (1898), and even *The Interpretation of Dreams* (1900, p. 130)]. One has to consider various factors and particularly the difficulties he had to face related to the cultural environment in which he was living. To claim, for instance, that "heredity is the seduction by the father", as he wrote to Fliess on 6 December 1896 (Masson, 1985, p. 212), was a revolutionary statement considering what his colleagues were claiming concerning the aetiology of hysteria and other disturbances, referring themselves only to constitutional factors and degeneracy—although Freud was at that time relying on his views concerned with the actual traumatic seduction suffered by his patients

in their childhood. To claim that normal development and mental disturbances in the adult later on were based on the existence of a repressed autonomous phantasy life tinged with sexual phantasies would, as we know, have exposed Freud to formidable criticism also. It was not an easy situation in which to find oneself Freud (1925a). See also the very important observations made by Laplanche & Pontalis (1968), this collection, pp. 118–120.

15. See, for instance, the *Three Essays on the Theory of Sexuality* (1905a, p. 176): "[The] germs of sexual impulses are already present in the new-born child". Notice, nevertheless, that Freud speaks here of impulses, not phantasies; although further on he writes: "The sexual life of children usually emerges in a form accessible to observation round about the third or fourth year of life" (*ibid.*, pp. 176–177).

16. It is interesting to remember that in the case of hysterics Freud very often mentioned the existence of a sort of passive phase in their childhood, before he abandoned the theory of actual trauma. In the case of obsessive patients he placed more emphasis on an active phase and experience, which, nevertheless, were preceded by a passive attitude and passive experience, too. This was mainly due to his conviction of the active impact of the sexual trauma on a sort of dormant child's sexuality (Freud, 1905a; Strachey [Editorial note], *S.E.*, 7, p. 128, Freud, 1906). It is true that with the abandonment of the theory of the sexual trauma and the hypothesis of the existence of the autonomous sexual phantasies in the child Freud's attitude towards activity and passivity changed. Yet one has the impression that something of that old conviction, particularly concerning the dormant sexuality of the child and therefore also the child's phantasy life, remained in Freud even later on—especially as far as the slowness with which he imagined sexual phantasies started to be *actively* present and used by the baby and the child even in normal development.

17. Melanie Klein (1944; see King & Steiner, 1991, p. 754) pointed out, for instance, that Freud himself had corrected his previous views concerning a particular moment of development in the child in his 1910 corrected version of the *Three Essays* (1905a, p. 194). Freud said that he had to change his views concerning auto-eroticism as being a separated moment in time *vis-à-vis* the phases of object love. That, according to Klein, was seriously putting into question the rigid view related to the existence of a pure primary narcissistic phase without any object relationship, postulated by Anna Freud, and also the objectless nature of Freud's notion of hallucinatory wish fulfilment as understood by Anna Freud and her co-workers.

18. It is impossible here to refer in detail to how, for instance, Freud came to

these conclusions in the case of the Wolf Man. For this was a case which seemed to condense Freud's theory concerning the existence of primal phantasies and the role played both by the direct observation of the coitus between the parents, the possible observation of copulations between animals (dogs) and the actual seduction by his sister. All this happened at different times in the development of the patient. Hence the enormous complication and the constant "nachträglich" effect of many of these events. See the chronology of the patient's life as finally established by Freud (p. 121) just to have an idea of the complexity of these issues in Freud's notion of time (see further Green, 2001).

19. See, for instance what Freud claims at a certain moment:

> They share this character of indestructibility with all other mental acts which are truly unconscious, i.e. which belong to the system *Ucs* only. These are paths which have been laid down once and for all, which never fall into disuse and which, whenever an unconscious excitation re-cathects them, are always ready to conduct the excitatory process to discharge. If I may use a simile, they are only capable of annihilation in the same sense as the ghosts in the underworld of the Odyssey—ghosts which awoke to new life as soon as they tasted blood. [1900, p. 553n.]

20. Incidentally, this is one of the rare cases in which Freud uses *Instinkt* (instinct) and not *Trieb* (drive) (Freud, 1918, p. 156); see further Strachey's discussion on *Trieb* and *Instinkt* in his Editorial Note to "Instincts and their vicissitudes" (Freud, 1915d).

21. See, for instance, the view adopted by the Sandlers in their 1994 paper concerning the validity of Freud's topographical model *vis-à-vis* the American ego psychology school. Contrary to the opinion of the latter, the Sandlers thought that Freud's structural model did not succeed completely in replacing the topographical model.

22. In a previous paper of 1986 entitled "The gyroscopic function of unconscious fantasy" the Sandlers were still spelling the word with an "f", as is done in America. When they refer to this 1986 paper in their 1994 paper the reader will notice that they spell phantasy with an "f". This may have been a misprint.

23. It is indeed rather curious that Laplanche and Pontalis—like Perron incidentally—who are so extremely careful in reconstructing the vicissitudes related to the term "fantasy" and its relationship to the Oedipus complex, omitted in their exploration of the Freud–Fliess correspondence (Masson, 1985) to quote a statement like this, which with striking lucidity and anticipation seems to condense many of Freud's, and even of post-Freudian object-related theorists', views concerning the role played by aggression and depression in what Freud

later on called the Oedipus complex (Letter, Freud to Fliess, 31 May 1897, Masson, 1985):

> Hostile impulses against parents (a wish that they should die) are also an integrating constituent of neuroses. (...) These impulses are repressed at periods when compassion for the parents is aroused—at times of their illness or death. On such occasions it is a manifestation of mourning to reproach oneself for their death (so-called melancholia). (...) It seems as though this death wish is directed in sons against their fathers and in daughters against their mothers. [p. 250]

24. Laplanche and Pontalis were the first to stress the link between Draft L of the letter to Fliess dated by Freud 2 May 1897 (Masson, 1985, p. 240), where Freud mentioned for the first time his *Urszenen* as a sort of structural underpinning to the patient's symptoms and subjectivity, and what more or less 20 years later he will call *"Urphantasien"*. Although in this letter Freud still referred to real primal, traumatic sexual events, he already mentioned that these *Urszenen* are limited in number.

25. One should also not forget the work of Pfeiffer. He was a student of Ferenczi's during the years in which Klein, too, was in analysis with Ferenczi. He published a very interesting and too often ignored paper, "Äusserungen infantilerotischer Triebe im Spiel", which Klein knew, on the importance of children's play and play in general, in psychoanalysis. Freud himself published the paper in *Imago* (Pfeiffer, 1919).

26. The reader should recall what I have called attention to concerning Ferenczi and his interest in Lamarck's theories and phylogenetic issues during the period of the First World War. In her 1923b paper Klein reminds the reader that Ferenczi thought that the phantasies of returning to the womb of the mother through coitus—which she also found in her small patients too—had a phylogenetic origin (see p. 61n.).

27. Something similar will be claimed by Melanie Klein in 1952, in a paper entitled "On observing the behaviour of young infants". There Klein, comparing her views with those of Freud expressed in his *Outline of Psycho-Analysis* (1940) concerning the importance of the baby's relationship to the breast, insists on "the fact that at the beginning of post-natal life an unconscious knowledge of the breast exists and that feelings towards the breast are experienced can only be conceived of as a phylogenetic inheritance" (Klein, 1952, p. 117).

28. According to Melanie Klein, even the primitive superego has to be antedated in comparison with what Freud had claimed. Although Freud did not accept all Klein's views in relation to this, he nevertheless agreed that the superego of the child, and the phantasies related to it, do not coincide with the actual reality of the parents as external objects.

In other words, the child's superego is much more rigid and distorted and "phantasmatic" (Freud, 1930, p. 78).

29. See Strachey's Editorial Note to "Instincts and their vicissitudes" (Freud, 1915d, p. 72).

30. Isaacs is quoting from a 1932 (Hogarth Press) edition of the *New Introductory Lectures*. The *S.E.* version reads: "We picture it [the id] as being open at its end to somatic influences, and as there taking up into itself instinctual needs which find their psychical expression in it..." (p. 73).

31. I cannot quote Money-Kyrle extensively here, but there is no doubt in my mind that in stressing a sort of revival in his own terms of the old theory of the innate idea, discarding Lamarck's theory of the inherited memories and experience in his emphasizing that the baby creates a sort of phantasy expectation of an object which in the outside world can match his expectations, or in emphasizing that it is through the way the baby re-introjects his innate phantasies that he can *transform* or not transform them, Money-Kyrle has put forward many ideas which Bion went on to reshape in his own language, introducing the theory of preconceptions waiting to be matched by an experience or the containment and transformations of projected phantasies. Money-Kyrle, following Klein, Isaacs, and the views of his colleagues during these years, privileges, as the first phantasies accessible to the baby, mother's breast, nipple, followed very soon by those related to the male genital and the intercourse between the parents. One could ask oneself, nevertheless, whether it would be more plausible to claim that all these phantasies are already present from the beginning, although in an extremely confused way—even those related to the father—waiting, to use Bion's language, to be matched and saturated by the external world. After all, even as far as the mother is concerned, there is not somebody like that without her implicit or explicit phantasies and the relationship between her and the present or absent father of her child and her own father and mother. And the same could be stated concerning the father of the baby as far as his unconscious phantasies related to his own mother and father and his wife are concerned. All of this complex interaction of unconscious phantasies appears to affect the baby from the beginning of life.

References

Bion, W. (1962). *Learning from Experience*. London: Tavistock.
Breuer, J., & Freud, S. (1893–1895). *Studies on Hysteria. S.E.*, 2.

Burdy, M. W. (1927). The theory of imagination in Classical and medieval thought. *University of Illinois Studies in Language and Literature*, 12: 183–472.

Coleridge, T. (1975 [1817]). *Biographia Literaia* or *Biographical Sketches of my Literary Life and Opinion*. G. Watson (Ed.). London: Dent.

Engell, J. (1981). *The Creative Imagination: Enlightenment to Romanticism*. Cambridge, MA: Harvard University Press.

Falzeder, E., & Brabant, E. (Eds.) (1996). *The Correspondence of Sigmund Freud and Sandór Ferenczi, Volume 2*. Cambridge, MA & London: Harvard University Press.

Ferenczi, S. (1924). *Thalassa: A Theory of Genitality*. New York: The Psychoanalytic Quarterly, Inc. [reprinted London: Karnac, 1989].

Freud, S. (1895). Project for a scientific psychology. *S.E.*, 1: 283–397.

Freud, S. (1896) The aetiology of hysteria. *S.E.*, 3: 189–221.

Freud, S. (1898). Sexuality in the aetiology of the neuroses. *S.E.*, 3: 261–285.

Freud, S. (1899). Screen memories. *S.E.*, 3: 301–322.

Freud, S. (1900). *The Interpretation of Dreams*. *S.E.*, 4–5.

Freud, S. (1905a). *Three Essays on Sexuality*. *S.E.*, 7: 125–243.

Freud, S. (1905b). Fragment of an analysis of a case of hysteria. *S.E.*, 7: 2–122.

Freud, S. (1906). My views on the part played by sexuality in the aetiology of the neuroses. *S.E.*, 7: 271–279.

Freud, S. (1907). *Delusions and Dreams in Jensen's "Gradiva"*. *S.E.*, 9: 3–95.

Freud, S. (1908a). Hysterical phantasies and their relationship to bisexuality. *S.E.*, 9: 157–166.

Freud, S. (1908b). Creative writers and day dreaming. *S.E.*, 9: 142–153.

Freud, S. (1908c). On sexual theories of children. *S.E.*, 9: 207–226.

Freud, S. (1909). Analysis of a phobia in a five-year-old boy. *S.E.*, 10: 3–147.

Freud, S. (1910). A special type of choice of object made by men. *S.E.*, 11: 164–175.

Freud, S. (1911). Formulations on the two principles of mental functioning. *S.E.*, 12: 218–226.

Freud, S. (1912). A note on the unconscious in psychoanalysis. *S.E.*, 12: 257–266.

Freud, S. (1912–1913). *Totem and Taboo*. *S.E.*, 13: 1–162.

Freud, S. (1914). On narcissism: an introduction. *S.E.*, 14: 69–102.

Freud, S. (1915a). Repression. *S.E.*, 14: 143–158.

Freud, S. (1915b). The unconscious. *S.E.*, 14: 161–215.

Freud, S. (1915c). A case of paranoia running counter to the psycho-analytic theory of the disease. *S.E.*, *14*: 262–272.

Freud, S. (1915d). Instincts and their vicissitudes. *S.E.*, *14*: 111–140.

Freud, S. (1916–1917). *Introductory Lectures on Psychoanalysis. S.E.*, *15–16*.

Freud, S. (1918). Aus der Geschichte einer infantilen Neurose. *Gesammelte Werke*, *12*: 29–157.

Freud, S. (1918b). From the history of an infantile neurosis. *S.E.*, *17*: 3–123.

Freud, S. (1923). *The Ego and the Id. S.E.*, *19*: 3–66.

Freud, S. (1924). The loss of reality in neurosis and psychosis. *S.E.*, *19*: 183–187.

Freud, S. (1925a). *An Autobiographical Study. S.E.*, *20*: 3–74.

Freud, S. (1925b). Negation. *S.E.*, *19*: 235–239.

Freud, S. (1926). *Inhibitions, Symptoms and Anxiety. S.E.*, *20*: 77–174.

Freud, S. (1930). *Civilisation and Its Discontents. S.E.*, *21*: 59–145.

Freud, S. (1933). *New Introductory Lectures on Psycho-Analysis. S.E.*, *22*: 3–182.

Freud, S. (1940 [1938]). *An Outline of Psycho-Analysis. S.E.*, *23*: 141–207.

Gay, P. (1988). *Freud: A Life for Our Time*. London & New York: Papermac.

Green, A. (1999). On discriminating and not discriminating between affect and representation. *International Journal of Psychoanalysis*, *80*: 277–316.

Green, A. (2001). *Life Narcissism Death Narcissism*. London: Free Association Books.

Grimm, J., & Grimm, W. (1889). *Deutsches Wörterbuch*. Leipzig: Hirzel.

Grosskurth, P. (1986). *Melanie Klein: Her World and her Work*. London: Hodder & Stoughton.

Grubrich-Simitis, I. (Ed.) (1987). *A Phylogenetic Fantasy: Overview of the Transference Neuroses*. A. Hoffer & P. T. Hoffer (Trans.). Cambridge, MA: Belknap Press of Harvard University Press.

Grubrich-Simitis, I. (1993). *Back to Freud's Texts: Making Silent Documents Speak*. P. Slotkin (Trans.). New Haven & London: Yale University Press.

Hayman, A. (1994). Some remarks about the Controversial Discussions. *International Journal of Psycho-Analysis*, *75*: 343–358.

Isaacs, S. (1948 [1943]). On the nature and function of phantasy. In: M. Klein, P. Heimann, S. Isaacs & J. Riviere (Eds.), *Developments in Psychoanalysis* (pp. 67–121). London: Hogarth Press and The Institute of Psycho-Analysis, 1952.

Jones, E. (1957). *The Life and Work of Sigmund Freud, Volume 3*. London: Hogarth Press.

Joseph, B. (1989). *Psychic Equilibrium and Psychic Change*. London: Routledge.

Kant, I. (1839 [1798]). *Anthropologie in pragmatischer Hinsicht, Volume 10*. G. Hartenstein (Ed.). Leipzig: Rodes & Bauman.

Kaplan, K., & Solms, M. (2000). *Clinical Studies in Neuropsychoanalysis*. London: Karnac Books.

King, P., & Steiner, R. (1991). *The Freud–Klein Controversies 1941–1945*. London & New York: Tavistock/Routledge.

Klein, M. (1921). The development of a child. In: Klein (1975), *Volume 1* (pp. 4–13).

Klein, M. (1923a). The role of the school in the libidinal development of the child. In: Klein (1975), *Volume 1* (pp. 59–76).

Klein, M. (1923b). Early analysis. In: Klein (1975), *Volume 1* (pp. 77–105).

Klein, M. (1925). A contribution to the psychogenesis of tics. In: Klein (1975), *Volume 1* (pp. 106–127).

Klein, M. (1926). The psychological principles of early analysis. In: Klein (1975), *Volume 1* (pp. 128–138).

Klein, M. (1927). Criminal tendencies in normal children. In: Klein (1975), *Volume 1* (pp. 170–185).

Klein, M. (1931). A contribution to the theory of intellectual inhibition in children. In: Klein (1975), *Volume 1* (pp. 236–247).

Klein, M. (1935). A contribution to the psychogenesis of manic-depressive states. In: Klein (1975), *Volume 1* (pp. 262–289).

Klein, M. (1936). Weaning. In: Klein (1975), *Volume 1* (pp. 290–305).

Klein, M. (1937). *Love, Guilt and Reparation*. In: Klein (1975), *Volume 1* (pp. 306–343).

Klein, M. (1944). The emotional life and the ego development of the infant, with special reference to the depressive position. In: P. King & R. Steiner (Eds.), *The Freud–Klein Controversies 1941–1945* (pp. 752–797). London: Routledge, 1991.

Klein, M. (1946). Notes on some schizoid mechanisms. In: Klein (1975), *Volume 3* (pp. 1–24).

Klein, M. (1952). On observing the behaviour of young infants. In: Klein (1975), *Volume 3* (pp. 94–121).

Klein, M. (1957). *Envy and Gratitude*. In: Klein (1975), *Volume 3* (pp. 176–235).

Klein, M. (1975). *The Writings of Melanie Klein, Volume 1: Love, Guilt and*

Reparation; Volume 3: Envy and Gratitude and Other Essays. London: Hogarth Press & The Institute of Psycho-Analysis.

Kristeva, J. (2000). *Le Génie Féminine: Mélanie Klein.* Paris: Fayard.

Laplanche, J. (1999). *Essays on Otherness.* London: Routledge.

Laplanche, J., & Pontalis, J.-B. (1968). Fantasy and the origins of sexuality. *International Journal of Psycho-Analysis, 49*: 1–18.

Laplanche, J., & Pontalis, J.-B. (1973). *The Language of Psychoanalysis.* London: Hogarth Press & The Institute of Psychoanalysis.

Lepschy, G. (1986). Fantasia e immaginazione. *Lettere Italiane, 1*: 1–39.

Masson, J. M. (Ed.) (1985). *The Complete Letters of Sigmund Freud to Wilhelm Fliess (1887–1904).* J. M. Masson (Trans.). Cambridge, MA: Belknap Press of Harvard University Press.

Money-Kyrle, R. E. (1961). Instinct in the child. In: *Man's Picture of his World* (pp. 42–59). London: Duckworth.

Perron, R. (2001). The unconscious and primal phantasies. *International Journal of Psychoanalysis, 82*: 583–595.

Pfeiffer, S. (1919). Äusserungen infantil-erotischer Triebe in Spielen. *Imago, 5*: 243–282.

Ritvo, L. (1990). *Darwin's Influence on Freud: A Tale of Two Sciences.* New Haven & London: Yale University Press.

Roudinesco, E. (1994). *Histoire de la Psychanalyse en France, Volume 2.* Paris: Fayard.

Rosenfeld, H. (1965). *Psychotic States.* London: Hogarth Press and The Institute of Psycho-Analysis.

Rosenfeld, H. (1986). *Impasse and Interpretation.* London: Routledge and The Institute of Psycho-Analysis.

Safuan, M. (1968). *Le Structuralisme en Psychanalyse.* Paris: Editions du Seuil.

Sandler, J., & Sandler, A.-M. (1984). The past unconscious, the present unconscious and the interpretation of the transference. *Psychoanalytic Inquiry, 4*: 367–399.

Sandler, J., & Sandler, A.-M. (1986). The gyroscopic function of unconscious fantasy. In: D. Feinsilver (Ed.), *Toward a Comprehensive Model for Schizophrenic Disorders* (pp. 109–124). Hillsdale, New York: Analytic Press.

Sandler, J., & Sandler, A.-M. (1987). The past unconscious, the present unconscious and the vicissitudes of guilt. *International Journal of Psycho-Analysis, 68*: 331–341.

Sandler, J., & Sandler, A.-M. (1994). Phantasy and its transformations: a contemporary Freudian view. *International Journal of Psycho-Analysis, 75*: 387–394.

Sandler, J., & Sandler, A.-M. (1998). *Internal Objects Revisited*. London: Karnac Books.

Sandler, J. *et al.* (1997). *Freud's Models of the Mind: An Introduction*. London: Karnac Books.

Segal, H. (1952). A psychoanalytic approach to aesthetics. In: *The Work of Hanna Segal* (pp. 185–205). New York: Aronson, 1981.

Segal, H. (1957). Notes on symbol formation. In: *The Work of Hanna Segal* (pp. 121–136). New York: Aronson, 1981.

Segal, H. (1962). *Introduction to the Work of Melanie Klein*. London: Tavistock.

Segal, H. (1991). *Dream, Phantasy, Art*. London: Tavistock/Routledge.

Segal, H. (1994). Phantasy and reality. *International Journal of Psycho-Analysis*, 75: 395–401.

Segal, H. (1998). Untitled, unpublished paper given at the conference for the author's 80th birthday, September 1998.

Segal, H. (2001). Changing models of the mind. In: C. Bronstein (Ed.), *Kleinian Theory: A Contemporary Perspective* (pp. 187–205). Philadelphia & London: Whurr Publications.

Solms, M. (1997). Do unconscious phantasies really exist? Unpublished paper based on a public lecture at the Institute of Psycho-Analysis, 14 September 1996; presented to the 1952 Club of the British Psychoanalytical Society, 10 June 1997.

Starobinski, J. (1970). Pour une histoire du concept de l'imagination. In: *L'Oeil Vivant, 2: La Relation Critique* (pp. 173–195). Paris: Gallimard.

Steiner, R. (1975). *La Teoria del Simbolo Nell'Opera di Melanie Klein*. Torino: Boringhieri.

Steiner, R. (1987). Paths to Xanadu ... *International Review of Psycho-analysis*, 15: 415–454.

Steiner, R. (1994). In Vienna veritas? *International Journal of Psycho-Analysis*, 75: 511–583.

Steiner, R. (1998). Unpublished paper given at the Anna Freud Centre to comment on J. and A.-M. Sandler's *Internal Objects Revisited* (Sandler & Sandler, 1998), July 1998.

Steiner, R. (1999). Who influenced whom? and how? *International Journal of Psychoanalysis*, 80: 367–375.

Steiner, R. (2000a). Introduction. In: I. Grubrich-Simitis (Ed.), *S. Freud: Psychopathologie des Alltagslebens*. Frankfurt am Main: Fischer Verlag.

Steiner, R. (2000b). *Tradition Change and Creativity in Psychoanalysis*. London: Karnac Books.

Steiner, R. (2000c). Introduction to A. Green & D. Stern. In: J. Sandler, A.-M. Sandler & R. M. Davies (Eds.), *Clinical and Observational Psychoanalytic Research: Roots of a Controversy* (pp. 1–17). London: Karnac Books.

Strachey, J. (1966). Glossary of technical terms. *S.E., 1*: xxiii–xxvi.

Strachey, J. (1968). Editorial note to S. Freud (1905a) *Three Essays on the Theory of Sexuality, S.E., 7*: 126–129.

Strachey, J. (1968). Editorial note to S. Freud (1911) Formulation on the two principles of mental functioning. *S.E., 12*: 215–216.

Formulations on the two principles of mental functioning

Sigmund Freud

W e have long observed that every neurosis has as its result, and probably therefore as its purpose, a forcing of the patient out of real life, an alienating of him from reality.[1] Nor could a fact such as this escape the observation of Pierre Janet; he spoke of a loss of the "function of reality" as being a special characteristic of neurotics, but without discovering the connection of this disturbance with the fundamental determinants of neurosis.[2] By introducing the process of repression into the genesis of the neuroses we have been able to gain some insight into this connection. Neurotics turn away from reality because they find it unbearable—either the whole or parts of it. The most extreme type of this turning away from reality is shown by certain cases of hallucinatory psychosis which seek to deny the particular event that occasioned the outbreak of their insanity (Griesinger).[3] But in fact every neurotic does the same with some fragment of reality.[4] And we are now confronted with the task of investigating the development of the relation of neurotics and of mankind in general to reality, and in this way of bringing the psychological significance of the real external world into the structure of our theories.

In the psychology which is founded on psychoanalysis we have become accustomed to taking as our starting-point the unconscious mental processes, with the peculiarities of which we have become acquainted through analysis. We consider these to be the older, primary processes, the residues of a phase of development in which they were the only kind of mental process. The governing purpose obeyed by these primary processes is easy to recognise; it is described as the pleasure-unpleasure principle, or more shortly the pleasure principle.[5] These processes strive towards gaining pleasure; psychical activity draws back from any event which might arouse unpleasure. (Here we have repression.) Our dreams at night and our waking tendency to tear ourselves away from distressing impressions are remnants of the dominance of this principle and proofs of its power.

I shall be returning to lines of thought which I have developed elsewhere[6] when I suggest that the state of psychical rest was originally disturbed by the peremptory demands of internal needs. When this happened, whatever was thought of (wishes for) was simply presented in a hallucinatory manner, just as still happens today with our dream-thoughts every night.[7] It was only the non-occurrence of the expected satisfaction, the disappointment experienced, that led to the abandonment of this attempt at satisfaction by means of hallucination. Instead of it, the psychical apparatus had to decide to form a conception of the real circumstances in the external world and to endeavour to make a real alteration in them. A new principle of mental functioning was thus introduced; what was presented in the mind was no longer what was agreeable but what was real, even if it happened to be disagreeable.[8] This setting-up of the *reality principle* proved to be a momentous step.

(1) In the first place, the new demands made a succession of adaptations necessary in the psychical apparatus, which, owing to our insufficient or uncertain knowledge, we can only retail very cursorily. The increased significance of external reality heightened the importance, too, of the sense-organs that are directed towards that external world, and of the *consciousness* attached to them. Consciousness now learned to comprehend sensory qualities in addition to the qualities of pleasure and unpleasure which hitherto had alone been of interest to it. A special function was instituted which had periodically to search the external world, in order that its

data might be familiar already if an urgent internal need should arise—the function of *attention*.[9] Its activity meets the sense-impressions half way, instead of awaiting their appearance. At the same time, probably, a system of *notation* was introduced, whose task it was to lay down the results of this periodical activity of consciousness—a part of what we call *memory*.

The place of repression, which excluded from cathexis as productive of unpleasure some of the emerging ideas, was taken by an *impartial passing of judgement*,[10] which had to decide whether a given idea was true or false—that is, whether it was in agreement with reality or not—the decision being determined by making a comparison with the memory-traces of reality.

A new function was now allotted to motor discharge, which under the dominance of the pleasure principle, had served as a means of unburdening the mental apparatus of accretions of stimuli, and which had carried out this task by sending innervations into the interior of the body (leading to expressive movements and the play of features and to manifestations of affect). Motor discharge was now employed in the appropriate alteration of reality; it was converted into *action*.

Restraint upon motor discharge (upon action), which then became necessary, was provided by means of the process of *thinking*, which was developed from the presentation of ideas. Thinking was endowed with characteristics which made it possible for the mental apparatus to tolerate an increased tension of stimulus while the process of discharge was postponed. It is essentially an experimental kind of acting, accompanied by displacement of relatively small quantities of cathexis together with less expenditure (discharge) of them.[11] For this purpose the conversion of freely displaceable cathexes into "bound" cathexes was necessary, and this was brought about by means of raising the level of the whole cathectic process. It is probable that thinking was originally unconscious, in so far as it went beyond mere ideational presentations and was directed to the relations between impressions of objects, and that it did not acquire further qualities, perceptible to consciousness, until it became bound to verbal residues.[12]

(2) A general tendency of our mental apparatus, which can be traced back to the economic principle of saving expenditure [of energy],

seems to find expression in the tenacity with which we hold on to the sources of pleasure at our disposal, and in the difficulty with which we renounce them. With the introduction of the reality principle one species of thought-activity was split off; it was kept free from reality-testing and remained subordinated to the pleasure principle alone.[13] This activity is *phantasying*, which begins already in children's play, and later, continued as *day-dreaming*, abandons dependence on real objects.

(3) The replacement of the pleasure principle by the reality principle, with all the psychical consequences involved, which is here schematically condensed into a single sentence, is not in fact accomplished all at once, nor does it take place simultaneously all along the line. For while this development is going on in the ego-instincts, the sexual instincts become detached from them in a very significant way. The sexual instincts behave auto-erotically at first; they obtain their satisfaction in the subject's own body and therefore do not find themselves in the situation of frustration which was what necessitated the institution of the reality principle; and when, later on, the process of finding an object begins, it is soon interrupted by the long period of latency, which delays sexual development until puberty. These two factors—auto-erotism and the latency period—have as their result that the sexual instinct is held up in its psychical development and remains far longer under the dominance of the pleasure principle, from which in many people it is never able to withdraw.

In consequence of these conditions, a closer connection arises, on the one hand, between the sexual instinct and phantasy and, on the other hand, between the ego-instincts and the activities of consciousness. Both in healthy and in neurotic people this connection strikes us as very intimate, although the considerations of genetic psychology which have just been put forward lead us to recognise it as a *secondary* one. The continuance of auto-erotism is what makes it possible to retain for so long the easier momentary and imaginary satisfaction in relation to the sexual object in place of real satisfaction, which calls for effort and postponement. In the realm of phantasy, repression remains all-powerful; it brings about the inhibition of ideas *in statu nascendi* before they can be noticed by consciousness, if their cathexis is likely to occasion a release of unpleasure. This is the weak spot in our psychical organisation; and it can be employed to bring back under the dominance of the pleasure principle thought-processes which had already become rational. An essential part of the psychical disposition to neurosis thus lies in the delay in educating the sexual instincts to pay regard to reality and, as a corollary, in the conditions which make this delay possible.

(4) Just as the pleasure-ego can do nothing but *wish*, work for a yield of pleasure, and avoid unpleasure, so the reality ego need do nothing but strive for what is *useful* and guard itself against damage.[14] Actually the substitution of the reality principle for the pleasure principle implies no deposing of the pleasure principle, but only a safeguarding of it. A momentary pleasure, uncertain in its results, is given up, but only in order to gain along the new path an assured pleasure at a later time. But the endopsychic impression made by this substitution has been so powerful that it is reflected in a special religious myth. The doctrine of reward in the after-life for the—voluntary or enforced—renunciation of earthly pleasures is nothing other than a mythical projection of this revolution in the mind. Following consistently along these lines, *religions* have been able to effect absolute renunciation of pleasure in this life by means of the promise of compensation in a future existence; but they have not by this means achieved a conquest of the pleasure principle. It is *science* which comes nearest to succeeding in that conquest; science too, however, offers intellectual pleasure during its work and promises practical gain in the end.

(5) *Education* can be described without more ado as an incitement to the conquest of the pleasure principle, and to is replacement by the reality principle; it seeks, that is, to lend its help to the developmental process which affects the ego. To this end it makes use of an offer of love as a reward from the educators; and it therefore fails if a spoilt child thinks that it possesses that love in any case and cannot lose it whatever happens.

(6) *Art* brings about a reconciliation between the two principles in a peculiar way. An artist is originally a man who turns away from reality because he cannot come to terms with the renunciation of

instinctual satisfaction which it at first demands, and who allows his erotic and ambitious wishes full play in the life of phantasy. He finds the way back to reality, however, from this world of phantasy by making use of special gifts to mould his phantasies into truths of a new kind, which are valued by men as precious reflections of reality. Thus in a certain fashion he actually becomes the hero, the king, the creator, or the favourite he desired to be, without following the long round-about path of making real alterations in the external world. But he can only achieve this because other men feel the same dissatisfaction as he does with the renunciation demanded by reality, and because that dissatisfaction, which results from the replacement of the pleasure principle by the reality principle, is itself a part of reality.[15]

(7) While the ego goes through its transformation from a *pleasure-ego* into a *reality-ego*, the sexual instincts undergo the changes that lead them from their original auto-erotism through various intermediate phases to object-love in the service of procreation. If we are right in thinking that each step in these two courses of development may become the site of a disposition to later neurotic illness, it is plausible to suppose that the form taken by the subsequent illness (the *choice of neurosis*) will depend on the particular phase of the development of the ego and of the libido in which the dispositional inhibition of development has occurred. Thus unexpected significance attaches to the chronological features of the two developments (which have not yet been studied), and to possible variations in their synchronisation.[16]

(8) The strangest characteristic of unconscious (repressed) processes, to which no investigator can become accustomed without the exercise of great self-discipline, is due to their entire disregard of reality-testing; they equate reality of thought with external reality, and wishes with their fulfilment—with the event—just as happens automatically under the dominance of the ancient pleasure principle. Hence also the difficulty of distinguishing unconscious phantasies from memories which have become unconscious.[17] But one must never allow oneself to be misled into applying the standards of reality to repressed psychical structures, and on that account, perhaps, into undervaluing the importance of phantasies in

the formation of symptoms on the ground that they are not actualities, or into tracing a neurotic sense of guilt back to some other source because there is no evidence that any actual crime has been committed. One is bound to employ the currency that is in use in the country one is exploring—in our case a neurotic currency. Suppose, for instance, that one is trying to solve a dream such as this. A man who had once nursed his father through a long and painful mortal illness, told me that in the months following his father's death he had repeatedly dreamt that *his father was alive once more and that he was talking to him in his usual way. But he felt it exceedingly painful that his father had really died, only without knowing it.* The only way of understanding this apparently nonsensical dream is by adding "as the dreamer wished" or "in consequence of his wish" after the words "that his father had really died", and by further adding "that he [the dreamer] wished it" to the last words. The dream-thought then runs: it was a painful memory for him that he had been obliged to wish for his father's death (as a release) while he was still alive, and how terrible it would have been if his father had had any suspicion of it! What we have here is thus the familiar case of self-reproaches after the loss of someone loved, and in this instance the self-reproach went back to the infantile significance of death-wishes against the father.[18]

The deficiencies of this short paper, which is preparatory rather than expository, will perhaps be excused only in small part if I plead that they are unavoidable. In these few remarks on the psychical consequences of adaptation to the reality principle I have been obliged to adumbrate views which I should have preferred for the present to withhold and whose justification will certainly require no small effort. But I hope it will not escape the notice of the benevolent reader how in these pages too the dominance of the reality principle is beginning.

Notes

1. [The idea, with the phrase "flight into psychosis", is already to be found in Section III of Freud's first paper on "The Neuro-Psychoses of Defence" (1894a). The actual phrase "flight into illness" occurs in his paper on hysterical attacks (1909a), *P.F.L.*, **10**, 99 and 100 n.1.]

2. Janet, 1909.
3. [W. Griesinger (1817–68) was a well-known Berlin psychiatrist of an earlier generation, much admired by Freud's teacher, Meynert. The passage alluded to in the text is no doubt the one mentioned by Freud three times in *The Interpretation of Dreams* (1900a), *P.F.L.*, **4**, 163, 214 and 326 n., and again in Chapter VI of the book on jokes (1905c), ibid., **6**, 228. In this passage Griesinger (1845, 89) drew attention to the wish-fulfilling character of both psychoses and dreams.]
4. Otto Rank (1910) has recently drawn attention to a remarkably clear pre-vision of this causation shown in Schopenhauer's *The World as Will and Idea* [Volume 11 (Supplements), Chapter 32].
5. [This seems to be the first appearance of the actual term "pleasure principle". In *The Interpretation of Dreams* it is always named the "unpleasure principle" (e.g. *P.F.L.*, **4**, 759.]
6. In the General Section of *The Interpretation of Dreams* [i.e. in Chapter VII. See in particular *P.F.L.*, **4**, 718–21 and 757 ff.]
7. The state of sleep is able to re-establish the likeness of mental life as it was before the recognition of reality, because a prerequisite of sleep is a deliberate rejection of reality (the wish to sleep).
8. I will try to amplify the above schematic account with some further details. It will rightly be objected that an organisation which was a slave to the pleasure principle and neglected the reality of the external world could not maintain itself alive for the shortest time, so that it could not have come into existence at all. The employment of a fiction like this is, however, justified when one considers that the infant—provided one includes with it the care it receives from its mother—does almost realise a psychical system of this kind. It probably hallucinates the fulfilment of its internal needs; it betrays its unpleasure, when there is an increase of stimulus and an absence of satisfaction, by the motor discharge of screaming and beating about with its arms and legs, and it then experiences the satisfaction it has hallucinated. Later, as an older child, it learns to employ these manifestations of discharge intentionally as methods of expressing its feelings. Since the later care of children is modelled on the care of infants, the dominance of the pleasure principle can really come to an end only when a child has achieved complete psychical detachment from its parents. A neat example of a psychical system shut off from the stimuli of the external world, and able to satisfy even its nutritional requirements autistically (to use Bleuler's term [1912]}, is afforded by a bid's egg with its food supply enclosed in its shell; for it, the care provided by its mother is limited to the provision of warmth. I shall not regard it as a correction, but as an amplification of the schematic picture under discussion, if it is insisted

that a system living according to the pleasure principle must have devices to enable it to withdraw from the stimuli of reality. Such devices are merely the correlative of "repression", which treats internal unpleasurable stimuli as if they were external—that is to say, pushes them into the external world.

9. [Some remarks on Freud's views about attention will be found in an Editor's footnote to "The Unconscious" (SE Vol.11, p. 196).]

10. [This notion, often repeated by Freud, appears as early as in the first edition of his book on jokes (1905c, Chapter VI; *P.F.L.* **6**, 233 and n.2) and is examined more deeply in his late paper on "Negation" (1925h, SE Vol.11 p. 438. Cf also "The Unconscious" (1915e, ibid. p. 190).

11. [This important theory had been put forward by Freud in *The Interpretation of Dreams* (1900a), *P.F.L.* **4**, 758–9, and more clearly in *Jokes* (1905c), ibid., **6**, 251 and n 2, as well as in "Negation" (1925h), p. 440 and n.– below, where further references are given.]

12. [Cf. *The Interpretation of Dreams* (1900a), *P.F.L.*, **4**, 729–30, 771n and 779. This is further developed in Section VII of "The Unconscious" (1915e, SE. Vol.11, p. 208).

13. In the same way, a nation whose wealth rests on the exploitation of the produce of its soil will yet set aside certain areas for reservation in their original state and for protection from the changes brought about by civilisation. (E.g. Yellowstone Park.) [Cf. the discussions of phantasies in "Creative Writers and Day-Dreaming" (1908e), *P.F.L.*, **14**, 129, and in "Hysterical Phantasies and their Relation to Bisexuality" (1908a), *P.F.L.*, **10**, 87ff. The term *"Realitätsprüfung"* seems to make its first appearance in this sentence.]

14. The superiority of the reality-ego over the pleasure-ego has been aptly expressed by Bernard Shaw in these words: "To be able to choose the line of greatest advantage instead of yielding in the direction of least resistance." (*Man and Superman: A Comedy and a Philosophy*.) [A remark made by Don Juan towards the end of the Mozartean interlude in Act III. A much more elaborate account of the relations between the "pleasure-ego" and the "reality-ego" is given in "Instincts and their Vicissitudes" (1915c, SE 11, pp. 132–4.]

15. Cf the similar position taken by Otto Rank (1907). [See also "Creative Writers and Day-Dreaming" (1908e), *P.F.L.*, **14**, 129, as well as the closing paragraph of Lecture 23 of the *Introductory Lectures* (1916–17), *P.F.L.*, **1**, 423–4.]

16. [This theme is developed in "The Disposition to Obsessional Neurosis" (1913i), *P.F.L.*, **10**, 142 ff.]

17. [This difficulty is discussed at length in the later part of Lecture 23 of the *Introductory Lectures* (1916–17), *P.F.L.*, **1**, 414 ff.]

18. [This dream was added to the 1911 edition of *The Interpretation of Dreams* (1900a), *P.F.L.*, **4**, 559–60, soon after the publication of the present paper.]

CHAPTER TWO

Phantasy and its transformations: a contemporary Freudian view

Joseph Sandler and Anne-Marie Sandler

Now that half a century has passed since the Freud–Klein Controversies (reported by King & Steiner, 1991), we are in a position to look back and see that the controversies within the British Society are significantly different now from what they were then, although in a certain sense they are, of course, derivatives of the conflicts of the past. Inevitably, over the past 50 years the different groups in the Society have influenced one another, and there can be little doubt that much of the impetus for this cross-fertilisation has come from the systematic discussion of clinical material, with the fine details of psychoanalytic theory taking second place. So, for many members of the Contemporary Freudian group, much greater emphasis has been put, over the years, on the importance of the earliest internal influences on the child's development, on the existence of transference phantasies, anxieties and resistances from the outset of the analysis, and on the need for these to be interpreted from the beginning. In this context, the understanding of processes of projection and externalisation in the transference has been significantly appreciated. Similarly, in the Klein group, we have seen a decreased emphasis on the early interpretation of deep anxieties and, as Elizabeth Spillius (1988) has pointed out, less stress is being laid on destructiveness, there is less use of concrete part-object language, and a variety of other changes. To Spillius's list of changes we would add our impression that the concepts of defence mechanisms (as opposed to defensive phantasies), and of resistance, are beginning to be discerned in Kleinian presentations, just as the notion of projective identification can be seen in the writings of some members of the Independent and Contemporary Freudian groups.

The views of the object-relations theorists in the Group of Independent Analysts have certainly affected the thinking of many in the Contemporary Freudian group. It is now widely accepted that the psychoanalytic view of motivation cannot be simply reduced to sexual and aggressive drives or their derivatives, and the link between motivation—both conscious and unconscious—and the tie to the object has been given increasing importance. The work of Donald Winnicott has also had a profound effect on Freudian thinking about infant development and infant–mother relationships. We cannot comment on the changes which have occurred in the Group of Independent Analysts under the influence of the Contemporary Freudian and the Klein groups, although we have no doubt that they are significant. Our reason for saying this is that the Independent Group consists of analysts, each of whom wishes to be independent of the two other groups, and as a consequence the views of its members are very diverse.

However, in spite of all these changes, some fundamental differences between the groups remain. While we shall put what follows in mainly theoretical terms, the differences between us still reflect, as we see them, important differences in approach both to psychoanalytic theory and technique.

At a meeting of the British Society on 13 January 1943, as part of the "Controversial Discussions", Susan Isaacs presented her paper on "The nature and function of phantasy" (in King & Steiner, 1991). As we have heard, she pointed out in that paper that the meaning of the word "phantasy" had been extended over the preceding years. She concluded that "the psychoanalytical term 'phantasy' essentially connotes unconscious mental content, which may seldom or never become conscious", and went on to extend the concept of unconscious phantasy even further than before, to include practically every variety of unconscious mental content, both knowable and unknowable—an extension which was a central point of disagreement in the controversial discussions, as Anne Hayman has shown us in her excellent and comprehensive presentation at this Conference (Hayman, 1994).

The extension of psychoanalytic concepts beyond their original meaning has been a frequent occurrence in the history of psychoanalysis, and this can serve a useful function in the advancement of psychoanalytic thinking. Such concepts can be referred to as "elastic",[1] but elastic concepts can only be stretched up to a certain point before they snap. In our view, this has occurred in relation to unconscious phantasy, resulting in a number of conceptual and clinical problems, some of which we shall try to address today.

We may all be clear about the role and function of conscious phantasies or daydreams in our mental life, but the concept of unconscious phantasy has suffered from a major ambiguity in regard to the meaning of the term "unconscious". You will recall that in Freud's topographical theory of the mind a firm distinction was made between the systems Preconscious (Pcs) and Unconscious (Ucs). While the system Unconscious contained childhood libidinal wishes that had been repressed, and which were subject to primary process functioning, the Preconscious was seen as following quite different principles. Further, although the Preconscious was regarded as being the repository of thoughts, wishes and ideas which were able to be called into consciousness relatively freely, Freud also postulated a censorship between the Preconscious and Conscious systems, as well as attributing the capacity for reality-testing to the Preconscious (1915).

The existence of a censorship between the Preconscious and consciousness, in addition to the censorship between the system Unconscious and the Preconscious, was referred to by Freud on a number of occasions. In 1915 he spoke of "a new frontier of censorship", going on to say that

> the first of these censorships is exercised against the Ucs itself, and the second against its Pcs derivatives. One might suppose that in the course of individual development the censorship had taken a step forward ... in psychoanalytic treatment the existence of the second censorship, located between the systems Pcs and Cs, is proved beyond question (1915, p. 193).

Descriptively speaking, the Preconscious can be considered to be unconscious, although the two systems were regarded as being governed by completely different rules, and this has made things rather complicated. They were complicated still further by the introduction of the structural theory in 1923, when it became (and still is) common usage to refer to the id and the unconscious parts of the ego and superego as "the unconscious". All of this has contributed to the confusion surrounding the meaning of unconscious phantasy. In one sense, unconscious phantasy can be taken to refer to early phantasies of the child which had subsequently been repressed into the system Unconscious of the topographical theory, a system contrasted with the systems Preconscious and Conscious, distinguished from them by its functioning according to the primary process, and characterised by timelessness, by the equality of opposites, and so forth. On the other hand, unconscious phantasy can be preconscious phantasy, showing a degree of secondary-process thinking and awareness of reality. It is perhaps because of the widening gap between our clinical observations and current psychoanalytic theories that we still make use of the concept of the unconscious alongside our other concepts, and it is important to know that the meaning of this term changes according to the context in which it is used. What has happened is that the adjective "unconscious" has been transformed into a noun.[2] As a consequence, the conceptual distinction between the system Unconscious and the system Preconscious has tended to be lost, the two systems becoming confused; and this confusion is still to be found in the writings of some of our most distinguished psychoanalytic writers.[3]

Because it is inevitable that the term "unconscious" will continue to refer to "all that is unconscious", we need to find a way to distinguish between the two sorts of unconscious phantasy we have been discussing. What we want to put forward is a frame of reference that will allow us to make such a distinction, and to take into account the clinical observation that the products of preconscious functioning are themselves often subject to repression or are otherwise defended against and prevented from reaching consciousness. The best examples of such preconscious content being defended against are unconscious transference thoughts and phantasies, in which unconscious secondary-process thinking is certainly involved.

We hope that we have been able to make the point that there are two broad classes of unconscious phantasies, and we shall try to show that the distinction between the two is not only theoretically but also clinically relevant. As it is clear that the term "the unconscious" is here to stay, it seems convenient to make use of a distinction which we have elaborated in a number of previous papers (Sandler & Sandler, 1983), (1984), (1986). This is the distinction between the past unconscious and the present unconscious, and consequently a distinction between phantasies in the past unconscious and phantasies in the present unconscious.

Phantasies in the past unconscious are those which are believed to occur in the first years of life, and which can be thought of as existing behind the so-called repression barrier (i.e. behind Freud's "first censorship"). The repression barrier is responsible for the infantile amnesia, and we are all aware of how little can be remembered from the first four or five years of life. What we do remember or recall in analysis tends to be in the form of isolated fragments which have been revised in the process of later remembering—if they have coherence, this has usually been added later. In addition, much that is recalled from the first few years has been acquired second-hand. The phantasies of the past unconscious are constructs which are extremely important for our psycho-analytic work, but our conception of the past unconscious comes from reconstruction, and the phantasies we assume to exist in the past unconscious are our reconstructions based upon the patient's analytic material, on our interpretation of the past, interpretations which are rooted in our psychoanalytic theory of mental functioning and our theory of child development.[4]

That part of the unconscious which we can refer to as the present unconscious can be thought of as having a very different type of functional organisation, and is in many ways similar to the system Preconscious of Freud's topographical model. It is the realm of current unconscious subjective experience. Phantasies in the present unconscious—especially here-and-now unconscious transference phantasies—are much more accessible to our analytic work. As wishful impulses and phantasies arise in the present unconscious-phantasies which can be considered to be in part derivatives of the past unconscious—they have to be dealt with by the person of the present, by the adult part of the person. One can put it thus: "Whereas the past unconscious acts and reacts according to the past, the present unconscious is concerned with maintaining equilibrium in the present ..." (Sandler & Sandler, 1984, p. 372). These phantasy derivatives of the past can be regarded as being different in structure from the phantasies of early childhood, from the phantasies which date from before the construction of the repression barrier and the resulting infantile amnesia. The phantasies in the present unconscious are more closely linked with representations of present-day persons, and are subject to a higher level of unconscious secondary-process functioning. Thus it follows that unconscious transference phantasies exist in the present unconscious, not in the past unconscious.

The phantasies or impulses arising in the present unconscious, to the extent that they arouse conflict, disturb the equilibrium of the present unconscious and, accordingly, have to be dealt with outside consciousness, have to be modified, disguised or repressed. It is here that the whole range of the mechanisms of defence, and indeed all sorts of other compensatory mechanisms, come in. These mechanisms serve to disguise the unconscious wishful phantasy by means of manipulations of the self and object representations involved in the phantasy. Parts of the self representation involved will be split off and displaced to the object representation (projection and projective identification), and parts of the object representation absorbed into the representation of the self (a process analogous to identification). All this is a reflection of what has been called the stabilising function of unconscious phantasy. This function involves a response in the present unconscious to all sorts of affective disturbances of inner equilibrium, whatever the sources of these disturbances may be (Sandler, 1986): (Sandler & Sandler, 1986).

Although an unconscious phantasy may have been substantially modified within the present unconscious in order to render it less disruptive, its path to the surface, to conscious awareness, may be impeded by a resistance due to what has been referred to earlier in this paper as the "second censorship", that is, the censorship spoken of by Freud as existing between the systems Preconscious and Conscious. In the present frame of reference this has been located between the present unconscious and consciousness. This censorship has been described as having as its fundamental motivation the avoidance of conscious feelings of shame, embarrassment and humiliation. Developmentally, it can be linked first with the step of substituting conscious phantasising for play, and the need to keep such phantasies secret. What happens then has been described as follows:

> As the child develops the increasing capacity to anticipate the shaming and humiliating reactions of others (with all the additions he has made to his expectations arising from his own projections), so he will become his own disapproving audience and will continually internalise the social situation in the form of the second censorship. Only content that is acceptable will be permitted through to consciousness. It must be plausible and not ridiculous or "silly". In a way the second censorship is much more of a narcissistic censorship than the first, but the narcissism involved often tends to centre around fears of being laughed at, as being thought to be silly, crazy, ridiculous or childish—essentially fears of being humiliated (Sandler & Sandler, 1983, pp. 421–2).

A very simple—and much simplified—example of a patient in analysis with one of us (J. S.) may be useful to illustrate the points made in the paper in a very general way. A male patient came a few minutes late to his session and complained about the fact that his girlfriend had not permitted him to use his alarm clock to wake in time for his analysis because it work her as well, so he had woken late. He thought that she had been very selfish. He had taken a minicab to come to the analysis, but the car was very uncomfortable—the springs were bad, and the driver had driven over every pothole in the road. He then went on to tell the analyst how badly he had been treated by his employer. He had been given so much to do that he had to work late the previous evening, and his employer didn't seem to care about his well-being at all. The employer had work which he had to do himself, but had at the last moment left it to the patient to do. He would complain at work but didn't want to lose his job. (These associations were, of course, those which the patient had permitted to enter his consciousness and could report in the analysis.) The analyst then commented that perhaps the patient was also angry with him for having mentioned on the previous day the dates when he would be taking his holiday. The analyst reminded him of how surprised the patient had been that analysis was stopping earlier than expected, and suggested that he was in conflict about his anger with the analyst because he thought that the analyst would get angry and replace him with another patient. On the other hand, he resented his not being allowed to fix the dates just as he resented his girlfriend not allowing him to use an alarm clock. He must have been feeling that the analyst was giving him a rough ride, just as the minicab driver did, but perhaps in fact he wanted to make things rough for the analyst in order to get even. (This interpretation was directed towards the underlying current unconscious transference phantasy that the analyst was treating him badly and to the wish to retaliate). The patient fell silent for a minute and then exploded with anger. "You're damn right", he said, "you boss me about, telling me when I can come and when I can't". He proceeded to elaborate on this theme, saying how times should be arranged to suit his own needs, but ending with the comment that the analyst would probably throw him out because he had been so rude. Days later, it was possible to reconstruct what had gone on in the transference in terms of the patient's interaction with his father during the oedipal period, and after some months we could trace this pattern to a significantly earlier aspect of his relationship with his mother.

We want to emphasise the need to interpret what is most dominant and affectively-laden in the present unconscious rather than to talk about the past. The patient was in resistance due to his transference conflict in the here-and-now, and it was this conflict which had to be interpreted. Reconstruction of the past, i.e. of the past unconscious, is more appropriate once the resistances in the here-and-now have been analysed. In the present instance, the patient had not been able to allow into his consciousness the transference phantasy which was active in his present unconscious (that the analyst was giving him a rough time), but had defensively displaced it in his associations on to his employer and the cab driver. This defensive displacement was much more consciousness-syntonic than the unconscious transference thoughts. Later it was also possible to see, through the transference-countertransference interaction, how he had almost certainly had a hand in provoking both his employer and his girlfriend into acting as they did.[5]

Our purpose in presenting this rather ordinary fragment of analysis was simply to illustrate the conceptual difference between the past and present unconsciouses, and the clinical value of making this particular theoretical differentiation. However, we also wanted to lay the ground for concluding this paper by referring briefly to a concept mentioned earlier, that is, the stabilising function of unconscious phantasy.[6]

The products of the stabilising function of unconscious phantasy may, of course, find their way into consciousness, modified to a greater or lesser extent by the second censorship, and can show themselves as any type of derivative. (The derivative of the censored phantasy in the present unconscious need not necessarily be in the form of a conscious daydream or free associations in analysis.) But, in any case, in order to pass the second censorship, the products of the stabilising function have to be modified further—must have to undergo a sort of secondary revision—in order to be made plausible, non-silly, non-stupid (except in specially-licensed forms such as dreams and humour).

In the very active work that occurs continuously in the present unconscious, a great deal of phantasy dialogue is involved. This dialogue can be said to be with one's introjects (Sandler & Sandler, 1978), but more precisely, they are dialogues in phantasy with the representatives of one's introjects in one's unconscious phantasy life.[7]

The central point in the "stabilising" or "gyroscopic" regulation of unconscious phantasy is the maintenance of safety and well-being in the face of disruptive urges of various kinds (Sandler, 1986); (Sandler & Sandler 1986). What is organised into the form of unconscious phantasy we are describing serves the function of creating and maintaining a feeling of self-preservation. In doing this, defences are used in relation to the self and object representations involved in the phantasy. These defences may be all sorts of projections, identifications and projective identifications, displacements, externalisations, as well as reversals of one kind or another.

It would appear that the extent to which this occurs only began to be realised in the mid-1930s with the analysis of those resistances in which defensive displacement between self and object representations occurred in the general context of transference. Anna Freud had written of combined projection and identification in so-called altruistic surrender—living through another—and of identification with the aggressor as a defence, in The Ego and the Mechanisms of Defence in 1936. Then, in 1946, Melanie Klein put forward her concept of projective identification. Although the latter concept has been used in an extremely broad way, we have all become more aware of the defences that make use of displacements between self and object representations. It is these displacements that will occur in the process of creating unconscious stabilising phantasies that restore the person's feeling of cohesion and of integrity of the self.

Finally, it should be said that one thing is certain about the concept of unconscious phantasy, whether we use it as introduced by Freud or in some modified form: psychoanalysis cannot do without it.

Notes

1. In writing on the value of the elasticity of certain psychoanalytic concepts, I (J.S.) suggested that "Elastic concepts play a very important part in holding psychoanalytic theory together. As psychoanalysis is made up of formulations at various levels of abstraction, and of part-theories which do not integrate well with one another, the existence of pliable, context-dependent concepts allows an overall framework of psychoanalytic theory to be spelled out, but can only articulate with similar part-theories if they are not tightly connected, if the concepts which form the joints are flexible ... The elastic and flexible concepts take up the strain of theoretical change, absorbing it while more organised newer theories can develop" (Sandler, 1983, p. 36).
2. In Freud's last work, An Outline of Psycho-Analysis, published just three years before the controversial discussions, he remarked, "The theory of the three qualities of what is psychical [he refers here to the qualities unconscious, preconscious and conscious] ... seems likely to be a source of limitless confusion rather than a help towards clarification" (1940, p. 161).
3. One of the factors fostering the tendency to absorb the notion of the unconscious ego and superego of the structural theory into the notion of "the unconscious" is the fact that Freud's structural theory did not succeed in completely and successfully relacing the topographical model (in spite of the claims of the "ego psychologists").
4. In this conception the past unconscious represents more than the person's id or the system Unconscious of the topographical model. Inasmuch as it represents "the child within" (Sandler, 1984) it can be regarded as far more developmentally complex, involving age-appropriate (but at best preoperational) secondary processes as well as primary process functioning.
5. This provocation could be called a form of projective identification, but

my own view is that the term should be used specifically for the provocative externalisation of a split-off aspect of the self representation (rather than an aspect of the object representation) for purposes of defence.

6. In an earlier publication (Sandler & Sandler, 1986) this was referred to as the "gyroscopic" function of unconscious phantasy. This section draws on material published there and in a further paper (Sandler, 1986).

7. There is always a pressure to anchor the phantasies in the present unconscious in reality. In some way we try to actualise our unconscious wishful phantasies (Sandler, 1976a), (1976b), but we need to do this in a way which is plausible to us. We make extensive use of what is perhaps the most overworked function of the mental apparatus, i.e. rationalisation, in order to make our implausible actions plausible to ourselves and to others. We have to anchor, to externalise, to fit our unconscious phantasies into reality in one way or another. In this context "psychotic" phantasies do not represent the direct emergence of the past unconscious, but rather the fact that the psychotic (or borderline) patient's style of rationalisation and vision of reality, as well as his understanding of the way other people's minds function, are different from and alien to our own as a consequence of impaired or deviant reality-testing.

References

Freud, A. (1936). *The Ego and the Mechanisms of Defence*. London: Hogarth Press.

Freud, S. (1915). The unconscious. *S.E., 14*.

Freud, S. (1923). *The Ego and the Id. S.E., 19*.

Freud, S. (1940). *An Outline of Psycho-Analysis. S.E., 23*.

Hayman, A. (1994). Some remarks about the Controversial Discussions. *Int. J. Psychoanal., 75*: 345–361.

Isaacs, S. (1943). The nature and function of phantasy. In: P. King & R. Steiner (Eds), *The Freud-Klein Controversies: 1941–45* (pp. 264–321). London & New York: Routledge, 1991.

King, P., & Steiner, R. (Eds) (1991). *The Freud-Klein Controversies: 1941–45*. London & New York: Routledge.

Klein, M. (1946). Notes on some schizoid mechanisms. *Int. J. Psychoanal., 27*: 99–110.

Sandler, J. (1976a). Dreams, unconscious fantasies and "identity of perception". *Int. J. Psychoanal., 3*: 33–42.

Sandler, J. (1976b). Countertransference and role-responsiveness. *Int. J. Psychoanal.*, *3*: 43–47.

Sandler, J. (1983). Reflections on some relations between psychoanalytic concepts and psychoanalytic practice. *Int. J. Psychoanal.*, *64*: 35–45.

Sandler, J. (1984). The id—or the child within. In: J. Sandler (Ed.), *Dimensions of Psychoanalysis*. London: Karnac.

Sandler, J. (1986). Reality and the stabilising function of unconscious fantasy. *Bulln. Anna Freud Centre*, *9*: 177–194.

Sandler, J., & Sandler, A.-M. (1978). On the development of object relationships and affects. *Int. J. Psychoanal.*, *59*: 285–296.

Sandler, J., & Sandler, A.-M. (1983). The "second censorship", the "three box model" and some technical implications. *Int. J. Psychoanal.*, *64*: 413–425.

Sandler, J., & Sandler, A. (1984). The past unconscious, the present unconscious, and interpretation of the transference. *Psychoanal. Inq.*, *4*: 367–399.

Sandler, J., & Sandler, A.-M. (1986). The gyroscopic function of unconscious fantasy. In: D. B. Feinsilver (Ed.), *Towards a Comprehensive Model for Schizophrenic Disorders*. Hillsdale, NJ: The Analytic Press.

Sandler, J., & Sandler, A.-M. (1987). The past unconscious, the present unconscious and the vicissitudes of guilt. *Int. J. Psychoanal.*, *68*: 331–341.

Spillius, E. B. (Ed.) (1988). *Melanie Klein Today: Vol. 2, Mainly Practice*. London & New York: Routledge.

CHAPTER THREE

Do unconscious phantasies really exist?[1]

Mark Solms

I n psychoanalysis today, different analysts use the term "unconscious phantasy" to refer to different things. This is bound to lead to confusion. In this paper I will use the term in the sense that Melanie Klein and her followers used it—with the aim of clarifying *from a Freudian point of view* what this thing that they call "unconscious phantasy" actually is, and whether it really exists.

"Do unconscious phantasies really exist?" This is not an idle question. When we use the word "phantasy", we do so in order to contrast it with something that we call "reality". That is the conventional meaning of the word "phantasy". We say: that thing is not real, it is only a phantasy. But unconscious phantasy is also supposed to be the basic stuff of what psychoanalysis is about. Unconscious phantasies (in the Kleinian sense of the term) are the essential object of study of psychoanalytic research; and a principle aim of psychoanalytic therapy is to make our patients aware of the unconscious phantasies that lead them to do and feel the things that bring them into treatment in the first place.

Clearly, if phantasies are not real things, then everything that we do in this field makes little sense. But what do we mean when we say that something is not real? How exactly do we decide whether something is real or not?

To begin with, when we say that phantasies are not real, we mean that they don't have a *physical* existence in the world around us. In other words, we mean that we can't see them or hear them or touch them. If we can see or hear or touch something and, better still, smell it and taste it, too, then we have little doubt about its reality; if not, its reality is brought into question. So one criterion for deciding whether something is real or not is: if we can *perceive* it through one or more of our external sensory modalities, then it really exists. I will call this our first criterion of reality.

This simple, conventional criterion is complicated by the fact that some people see and hear things that nobody else can see or hear. In these cases, we say that there is something *wrong* with their sense of reality. We don't call their perceptions "perceptions", we call them "hallucinations". Accordingly, hallucinations, being something "not real", are included under the heading of phantasy. The first criterion of reality therefore stands; we can still maintain that only things that we actually perceive really exist. But we need to add a second, qualifying criterion: we must say that something is real if, first of all, you can actually perceive it, and, in addition, *everyone else can perceive it, too.*

But what about introspective perceptions? What about emotions, for example—the purest form of internal perception. Aren't they real? If you learn that you have won the National Lottery, and you feel an exquisite sense of joy, is that not something real? Nobody can seriously deny that things like "joy" really exist, even if a feeling of joy is not accessible to public scrutiny. You may be the only one who can actually feel your own sense of joy, but that doesn't make it a hallucination. Clearly we must concede that emotional feelings, too, are perceptions. They, too, refer to something real, notwithstanding the fact that they are introspective perceptions—that is to say, conscious perceptions of a type that other people around us cannot share. And the same applies to memories.

This obviously undermines my second criterion of reality. I said that things that you can perceive and everybody around you can also perceive deserve to be described as real. We therefore need to modify further the criteria of reality, in order to take account of the phenomenological reality of internal perceptions. In doing so we immediately come to the nub of some of the most difficult theoretical problems that we confront in psychoanalysis. We have to draw a distinction between *two kinds of reality*. We have to say that there are things that we perceive in the external world around us, through our external sensory modalities (such as vision and hearing), and, in addition, we have to say that there are other things that we perceive within our own selves, through our internal sensory modalities (such as our emotions and memories). These things are equally real, even though only the externally perceived ones are reliably available to public scrutiny. We distinguish between these two things by speaking of *external* as opposed to *internal* reality.

Freud found a place for this basic distinction in the way that we perceive the world in his theoretical model of the mind by saying that *consciousness registers perceptions on two sensory surfaces*. One perceptual surface of consciousness is externally directed and registers reality in the form of material objects (through our external sensory modalities), whereas the other perceptual surface is internally directed and registers reality in a psychical form (through internal sensory modalities). This is the basis of Freud's fundamental theoretical distinction between what he called "material reality" on the one hand and "psychical reality" on the other. This theoretical distinction runs through every subsequent psychoanalytic model of the mind, right up to the present day, notwithstanding all of the disagreements in regard to other matters that have sprung up along the way. For example, Wilfred Bion, who in some respects is far removed theoretically from Freud, reserved a central place in his model of the mind for the distinction between what he called "reality sensual" and "reality psychic".

In accordance with this fundamental theoretical distinction, which does little more than formalize our ordinary, everyday experience, we need to specify the *origin* of a perception before we know what we really mean when we say that it is real. If a perception is stimulated from the outside, and therefore is registered on the external sensory surface of consciousness, we say that it is *materially* real; whereas if the perception is stimulated from inside, and therefore is registered on the internal surface of consciousness, we say that it is *psychically* real. This matter of the origin of a perception clarifies the earlier complication that was raised by the problem of hallucinations. Although they appear subjectively to have their origin in the outside world, hallucinations actually have their origin within us. They are only psychically real. This is where the mechanism that we call "reality testing" comes in; it determines the origin of a perception, and—all being well—thereby classifies it as internal or external.

So the fundamental psychoanalytic concept of a "psychical reality" is completely synonymous with the concept of "inner reality" or an "internal world". The term "psychical reality" simply refers to the portion of reality that exists within us, the portion that we perceive by looking inwards, as opposed to the "material reality" that we perceive by looking outwards. The term "psychical reality" is therefore also synonymous with *subjective* as opposed to *objective* reality. Psychical reality exists within the subject, and is perceived in the intangible form of thoughts and feelings, whereas material reality exists outside of the subject, and is perceived in the tangible form of physical things (objects).

This distinction makes an enormous difference. Consider, for example, the difference between an external perception such as the objective perception of an alarm clock, and an internal perception such as the subjective feeling of depression. Because, as I said earlier, our external perceptions are shared by the people around us, we can all agree that something out there in the world at this point in time is indeed an alarm clock. In other words, we can all agree that it is not an hallucination. But who is to decide whether a feeling of depression that you perceive when you wake up one morning is an accurate perception of the things that are currently going on inside you? It is problematical to say that one person's feeling of depression is real whereas another person's depression is an hallucination.

With some modifications, the same applies to memories. If the two sole witnesses to an event recall that event completely differently, how do we decide whose memory is real? Here we have the essence of the current controversy about so-called "false memories". That controversy revolves around precisely the distinction that I am drawing here, between material (or objective) reality and psychical (or subjective) reality; that is, it revolves around the distinction between things that we believe to be real because we see them in front of us, and things that we believe to be real because we feel them inside ourselves. That is why I am saying that this distinction brings us to the nub of some of the most difficult theoretical problems that we confront in psychoanalysis.

Rather than deny the reality of things such as depression, we in psychoanalysis have attempted to incorporate them into our picture of the natural world. As I have said, we have done so by proposing (with Freud) that consciousness has two perceptual surfaces, one of which is directed outward and registers the world around us in the form of material objects, while the other is directed inward and registers the world within us in a psychical form. Just as physical scientists study the things that are perceived on the outer surface of consciousness, psychoanalysts study the things that are perceived on the inner surface of consciousness. On this basis, we proceed in the same way as any other science would in relation to any other object of study. We attempt to formulate a coherent understanding of the law-governed processes that organize our introspective perceptions, using appropriate methods. In so doing, we attempt to lay bare the natural processes that lie behind our internal perceptions, ultimately in order to be able to intervene in those processes, and thereby alter the quality of life (that is, the subjective experiences) of people who are troubled by them.

Although at first sight this seems to be an obvious and straightforward way to proceed, in fact it gives rise to some extremely difficult problems. The most important of them is this: when I say that the reality around us is represented on the external perceptual surface of consciousness, whereas the reality within us is represented on its internal perceptual surface, what do I actually mean by "the reality within us"? I have indicated that I mean by this phrase the internal processes that generate our thoughts and feelings. But isn't it *bodily* processes, and specifically *brain* processes, that generate our internal perceptions? And doesn't that imply that the "reality within us" is, in fact, the physical reality of the body and the brain? And if it is true that the reality within us is the physical reality of the brain—which is a reality that can be seen and touched just like any other physical object—then why did Freud find it necessary to postulate the spooky thing called "psychical reality", and make it the fundamental object of study of a whole new branch of science? This attitude to the reality within us (namely, that it is a part of the physical world) is held by a good many serious and thoughtful medical and scientific colleagues, who choose to study and treat things like emotions and hallucinations by way of physical entities like neurotransmitters.

In order to understand why psychoanalysts have chosen instead to postulate a "psychical reality", we must return to the observations that led us to postulate its existence in the first place. We started from the observation that our perceptions of the world included things like joy and depression, which have particular perceptual qualities. We observed, in addition, that perceptions of this type can only arise from within our own selves. We cannot hear or touch depression, we can only feel it within ourselves. Other things, such as alarm clocks, the sounds they make and the colours they assume, also have particular perceptual qualities—which we can only perceive through our external sensory organs. The sound of an alarm clock is quite unlike an emotion, and we can never feel the colour green arising from within us.[2] These self-evident observations reflect a basic fact about reality and the way that we perceive it. We can only perceive the world in a limited variety of ways, which correspond to the limited properties of our different sensory modalities—the sense of vision and touch and so on. Each of those modalities arises from a sensory apparatus which occupies a fixed position in space. For this reason, it is in the nature of the modality called vision, for example, that it can only perceive processes that are external to the subject; and it is in the nature of the modality called emotion that it can only perceive processes that are internal to the subject. Moreover, it is in the nature of the modality called vision that it can only represent the things it perceives in a particular way, that is, within the qualitative range that is appropriate to the visual sensory apparatus. In other words, it can only represent things in the form of light, colour, orientation, and so on. No matter what the actual properties might be of the thing that exists out there in the world, the visual modality can only represent that thing in a visual form, in the form of visual images.

Similarly, it is in the nature of the modality called emotion that it can only represent the things that it perceives in a particular way, that is, within the qualitative range that is appropriate to the emotional apparatus. In other words, it can only represent things in the form of pleasure and unpleasure and so on. No matter what the actual properties might be of the things that exist deep within us, the emotional modality can only represent them in an emotional form, in the form of emotional states.

Let me illustrate these principles by way of a simple example. If you place an alarm clock in front of somebody, he can see, hear, and touch it, and, if he wants to, he can smell and taste it, too. Each of his external sensory modalities registers a different aspect of the alarm clock, and represents it in its own particular way. As a result, the person doing the perceiving has five different representations of the thing that he calls an alarm clock. In accordance with convention, he would think of the alarm clock itself as being a combination of these five representations of it. But this is not strictly correct. Strictly speaking, it would be more correct for him to say that the alarm clock *itself* can never be perceived directly. The alarm clock itself is the *origin* of his five perceptual images of it; but it is not the images themselves. All that we can ever know about the alarm clock is the different perceptual *representations* of it that are generated by our five senses. If we had additional senses, we might be able to perceptually represent other properties of the alarm clock itself, and our image of what an alarm clock actually is might be completely different.

But we have to make do with what we have got; and on this basis we piece together our picture of the natural world by making inferences from our incomplete and untrustworthy perceptual representations of it; we attempt to know its real underlying properties. Of course, since we all do this all of the time, we do it without even realizing it. But when it comes to *scientific* observations we have to be more precise about what we really can and cannot know. That is why when a physicist, for example, looks at an alarm clock, or at one of its components, such as the quartz crystal that drives it, he is not content with a phenomenological description of its superficial, perceptual properties. Instead, he wants to know what *lies behind* the perceptual attributes of the object under examination. To this end, he makes use of artificial aids, such as electron microscopes, which extend the efficiency of his sense organs to the farthest possible extent, and he concludes that what *appears* to be a solid body of quartz is in fact made up of invisible entities, such as waves and energies, which possess certain fundamental properties and occupy certain relative positions.

Consider for a moment what all of this means for our attempts to define reality. I said previously that the first criterion for determining the reality of something depended upon whether or not we can actually perceive it. Now we have to significantly revise that criterion once again. We have to admit that it is not the things we perceive that are ultimately real, but rather the things that lie at the *origin* of our perceptions, the things that *lie behind* the perceptions. Moreover, the fundamental properties of those things can never be perceived directly, since we can never free ourselves from the decisive influence of the apparatus which is interposed *between* them and our perceptions of what we finally perceive. We can, therefore, only ever *infer* the fundamental properties of reality. We can never actually *perceive* them.

Not surprisingly, all of this applies to internal perceptions just as much as it does to external ones. We are capable of representing the things that occur inside of us in different ways, depending on the sensory channels that are used for that purpose. Something that is going on in the depths of our selves can be represented visually if we look at it, or it can be represented emotionally if we feel it. Whether we see or feel the thing that is occurring inside us simply depends on which perceptual modality we use to represent it. Thus one and the same thing—depression, for example—can be perceived as a subjective emotional state from one point of view and an objective chemical imbalance from another. If it is perceived through an internally directed perceptual modality (and registered on the inner surface of consciousness) it is a feeling state, whereas if it is perceived through an externally directed modality (and registered on the outer surface of consciousness) it is a material process.

In this respect the difference between our inner and outer perceptions is just the same as the differences between the various external sensory modalities. If one listens to something, one obtains one type of image of it, and if one looks at the same thing, one obtains a different type of image of it. Both images are perceptions of something real, although neither image is the underlying reality itself. However, given the fixed spatial orientation of the different sensory modalities, it so happens that one can only perceive one's *own* feeling states as feeling states, whereas the visual equivalent of those feelings, which take the form of neurochemical processes, can be scrutinized publicly. That is, the internal representation of your current inner state (your feelings) can be perceived by you alone, whereas the external representation of that same state (your neurochemistry) can be perceived by others around you. That is why we classify psychical perceptions (like memories and feelings) under the heading of internal reality, and material perceptions (like brains and chemicals) under the heading of external reality.

I will not delve into the complication introduced by the fact that we can *indirectly* perceive the feelings of another person as feelings in ourselves, by means of an intriguing process called "empathy". This process forms the basis of the modern concept of counter-transference, and suggests a surprisingly literal basis for the notion of a *"sixth sense"*. We become aware of aspects of our patients' experience by directing our attention *inwards*. This underlines the fact that the internal perspective on reality occupies a fixed position in space; feelings (including those belonging to other people) can only be felt internally.

Two important implications flow from all this. One is that the feeling of depression and the neurochemical process that corresponds to it are in fact two different perceptual representations of *the same underlying thing*. The other is that the unitary underlying thing that generates both of these perceptual realizations is in fact *neither* an emotional feeling *nor* a visual image. Behind both the emotional feeling of depression and the visual image of the chemical process that corresponds to it, there lies something else, *something which is independent of our perceptual modalities*, and which can, in itself, never be perceived directly. Our conscious perceptions of this underlying reality are, and can only be, indirect representations of it. In other words, behind the different varieties of conscious perception there lies the actual stuff of reality, which is in itself non-perceptual, and therefore *unconscious*.

This has significant implications for psychoanalysis. It implies that the things that we study in psychoanalysis are in fact the very same things that are studied by our colleagues in the neurological sciences. The differences between these disciplines arise only from the fact that they use different perceptual channels to study that unitary underlying thing. Psychoanalysts study the workings of the mind through internally directed perceptual channels, whereas our colleagues in the neurological sciences study it through externally directed channels. Each of these two approaches to the underlying reality of the mind has strengths and weaknesses of its own, and these derive directly from the functional properties and spatial orientations of the perceptual channels upon which they depend. In relation to the problem that we are considering it is essential for us to recognize the inescapable conclusion that the things that we study in psychoanalysis are *no less real* in themselves than the things that are studied by neuroscientists. It is only our perceptual vantage points that are different. The underlying reality is the same. And this is the reality that we study in psychoanalysis.

The following short passage is from Freud's posthumously published essay entitled *An Outline of Psycho-Analysis*, in which he rather beautifully summarizes the points that I have just been making:

> In our science as in the others the problem is the same: behind the attributes (qualities) of the object under examination which are presented directly to our perception, we have to discover something else which is more independent of the particular receptive capacity of our sense-organs and which approximates more closely to what may be supposed to be the real state of affairs. We have no hope of being able to reach the latter itself, since it is evident that everything new that we have inferred must nevertheless be translated back into the language of our perceptions, from which it is simply impossible to free ourselves. But herein lies the very nature and limitation of our science. It is as though we were to say in physics: "If we could see clearly enough we should find that what appears to be a solid body is made up of particles of such and such a shape and size occupying such and such relative positions." In the meantime we try to increase the efficiency of our sense-organs to the farthest possible extent by artificial aids; but it may be expected that all such efforts will fail to affect the ultimate outcome. Reality in itself will always remain "unknowable". [Freud, 1940 [1938], p. 196]

So that is the psychoanalytic method. It is an artificial aid which increases the efficiency of our internally directed perceptions to the farthest possible extent—just like the microscope does for the externally directed modality of vision—and it thereby enables us to perceive as clearly and accurately as possible the actual things that exist within us. But still the picture that we are left with is incomplete and untrustworthy, and still it is limited by the fundamental parameters of internal perception, from which it is simply impossible to free ourselves.

Before I pull the strands of my argument together, in order to clarify its implications for the problem of unconscious phantasy, I would like to take stock of the picture that has emerged so far. One way of studying the internal workings of the human mind is to examine it in the form in which it is represented materially, through our external perceptual apparatus—that is, as an anatomical phenomenon. Another way of studying the internal workings of the human mind is to examine it as it is represented psychically, through our internal perceptual apparatus, in the form of our subjective awareness. Either way, the thing that we are studying is entirely real. The scientific limitations that we face arise from the fact that we can only study that real thing *indirectly*, by way of the incomplete and untrustworthy images of which our perceptual modalities are capable. *We in psychoanalysis study the human mind from the vantage point of subjective perception. We do this because that is where our patients locate their suffering, and because that is the perceptual window on the reality of the human being that science has hitherto neglected.* If you think about the relationship between our perceptions of reality and reality itself, and liken this situation to the tale about the blind men and the elephant, then I am sure you will agree that there are significant advantages to be gained from studying the underlying reality within us from as many different vantage points as possible.

When Freud first began to study this portion of reality from the vantage point of introspective awareness, around 100 years ago, we obtained our initial bearings by relying on a simple map of our subject matter—which did little more than formalize the starting points of our investigation and attach scientific names to them. We pictured the mind as a compound apparatus, the most superficial portion of which was the inner surface of consciousness, which registered the processes going on within the mind in the form of subjective perceptions. Freud called this superficial surface the "system Conscious", and he called the hidden interior the "system Unconscious". These names signify the fundamental difference between the two systems—namely, that one of them cannot be perceived. With this simple map, he set about the arduous task of trying to infer what the properties of the hidden, unconscious reality of the mind must be in order for it to generate the manifest, conscious perceptions that it does. One of the first things that struck him in this regard was the fact that our subjective conscious perceptions—unlike our visual perceptions, for example—formed incomplete sequences, which were causally discontinuous. He therefore decided to study these breaks in the causal sequence, in order to isolate their typical antecedents and consequences. On this basis, he attempted to reconstruct the missing links in the psychical chain. His aim was to gain some impression of the *complete* sequence of underlying mental events.

In doing so, he was driven to conclude that the breaks in the sequence of perception did not occur randomly: he observed, for example, that the missing bits tended to be unpleasant, from the viewpoint of the perceiving subject. He also observed that whenever he tried to fill in the gaps by communicating the missing bits to the perceiving subject, the thoughts and feelings in question were immediately ejected once more from perceptual awareness. Freud called this clinical phenomenon "resistance". On this basis, he began to construct a theoretical picture of what the functional properties of the underlying processes must be. He observed, for example, that the underlying processes functioned according to a basic principle whereby all psychical material that was likely to arouse unpleasurable thoughts and feelings was kept away from consciousness. Freud called this the "pleasure principle". Next he inferred that there must be a mechanism whereby this process of selective exclusion is achieved. He called this mechanism "repression". Then Freud looked at the exceptions to the rule that he had established; that is, he looked at the unpleasurable thoughts that *did* manage to enter perceptual awareness. This led him to distinguish between what he called the "primary and secondary processes" of the underlying apparatus (only the primary process obeys the pleasure principle exclusively). Proceeding in this way, piece by piece, and by continually revising his map, Freud gradually built up an extremely elaborate picture of how the underlying mental apparatus functioned. That is to say, he constructed a theoretical picture of what the perceptually unknowable reality must be that generates our subjective awareness.

According to that picture, the ultimate origins of the processes that end in subjective awareness are two fundamental biological forces, which ultimately cause the organism to react in all the different ways that it does in relation to the stimuli that impinge upon it. Freud called these the Life and Death "drives". These drives can never be perceived directly; they are theoretical entities, which we assume to be the fundamental properties of the uncon-scious—that is, of the unperceivable, underlying reality within us.

Between these fundamental drives and the superficial awareness of our thoughts and feelings lie a great many complex mechanisms, some of which I have already mentioned, such as reality-testing, repression, the pleasure principle, and the primary and secondary processes. Mechanisms such as these, which mediate between the innermost drives of the subject and the myriad stimuli that impinge upon it, are responsible for the great complexity of mental life.

I have said that the basic mechanisms of the mental apparatus which Freud inferred from the data of subjective awareness, such as those that I have just mentioned, are assumed to be the fundamental properties of the portion of reality that exists within us. These mech-anisms can also be studied from an anatomical or a physiological viewpoint; that is to say, they can also be studied via external perceptual channels, as physical things. But we in psychoanalysis do not do that; rather, we study them from the vantage point of the introspective portion of the perceptual apparatus. The important point is that even though all of these underlying processes are—in themselves—no less unconscious and unperceivable than the drives are, and can therefore never be known directly, they are, never-theless, the fundamental reality within us. That is to say, they are the ultimate origin of all our introspective perceptions. In this respect, they have the same status in psychoanalysis as things like waves and energies have in physics. Our knowledge of the internal reality within us ultimately consists of these theoretical things. And nothing could be more real than these things, even though our knowledge of them is far from secure.

We are approaching the heart of the matter. In recognition of the fact that we can never directly perceive those things that generate our internal perceptions, we in (Freudian) psychoanalysis have traditionally described them in abstract, non-experiential terms. When Freud invented his abstract, mechanistic language, known as metapsychology, he was attempting to describe the unknowable depths of the mind in a language that was—in the words of the quotation on p. 98 above—as far as possible "independent of the particular receptive capacity of our sense organs". The aim of doing this was, to quote Freud again, to "approximat[e] more closely to what may be supposed to be the real state of affairs". In other words, Freud used an abstract, non-experiential language in his descriptions of the hidden depths of the mind, in an admittedly futile attempt to escape what he called "the language of perception".

I say "admittedly futile", because it is in fact impossible to free ourselves from the language of perception. In other words, Freud's metapsychological language, too, inevitably relied upon perceptual images; that is why he so frequently had recourse to figurative analogies. As a result, we, the readers of these abstract, mechanical descriptions of the mind's internal workings, inevitably form images in our minds of the apparatus that Freud was describing. This was the origin of the all too common tendency of classical psychoanalysts to reify their concepts. There has been a pernicious tendency to think of the human mental apparatus as though it really were a machine. But the mind is not a machine; it is in itself—that is to say, in reality—something of which we are totally unable to form a picture. It is, in its essence, unperceivable. For that reason, we can describe it in many different ways. Some post-Freudian analysts, like Bion and Ignacio Matte-Blanco, for example, have endeavoured to render the mind in an even more abstract language than Freud did, and have relied upon quasi-mathematical descriptions. Other analysts, like Melanie Klein and after her Herbert Rosenfeld, Hanna Segal in particular, have taken a different tack. I am not sure to what extent she did so deliberately, but starting in the 1920s and 1930s, Melanie Klein gradually began to describe the inner workings of the mental apparatus *as if they were subjective experiences.*

This is what unconscious phantasy (in the sense that Melanie Klein used that term) actually is. *It is an attempt to describe the very same processes that Freud attempted to describe (in abstract, mechanistic terms), in the language of personal experience.* The living theatre of unconscious phantasy is nothing more and nothing less than a different way of depicting the unperceivable events that occur within the portion of reality that ultimately generates our subjective states of awareness.

This new way of depicting the mental apparatus has some advantages over the classical approach. There was an uncomfortable hiatus between Freud's descriptions of his clinical observations and his metapsychological explanations of them. In order to move from the one level of analysis to the other, it was necessary for the analyst to effect a translation from the language of personal experience into the language of scientific abstraction. I have already mentioned why Freud considered this translation to be necessary: he wanted to "discover something else which is more independent of the particular receptive capacity of our sense-organs and which approximates more closely to what may be supposed to be the real state of affairs". But Melanie Klein's approach had the advantage of being able to explain the patient's subjective experiences in a language that did not differ fundamentally from the language of the experiences themselves. This was a language that the patient himself could immediately identify with. As a result, the analyst could put his metapsychological inferences about what the patient was saying and doing directly to the patient, in the same language that the patient himself was using to depict his lived experiences. And, moreover, the analyst could later communicate exactly the same inferential descriptions to his colleagues, and in this way assimilate them directly into theory, without having to effect the unwelcome translations that I mentioned a moment ago. The effect was instantaneous; it was as if, suddenly, the unconscious had come to life. Where previously there were energies and forces and structures and the like, now there were simply experiences (extraordinary as those experiences might be). There were of course other advantages, and disadvantages, too,[3] of proceeding in this way. But I believe that the direct, experiential quality of the language of unconscious phantasy has played no small part in its gaining such popularity among modern psychoanalytic clinicians.

We must not forget, though, that the language of unconscious phantasy is *just another figurative language*. Unconscious phantasies can still never be perceived directly; they can still only ever be *inferred* from the data of conscious perception. As a result, some unconscious phantasies are bound to sound strange to the uninitiated. Any attempt to describe the deepest processes of the mind, which correspond in classical metapsychology to the seething cauldron of the drives, in the language of subjective awareness, will inevitably bear very little resemblance to the ordinary subjective experiences with which we are familiar, and which we are actually capable of perceiving. Likewise, the mental processes of the small infant, which in classical theory were almost devoid of secondary processes, are bound to sound strange when they are translated into the reflective language of adult experience. This was the cause of much of the controversy that occurred in the British Psychoanalytical Society in the 1940s, when Anna Freud and her supporters found it so hard to believe that small infants could actually have the thoughts and feelings that the Kleinians said they were having "in phantasy". The point is, though, as I hope I have made clear: they don't *actually* have them—or rather, I should say they *can't* actually have them; their unconscious mental processes themselves exist in some form of which they (and we) are by definition totally unable to form a direct perceptual image. What Melanie Klein and her supporters were describing were *inferences*, framed in a figurative language that they believed provided the most appropriate analogies, the closest possible approximations, of "the real state of affairs".

Even in the happiest of clinical circumstances, where an analysis facilitates explicit awareness of a previously unconscious phantasy, what the patient becomes aware of is not the unconscious phantasy *itself*. Rather, it is a conscious *representation* (or retranscription) of the phantasy itself. Unconscious phantasies remain forever unconscious, no matter what we call them and how we describe them. And this applies even if their modes of perceptual transformation into consciousness (and even the phantasies themselves) are altered by the process of analysis.

This is not to deny that some descriptions are more plausible than others, more commensurate with the perceivable data. But before one description can be compared with another, we need to distinguish between the *figurative language* and the *inferential content* of each description. The alternative is Babel.

So, as you can see, we have finally answered the question that the title of my paper posed for us. Do unconscious phantasies really exist? Well, yes and no. Yes, they *do* really exist in the sense that they are (more or less plausible) descriptions of the things that actually do make up the inner workings of our minds, and which really do cause us to think and feel our conscious thoughts and feelings. In this sense they are just as real as the waves and energies that physicists tell us cause matter to behave in the ways that it does, when we kick it or boil it or send it hurtling into outer space. But unconscious phantasies also *do not* really exist, because we can never perceive them directly. They are not *phenomenologically* real. They are and can only ever be *inferences* about what it is that really lies beyond the envelope of conscious awareness.

Significantly, in this respect, too, unconscious phantasies are no different from the waves and energies of the physicists. The only essential difference between them is the difference that I mentioned at the outset. I am referring to the fact that even the conscious perceptions that are derived from unconscious phantasies cannot be publicly verified. That is simply due to the spatial arrangement of the different perceptual modalities, as a result of which our personal, subjective experiences will always be personal and subjective. In this respect our scientific attempts to describe the inner workings of the mind from a subjective, psychical point of view will always fall short of our descriptions of its objective, material realization in the tissues of the brain. But then, again, the introspective approach has the significant virtue of looking at the things that go on inside us from the same point of view as our patients. And it is, as I have said, in their subjective experiences that our patients locate their suffering. And that, as I have also said already, is the greatest virtue of the concept of unconscious phantasy: it lays bare the causes of our patients' suffering in a language that the patients themselves can identify with, and it thereby renders the unthinkable thinkable.

Notes

1. Based on a public lecture presented at the Institute of Psycho-Analysis on 14 September 1996. Also presented to the 1952 Club of the British Psycho-Analytical Society on 10 June 1997.
2. We can, however, *remember* it. This occurs because we *internalize* our external impressions of the world. Once internalized, material objects become mental objects.
3. Theoretical reliance on a concept that is so broad as to include the whole of unconscious mental life (in all its complexity) has many drawbacks, the most obvious of which is a loss of conceptual differentiation and precision.

Reference

Freud, S. (1940 [1938]). *An Outline of Psycho-Analysis. S.E.*, 23: 141–207.

CHAPTER FOUR

Fantasy and the origins of sexuality[1]

Jean Laplanche and J. B. Pontalis

From its earliest day, psychoanalysis has been concerned with the material of fantasy. In the initial case of Anna O., Breuer was apparently content to plunge into the patient's inner world of imagination, into her "private theatre," in order to achieve catharsis through verbalization and emotive expression. "I used to visit her in the evening," he writes, "when I knew I should find her in her hypnosis, and I then relieved her of the whole stock of imaginative products which she had accumulated since my last visit (Breuer and Freud, p. 30)."

It is remarkable to note, when studying this case, how Breuer, unlike Freud, is little concerned to recover the elements of experience which might underlie these daydreams. The event which provoked the trauma is considered to contain an imaginary element, a hallucination leading to trauma. There is a circular relationship between the fantasy and the dissociation of consciousness which leads to the formation of an unconscious nucleus: fantasy becomes trauma when it arises from a special hypnoid state but, equally, the panic states it induces help to create this fundamental state by a process of autohypnosis.

If Breuer worked from within the world of imagination and tried to reduce its pathogenic force without reference to extrinsic factors, the same can be said of the methods of certain contemporary analysts, notably the followers of Melanie Klein. Firstly, the imaginary dramas underlying the verbal or behavioural material produced by the patient during the session—for instance, introjection or projection of the breast or penis, intrusions, conflicts or compromises with good or bad objects and so on—are made explicit and verbalized (no doubt in this case by the analyst (Klein, 1960)). A successful outcome to the treatment, if it does lead eventually to a better adaptation to reality, is not expected from any corrective initiative, but from the dialectic "integration" of the fantasies as they emerge. Ultimately, the introjection of the good object (no less imaginary than the bad), permits a fusion of the instincts in an equilibrium based on the predominance of the libido over the death instinct.

Fantasy, in German "Phantasie," is the term used to denote the imagination, and not so much the faculty of imagining (the philosophers' Einbildungskraft) as the imaginary world and its contents, the imaginings or fantasies into which the poet or the neurotic so willingly withdraws. In the scenes which the patient describes, or which are described to him by the analyst, the fantastic element is unmistakable. It is difficult therefore to avoid defining this world in terms of what it is not, the world of reality. This opposition antedates psychoanalysis by many centuries, but is liable to prove restrictive both to psychoanalytic theory and practice.

Psychoanalysts have fared rather badly with the theory itself, all too often basing it on a very elementary theory of knowledge.

Analysts such as Melanie Klein, with techniques devoid of any therapeutic intention, are, more than others, careful to distinguish between the contingent imagery of daydreams and the structural function and permanence of what they call "unconscious phantasies". (We shall discuss this distinction later.) Yet in the last resort they maintain that the latter are "false perceptions". The "good" and "bad" object should, for us, always be framed in quotation marks,[2] even though the whole evolution of the patient will occur within this framework.

Turning to Freud, we shall find a marked ambiguity of his conceptions as new avenues open out to him with each new stage in his ideas. If we start with the most accepted formulation of his doctrine, the world of fantasy seems to be located exclusively within the domain of opposition between subjective and objective, between an inner world, where satisfaction is obtained through illusion, and an external world, which gradually, through the medium of perception, asserts the supremacy of the reality principle. The unconscious thus appears to inherit the patient's original world, which was solely subject to the pleasure principle. The fantasy world is not unlike the nature reserves which are set up to preserve the original natural state of the country:

> With the introduction of the reality principle one species of thought-activity was split off; it was kept free from reality-testing and remained subject to the pleasure principle alone. This activity is "fantasying" (Freud, 1911, p. 222).

> The strangest characteristic of unconscious processes is due to their entire disregard of reality testing; they equate reality of thought with external actuality, and wishes with their fulfilment (Freud, 1911, p. 225).

This absence of the "standards of reality" in the unconscious may lead to its being depreciated as a lesser being, a less differentiated state.

In psychoanalytic practice any inadequacy of the conceptual background cannot fail to make itself felt. It is no purely formal necessity to recall how many techniques are founded on this opposition between the real and the imaginary, and which envisage the integration of the pleasure principle into the reality principle, a process which the neurotic is supposed to have only partially achieved. No doubt any analyst would find it incorrect to invoke "realities" external to the treatment, since the material must be developed in the context of the analyst-patient relationship, the transference. But unless we are careful, any interpretation of the transference: "You are treating me as if I ..." will imply the underlying "... and you know very well that I am not really what you think I am."

Fortunately we are saved by the technique: we do not actually make this underlying comment.[3] Speaking more fundamentally, the analytical rule should be understood as a Greek epoch, an absolute suspension of all reality judgments. This places us on the same level as the unconscious, which knows no such judgments. A patient tells us that he is an adopted child, and relates fantasies in which, while searching for his true mother, he perceives that she is a society woman turned prostitute. Here we recognize the banal theme of the "family romance", which might equally well have been composed by a child who had not been adopted. In the course of our "phenomenonological reduction" we should no longer make any distinction, except to interpret, as a "defence by reality", the documents which the patient brings to prove his adoption.[4]

Preoccupied, understandably, by the urge to discover at what level he was working, Freud does not come out so well when he has to justify the suspension of reality judgments in the course of treatment. At first he feels it almost his duty to show the patient what is under the counter. But, caught like the patient himself between the alternatives real-imaginary, he runs the double risk of either seeing the patient lose all interest in the analysis, if he is told that the material produced is nothing but imagination (Einbildung), or of incurring his reproaches later for having encouraged him to take his fantasies for realities (Freud, 1916–17, p. 368). Freud has recourse here to the notion of "psychical reality," a new dimension not immediately accessible to the analysand. But what does Freud mean by this term?

Frequently it means nothing more than the reality of our thoughts, of our personal world, a reality at least as valid as that of the material world and, in the case of neurotic phenomena, decisive. If we mean by this that we contrast the reality of psychological phenomena with "material reality" (Freud, 1916–17, p. 369), the reality of thought with "external actuality" (Freud, 1911, p. 225), we are in fact just saying that we are dealing with what is imaginary, with the subjective, but that this subjective is our object: the object of psychology is as valid as that of the sciences of material nature. And even the term itself, "psychical reality," shows that Freud felt he could only confer the dignity of object on psychological phenomena by reference to material reality, for he asserts that "they too possess a reality of a sort" (Freud, 1916–17, p. 368). In the absence of any new category, the suspension of reality judgments leads us once more into the "reality" of the purely subjective.

Yet this is not Freud's last word. When he introduces this concept of "psychical reality," in the last lines of the Interpretation of Dreams, which sums up his thesis that a dream is not a fantasmagoria, but a text to be deciphered, Freud does not define it as constituting the whole of the subjective, like the psychological field, but as a heterogeneous nucleus within this field, a resistant element, alone truly real, in contrast with the majority of psychological phenomena:

> Whether we are to attribute reality to unconscious wishes, I cannot say. It must be denied, of course, to any transitional or intermediate thoughts. If we look at unconscious wishes reduced to their most fundamental and truest shape, we shall have to conclude, no doubt, that psychical reality is a particular form of existence which is not to be confused with material reality.[5]

There are therefore three kinds of phenomena (or of realities, in the widest sense of the word): material reality, the reality of intermediate thoughts or of the psychological field, and the reality of unconscious wishes and their "truest shape": fantasy. If Freud, again and again, finds and then loses the notion of psychical reality, this is not due to any inadequacy of his conceptual apparatus: the difficulty and ambiguity lie in the very nature of its relationship, to the real and to the imaginary, as is shown in the central domain of fantasy.[6]

The years 1895–1899 which completed the discovery of psychoanalysis are significant not only because of the dubious battle taking place but also because of the oversimplified way in which its history is written.

If we read, for instance, Kris's introduction to the Origins of Psychoanalysis (Freud, 1950),[7] the evolution of Freud's views seems perfectly clear: the facts, and more especially Freud's own self-analysis, apparently led him to abandon his theory of seduction by an adult. The scene of seduction which until then represented for him the typical form of psychological trauma is not a real event but a fantasy which is itself only the product of, and a mask for, the spontaneous manifestations of infantile sexual activity. In his "History of the Psycho-Analytic Movement" Freud (1914) thus traces the development of his theory from his experience:

> If hysterical subjects trace back their symptoms to traumas that are fictitious, then the new fact which emerges is precisely that they create such scenes in fantasy, and this psychical reality requires to

be taken into account alongside practical reality. This reflection was soon followed by the discovery that these fantasies were intended to cover up the autoerotic activity of the first years of childhood, to embellish it and raise it to a higher plane. And now, from behind the fantasies, the whole range of a child's sexual life came to light.

Freud would, in these lines, be admitting his error in imputing to the "outside" something that concerns the "inside".

The very words, theory of sexual seduction, should arrest our attention: the elaboration of a schema to explain the aetiology of neuroses, and not the purely clinical observation of the frequency of the seduction of children by adults, nor even a simple hypothesis that such occurrences would preponderate among the different kinds of traumas. Freud was concerned theoretically to justify the connection he had discovered between sexuality, trauma, and defence: to show that it is in the very nature of sexuality to have a traumatic effect and, inversely, that one cannot finally speak of trauma as the origin of neurosis except to the extent that sexual seduction has occurred. As this thesis becomes established (1895–1897), the role of the defensive conflict in the genesis of hysteria, and of the defence in general, is fully recognized, although the aetiological function of trauma is not thereby reduced. The notions of defence and trauma are closely articulated one to the other: the theory of seduction, by showing how only a sexual trauma has the power to activate a "pathological defence" (repression) is an attempt to do justice to a clinically established fact (Studies on Hysteria), that repression concerns specifically sexuality.

We should consider a moment the schema propounded by Freud. The action of the trauma can be broken down into various time sequences and always implies the existence of at least two events. In the first scene, called "seduction scene," the child is subjected to a sexual approach from the adult ("attempt" or simply advances), without arousing any sexual excitation in himself. To try to describe such a scene as traumatic would be to abandon the somatic model of trauma, since there is neither an afflux of external excitation nor an overflow of the defences. If it can be described as sexual, it is only from the point of view of the external agent, the adult. But the child has neither the somatic requisites of excitation nor the representations to enable him to integrate the event:

although sexual in terms of objectivity, it has no sexual connotation for the subject, it is "presexually sexual" (Freud, 1950, letter 30). As for the second scene, which occurs after puberty, it is, one might say, even less traumatic than the first: being non-violent, and apparently of no particular significance, its only power lies in being able to evoke the first event, retroactively, by means of association. It is then the recall of the first scene which sets off the upsurge of sexual excitation, catching the ego in reverse, and leaving it disarmed, incapable of using the normally outward-directed defences, and thus falling back on a pathological defence, or "posthumous primary process"; the recollection is repressed.

If we dwell on concepts which might, at first sight, appear only of historic interest since they seem to presuppose an innocent child, without sexuality, thus contradicting undeniable later findings, it is not solely to outline the various stages of a discovery.

This explanatory schema, which Freud described as proton pseudos, is of remarkable value in considering the significance of human sexuality. In fact, it introduces two major propositions. On the one hand, in the first stage, sexuality literally breaks in from outside, intruding forcibly into the world of childhood, presumed to be innocent, where it is encysted as a simple happening without provoking any defence reaction—not in itself a pathogenic event. On the other hand, in the second stage, the pressure of puberty having stimulated the physiological awakening of sexuality, there is a sense of unpleasure, and the origin of this unpleasure is traced to the recollection of the first event, an external event which has become an inner event, an inner "foreign body", which now breaks out from within the subject.[8]

This is a surprising way to settle the question of trauma. The question often arises, whether it is an afflux of external excitation which creates the trauma or whether, on the contrary, it is the internal excitation, the drive, which, lacking an outlet, creates a "state of helplessness"[9] in the subject.

However, with the theory of seduction, we may say that the whole of the trauma comes both from within and without: from without, since sexuality reaches the subject from the other;[10] from within, since it springs from this internalised exteriority, this "reminiscence suffered by hysterics" (according to the Freudian formula), reminiscence in which we already discern what will be later named fantasy. This is an attractive solution, but it is liable to collapse when the meaning of each term deviates: the external towards the event, the internal towards the endogenous and biological.

Let us look at the seduction theory more positively and try to salvage its deeper meaning. It is Freud's first and sole attempt to establish an intrinsic relationship between repression and sexuality.[11] He finds the mainspring of this relationship, not in any "content", but in the temporal characteristics of human sexuality, which make it a privileged battlefield between both too much and too little excitation, both too early and too late occurrence of the event: "Here we have the one possibility of a memory subsequently producing a more powerful release than that produced by the corresponding experience itself" (Draft K). Hence the repartition of the trauma into two stages, as the psychological trauma can only be conceived as arising from something already there, the reminiscence of the first scene.

But how can we conceive the formation of this "already there," and how can this first scene, which is "pre-sexually sexual", acquire a meaning for the subject? Given a perspective which tends to reduce temporal dimensions to chronology, one must either embark on an infinite regression in which each scene acquires sexual quality solely through the evocation of an earlier scene without which it would have no meaning for the subject or, on the other hand, one must stop short arbitrarily at a "first" scene, however inconceivable it may be.

No doubt the doctrine of an innocent world of childhood into which sexuality is introduced by perverse adults is pure illusion: illusion, or rather a myth, whose very contradictions betray the nature. We must conceive of the child both as outside time, a bon sauvage, and as one already endowed with sexuality, at least in germ, which is ready to be awakened; we must accept the idea of an intrusion from without into an interior which perhaps did not exist as such before this intrusion; we must reconcile the passivity which is implied by merely receiving meaning from outside with the minimum of activity necessary for the experience even to be acknowledged, and the indifference of innocence with the disgust which the seduction is assumed to provoke. To sum up, we have a subject who is pre-subjectal, who receives his existence, his sexual existence, from without, before a distinction between within and without is achieved.

Forty years later Ferenczi (1933) was to take up the theory of seduction and give it analogous importance. His formulations are no doubt less rigorous than Freud's, but they have the advantage of filling out the myth with two essential ingredients: behind the facts, and through their mediation, it is a new language, that of passion, which is introduced by the adult into the infantile "language" of tenderness. On the other hand, this language of passion is the language of desire, necessarily marked by prohibition, a language of guilt and hatred, including the sense of annihilation linked with orgastic pleasure.[12] The fantasy of the primal scene with its character of violence shows the child's introjection of adult erotism.

Like Freud in 1895, Ferenczi is led to assign a chronological location to this intrusion, and to presuppose a real nature of the child before seduction. One might, on the other hand, be tempted to close the discussion once and for all by introducing the concept of myth: the seduction would become the myth of the origin of sexuality by the introjection of adult desire, fantasy and "language". The relationship of the myth to the time factor (the event) is present and, as it were, embedded in the myth itself. But we cannot rest there. This myth (or fantasy) of the intrusion of the fantasy (or myth) into the subject, cannot but occur to the organism, the little human being, at a point in time, by virtue of certain characteristics of his biological evolution, in which we can already distinguish what is too much or too little, too early (birth) and too late (puberty).

In 1897 Freud abandoned his theory of seduction. On September 21st he wrote to Fliess:

> I will confide in you at once the great secret that has been slowly dawning on me in the last few months: I no longer believe in my neurotica ...

He adduces a number of arguments. Some were factual: the impossibility of conducting analyses to their conclusion, that is, back to the first pathogenic event; even in the deepest psychosis—where the unconscious seems the most accessible—the key to the enigma is not available. Others were of a logical nature: one would have to generalize the father's perversity even beyond the cases of hysteria, since when hysteria supervenes it entails the intervention of other factors. On the other hand, and this is the point that interests us,

> ... there are no indications of reality in the unconscious, so that one cannot distinguish between the truth and fiction that is cathected with affect.

Two solutions are mentioned by Freud, either to consider fantasies of childhood as only the retroactive effect of a reconstruction performed by the adult (which would amount to the Jungian concept of retrospective fantasies (Zurückphantasieren) which Freud rejected), or to revert to the idea of hereditary predisposition. If this second possibility—which Freud admitted he had always "repressed"—returns to favour, it is because the search for the first scene has led to an impasse. But it is also because Freud, momentarily at a loss, did not succeed in isolating the positive element, lying beyond the realistic chronological approach, in the seduction theory. If the event evades us, then the alternative factor, constitution, is rehabilitated. Since reality, in one of its forms, is absent, and proves to be only fiction, then we must seek elsewhere for a reality on which this fiction is based.

When the historians of psychoanalysis tell us, picking up Freud's own version of his evolution, that the abandonment of the seduction theory in the face of facts cleared the ground for the discovery of infantile sexuality, they oversimplify a much more involved process. To a contemporary psychoanalyst, to Kris as to us, infantile sexuality is inseparable from the Oedipus complex. And in effect, at the very moment of the "abandonment" of seduction, we find three themes predominant in the correspondence with Fliess: infantile sexuality, fantasy, and the Oedipus complex. But the real problem lies in their interrelation. And we find that inasmuch as real trauma and the seduction scene have been effectively swept away,[13] they have not been replaced by the Oedipus complex but by the description of a spontaneous infantile sexuality, basically endogenous in development. Libidinal stages succeeding each other in a natural and regular evolution, fixation considered as an inhibition of development, genetic regression, form at least one of the perspectives suggested in the Three Essays on Sexuality (1905). In this direction, we must notice that the second Essay, on Infantile

Sexuality, discusses neither the Oedipus complex nor fantasy. An article which appeared at the same time as the Three Essays is typical of this point of view: in it Freud is able to discuss his "Views on the Part Played by Sexuality in the Aetiology of the Neuroses" (1906) without a single word about the Oedipus complex. The sexual development of the child is here defined as endogenous, and determined by the sexual constitution:

> Accidental influences derived from experience having thus receded into the background, the factors of constitution and heredity necessarily gained the upper hand once more; but there was this difference between my views and those prevailing in other quarters, that on my theory the "sexual constitution" took the place of a "general neuropathic disposition".

It may however be objected that it was also in 1897, at the very moment when he abandoned the seduction theory, that Freud in his self-analysis discovered the Oedipus complex. We should emphasize, though, that in spite of Freud's immediate recognition of its importance, the Oedipus complex was, for twenty years, to lead a marginal existence alongside his theoretical syntheses. It was deliberately set apart in a section devoted to "the choice of objects at puberty" (in the Three Essays), or to studies of "typical dreams" (in The Interpretation of Dreams). In our opinion the discovery of the Oedipus complex in 1897 was neither the cause of the abandonment of the seduction theory, nor clearly indicated as its successor. It seems much more probable that, being encountered in a "wild" form in the seduction theory, the Oedipus complex nearly suffered the same fate of being replaced by biological realism.

Freud himself recognized, much later, all that was positive and foreboding in the seduction theory: "here I had stumbled for the first time upon the Oedipus complex" (1925) or again,

> I came to understand that hysterical symptoms are derived from fantasies and not from real occurrences. It was only later that I was able to recognize in this fantasy of being seduced by the father the expression of the typical Oedipus complex ... (1933).[14]

At that time (1897) Freud had discarded on the one hand the idea, contained in the seduction theory, of a foreign body which introduces human sexuality into the subject from without, and, on the other hand, discovered that the sexual drive becomes active before puberty. But for some time he was not able to articulate the Oedipus complex with infantile sexuality. If the latter existed, as clinical observation undoubtedly proved, it could henceforward only be conceived as biological reality, fantasy being no more than the secondary expression of this reality. The scene in which the subject describes his seduction by an older companion is, in fact, a double disguise: pure fantasy is converted into real memory, and spontaneous sexual activity into passivity.[15] One is no longer justified in attributing psychical reality—in the stricter sense sometimes employed by Freud—to the fantasy, since reality is now totally attributed to an endogenous sexuality, and since fantasies are only considered to be a purely imaginary efflorescence of this sexuality.

Something was lost with the discarding of the seduction theory: beneath the conjunction and the temporal interplay of the two "scenes" there lay a pre-subjective structure, beyond both the strict happening and the internal imagery. The prisoner of a series of theoretical alternatives, subject-object, constitution-event, internal-external, imaginary-real, Freud was for a time led to stress the first terms of these "pairs of opposites".

This would suggest the following paradox: at the very moment when fantasy, the fundamental object of psychoanalysis, is discovered, it is in danger of seeing its true nature obscured by the emphasis on an endogenous reality, sexuality, which is itself supposed to be in conflict with a normative, prohibitory external reality, which imposes on it various disguises. We have indeed the fantasy, in the sense of a product of the imagination, but we have lost the structure. Inversely, with the seduction theory we had, if not the theory, at least an intuition of the structure (seduction appearing as an almost universal datum, which in any case transcended both the event and, so to speak, its protagonists). The ability to elaborate the fantasy was however, if not unknown, at least underestimated.

It would be taking a very limited view to describe as follows the evolution of Freud's ideas during the period around 1897: from historical foundation of the symptoms to the establishment of an ultimately biological theory, to the causal sequence, sexual constitution®fantasy®symptom. Freud never makes the theory entirely his own until he is obliged to present his aetiological views in systematic fashion. If we intended, which we do not, to present a step-by-step account of the development of his thought, we should have to distinguish at least two other currents in this central period.

The one derives from the fresh understanding of fantasy which is effective from 1896 onwards: fantasy is not merely material to be analysed, whether appearing as fiction from the very start (as in daydreaming) or whether it remains to be shown that it is a construction contrary to appearances (as in screen-memory), it is also the result of analysis, an end-product, a latent content to be revealed behind the symptom. From mnesic symbol of trauma, the symptom has become the stage-setting of fantasies (thus a fantasy of prostitution, of street-walking, might be discovered beneath the symptom of agoraphobia).

Freud now starts to explore the field of these fantasies, to make an inventory, and to describe their most typical forms. Fantasies are now approached from two aspects at once, both as manifest data and latent content; and, located thus at the crossroads, they acquire in due course the consistency of an object, the specific object of psychoanalysis. Henceforward analysis will continue to treat fantasy as "psychical reality" whilst exploring its variants and above all analysing its processes and structure. Between 1897 and 1906 appear all the great works which explore the mechanisms of the unconscious, that is to say, the transformations (in the geometric sense of the word) of fantasy, namely, The Interpretation of Dreams (1900), The Psychopathology of Everyday Life (1901), Jokes and their Relation to the Unconscious (1905).

But, and here is the third current, the development of Freudian research and psychoanalytic treatment display at the outset a regressive tendency towards the origin, the foundation of the symptom and the neurotic organization of the personality. If fantasy is shown to be an autonomous, consistent and explorable field, it leaves untouched the question of its own origin, not only with regard to structure, but also to content and to its most concrete details. In this sense nothing has changed, and the search for chronology, going backwards into time towards the first real, verifiable elements, is still the guiding principle of Freud's practice.

Speaking of one of his patients, he writes in 1899:

Buried deep beneath all his fantasies we found a scene from his primal period (before twenty-two months) which meets all requirements and into which all the surviving puzzles flow (Letter 126).

A little later we come across these lines, eloquent of his passion for investigation, pursued ever deeper and with certainty of success, and the resort to a third person, if necessary, to verify the accuracy of his enquiry:

> In the evenings I read prehistory, etc., without any serious purpose [our italics], and otherwise my only concern is to lead my cases calmly towards solution. ... In E's case the second real scene is coming up after years of preparation, and it is one that it may perhaps be possible to confirm objectively by asking his elder sister. Behind it there is a third, long-suspected scene. ... (Letter 127).

Freud defines these scenes from earliest infancy, these true scenes, as Urszenen (original or primal scenes). Later, as we know, the term will be reserved for the child's observation of parental coitus. The reference is to the discussion in From the History of a Childhood Neurosis (1918) of the relationship between the pathogenic dream and the primal scene on which it is based. When reading the first draft of the clinical account composed during "the winter of 1914/15, shortly after the end of treatment". one is struck by the passionate conviction which urges Freud, like a detective on the watch, to establish the reality of the scene down to its smallest details. If such concern is apparent so long after the abandonment of the seduction theory, it is surely a proof that Freud had never entirely resigned himself to accepting such scenes as purely imaginary creations. Although discarded as concerns the seduction scene, the question re-emerges in identical terms twenty years later, in the case of the observation of parental coitus by the Wolf Man. The discovery of infantile sexuality has not invalidated in Freud's mind the fundamental schema underlying the seduction theory: the same deferred action (Nachträglichkeit) is constantly invoked; we meet once more the two events (here the scene and the dream), separated in the temporal series, the first remaining un-understood and, as it were, excluded within the subject, to be taken up later in the elaboration of the second occasion.[16] The fact that the whole process develops in the first years of infancy affects nothing essential in the theoretical model.

It is well known that before publishing his manuscript Freud added, in 1917, two long discussions which showed that he was disturbed by the Jungian theory of retrospective fantasy (Zurück-phantasieren). He admits that since the scene is, in analysis, the culmination of a reconstruction, it might indeed have been constructed by the subject himself, but he nevertheless insists that perception has at least furnished some indications, even if it were only the copulation of dogs. ...

But, more particularly, just at the moment when Freud appears to lose hope of support from the ground of reality—ground so shifting on further enquiry—he introduces a new concept, that of the Urphantasien, primal (or original) fantasy. The need for a theoretical foundation has now undergone a veritable transmutation. Since it has proved impossible to determine whether the primal scene is something truly experienced by the subject, or a fiction, we must in the last resort seek a foundation in something which transcends both individual experience and what is imagined.

For us too it is only at a deferred date (nachträglich) that the full meaning of this new direction of Freud's thought becomes apparent. Nothing appears to be changed: there is the same pursuit of an ultimate truth, the same schema is used once more, the dialectic of the two successive historical events, the same dis-appointment—as if Freud had learned nothing—as the ultimate event, the "scene", disappears over the horizon. But simulta-neously, thanks to what we have described as the second current, there is the discovery of the unconscious as a structural field, which can be reconstructed, since it handles, decomposes and recomposes its elements according to certain laws. This will henceforward permit the quest for origins to take on a new dimension.

In the concept of original fantasy,[17] there is a continuation of what we might call Freud's desire to reach the bedrock of the event (and if this disappears by refraction or reduction, then one must look further back still), and the need to establish the structure of the fantasy itself by something other than the event.

The original fantasies constitute this "store of unconscious fantasies of all neurotics, and probably of all human beings" (Freud, 1915, p. 269). These words alone suggest that it is not solely the empirical fact of frequency, nor even generality, which characterises them. If "the same fantasies with the same content are created on every occasion" (1916, p. 370), if, beneath the diversity of individual fables we can recover some "typical" fantasies,[18] it is because the historical life of the subject is not the prime mover, but rather something antecedent, which is capable of operating as an organizer.

Freud saw only one possible explanation of this antecedence, and that was phylogenesis:

> It seems to me quite possible that all the things that are told to us in analysis as fantasy ... were once real occurrences in the primaeval times of the human family [what was factual reality would, in this case, have become psychological reality] and that children in their fantasies are simply filling in the gaps in individual truth with prehistoric truths.

Thus once again a reality is postulated beneath the elaborations of fantasy, but a reality which, as Freud insists, has an autonomous and structural status with regard to the subject who is totally dependent on it. He pursues this some considerable way, since he admits the possibility of discordance between the schema and individual experiences, which would lead to psychological conflict.[19]

It is tempting to accept the "reality" which inspires the work of imagination according to its own laws, as a prefiguration of the "symbolic order" defined by Levi-Strauss and Lacan in the ethnological and psychoanalytic fields respectively. These scenes, which Freud traces back in Totem and Taboo to the prehistory of man, are attributed by him to primaeval man (Urmensch), to the primal father (Urvater). He invokes them, less in order to provide a reality which escapes him in individual history, than to assign limits to the "imaginary" which cannot contain its own principle of organization.

Beneath the pseudo-scientific mask of phylogenesis, or the recourse to "inherited memory-traces", we should have to admit that Freud finds it necessary to postulate an organization made of signifiers anteceding the effect of the event and the signified as a whole. In this mythical prehistory of the species we see the need to create a pre-structure inaccessible to the subject, evading his grasp, his initiatives, his inner "cooking pot", in spite of all the rich ingredients our modern sorceresses seem to find there. But Freud is in fact caught in the trap of his own concepts; in this false synthesis by which the past of the human species is preserved in hereditarily transmitted patterns, he is vainly trying to overcome the opposition between event and constitution.

However we should not be in a hurry to replace the phylogenic explanation by a structural type of explanation. The original fantasy is first and foremost fantasy: it lies beyond the history of the subject but nevertheless in history: a kind of language and a symbolic sequence, but loaded with elements of imagination; a structure, but activated by contingent elements. As such it is characterized by certain traits which make it difficult to assimilate to a purely transcendental schema, even if it provides the possibility of experience.[20]

The text in which Freud first mentions primal fantasies ("A Case of Paranoia", 1915), leaves no doubt in this respect. In it he describes the case of a woman patient who declared that she had been watched and photographed while lying with her lover. She claimed to have heard a "noise", the click of the camera. Behind this delirium Freud saw the primal scene: the sound is the noise of the parents who awaken the child; it is also the sound the child is afraid to make lest it betray her listening. It is difficult to estimate its role in the fantasy. In one sense, says Freud, it is only a provocation, an accidental cause, whose role is solely to activate "the typical fantasy of overhearing, which is a component of the parental complex," but he immediately corrects himself by saying: "It is doubtful whether we can rightly call the noise 'accidental'. ... Such fantasies are on the contrary an indispensible part of the fantasy of listening." In fact, the sound alleged by the patient,[21] reproduces in actuality the indication of the primal scene, the element which is the starting point for all ulterior elaboration of the fantasy. In other words, the origin of the fantasy is integrated in the very structure of the original fantasy.

In his first theoretical sketches on the subject of fantasy, Freud stresses, in a way which may intrigue his readers, the role of aural perception.[22] Without placing too much importance on these fragmentary texts, in which Freud seems to be thinking more particularly of paranoid fantasies, one must consider why such a privileged position was accorded to hearing. We suggest there are two reasons. One relates to the sensorium in question: hearing, when it occurs, breaks the continuity of an undifferentiated perceptual field and at the same time is a sign (the noise waited for and heard in the night), which puts the subject in the position of having to answer to something. To this extent the prototype of the signifier lies in the aural sphere, even if there are correspondences in the other perceptual registers. But hearing is also—and this is the second reason to which Freud alludes explicitly in the passage—the history or the legends of parents, grandparents and the ancestors: the family sounds or sayings, this spoken or secret discourse, going on prior to the subject's arrival, within which he must find his way. Insofar as it can serve retroactively to summon up the discourse, the noise—or any other discrete sensorial element that has meaning—can acquire this value.

In their content, in their theme (primal scene, castration, seduction ...), the original fantasies also indicate this postulate of retroactivity: they relate to the origins. Like myths, they claim to provide a representation of, and a solution to, the major enigmas which confront the child. Whatever appears to the subject as something needing an explanation or theory, is dramatized as a moment of emergence, the beginning of a history.

Fantasies of origins: the primal scene pictures the origin of the individual; fantasies of seduction, the origin and upsurge of sexuality; fantasies of castration, the origin of the difference between the sexes.[23] Their themes therefore display, with redoubled significance, that original fantasies justify their status of being already there.

There is convergence of theme, of structure, and no doubt also of function: through the indications furnished by the perceptual field, through the scenarios constructed, the varied quest for origins, we are offered in the field of fantasy, the origin of the subject himself.

Since we encounter fantasy as given, interpreted, reconstructed or postulated, at the most diverse levels of psychoanalytic experience, we have obviously to face the difficult problem of its metapsychological status, and first of all, of its topography within the framework of the distinction between the unconscious, preconscious and conscious systems.

There are certain tendencies in contemporary psychoanalysis to settle the question by making a theoretical transposition, which seems inevitable in practice, between the fantasy as it presents itself for interpretation and the fantasy which is the conclusion of the work of analytic interpretation (S. Isaacs, 1948). Freud would thus have been in error in describing by the same term, Phantasie, two totally distinct realities. On the one hand there is the unconscious Phantasie, "the primary content of unconscious mental processes" (Isaacs), and on the other, the conscious or subliminal imaginings, of which the daydream is the typical example. The latter would be only a manifest content, like the others, and would have no more privileged relationship to unconscious Phantasie than dreams, behaviour, or whatever is generally described as "material". Like all manifest data, it would require interpretations in terms of unconscious fantasy.[24]

Freud's inspiration is shown by his persistent employment of the term Phantasie up to the end, in spite of the very early discovery that these Phantasien might be either conscious or unconscious. He wishes thereby to assert a profound kinship:

> The contents of the clearly conscious fantasies of perverts (which in favourable circumstances can be transformed into manifest beha- viour), of the delusional fears of paranoics) which are projected in a hostile sense on to other people), and of the unconscious fantasies of hysterics (which psychoanalysis reveals behind their symptoms)— all these coincide with one another even down to their details (Freud 1905, pp. 165–166).

That is to say, that the same content, the same activation can be revealed in imaginary formations and psychopathological struc- tures as diverse as those described by Freud, whether conscious or unconscious, acted out or represented, and whether or not there is a change of sign or permutation of persons.

Such an affirmation (1905) does not come from any so-called proto-Freud. It is of cardinal importance, particularly in the period 1906–1909, when much research was devoted to the subject. (In "Gradiva", "Creative Writers and Day-Dreaming", "Hysterical Fantasies and their Relation to Bisexuality", "On the Sexual Theories of Children", "Some General Remarks on Hysterical Attacks", "Family Romances",) At this time the unconscious efficacy of fantasy was fully recognised as, for instance, underlying the hysterical attack which symbolizes it. Freud however takes the conscious fantasy, the daydream, not only as paradigm, but as source. The hysterical fantasies which "have important connections with the causation of the neurotic symptoms" (we must be dealing with unconscious fantasies) have as "common source and normal prototype what are called the daydreams of youth" (Freud, 1908). In fact it is conscious fantasy itself which may be repressed and thus become pathogenic. Freud even considers fantasy as the privileged point where one may catch in the raw the process of transition from one system to another, repression, or the return of repressed material.[25] It is indeed the same mixed entity, the same "mixed blood" which, being so close to the limits of the unconscious, can pass from one side to the other, particularly as the result of a variation of cathexis.[26] It may be objected that Freud is not here taking fantasy at its deepest level, and that we are not dealing with a true fantasy, but simply with a subliminal reverie. But Freud does describe the process of dismissal as repression and the frontier of which he speaks is indeed that of the unconscious in the strict, topographical, sense of the term.

We do not of course deny that there are different levels of unconscious fantasy, but it is remarkable to note how Freud, when studying the metapsychology of dreams, discovers the same relationship between the deepest unconscious fantasy and the daydream: the fantasy is present at both extremities of the process of dreaming. On the one hand it is linked with the ultimate unconscious desire, the "capitalist" of the dream, and as such it is at the basis of that "zigzag" path which is supposed to follow excitation through a succession of psychological systems: "The first portion [of this path] was a progressive one, leading from the unconscious scenes of fantasies to the preconscious" (Freud, 1900, p. 574), where it collects "the day residues" or transference thoughts. But fantasy is also present at the other extremity of the dream, in the secondary elaboration which, Freud insists, is not part of the unconscious work of the dream, but must be identified "with the work of our waking thought." The secondary elaboration is an a posteriori reworking which takes place in the successive transformations which we impose on the story of the dream once we are awake. This consists essentially in restoring a minimum of order and coherence to the raw material handed over by the unconscious mechanisms of displacement, condensation and symbolism, and in imposing on this heterogeneous assortment a façade, a scenario, which gives it relative coherence and continuity. In a word, it is a question of making the final version relatively similar to a daydream.

Thus the secondary elaboration will utilize those ready-made scenarios, the fantasies or daydreams with which the subject has provided himself in the course of the day before the dream.

This is not necessarily to say that there is no privileged relationship between the fantasy which lies at the heart of the dream, and the fantasy which serves to make it acceptable to consciousness. Preoccupied by his discovery of the dream as the fulfilment of unconscious desire, it was no doubt natural for Freud to devalue anything close to consciousness which might appear to be defence and camouflage, in fact, the secondary elaboration.[27] But he quickly returns to a different appreciation:

> It would be a mistake, however, to suppose that these dream-façades are nothing other than mistaken and somewhat arbitrary revisions of the dream-content by the conscious agency of our mental life. ... The wishful fantasies revealed by analysis in night-dreams often turn out to be repetitions or modified versions of scenes from infancy; thus in some cases the façade of the dream directly reveals the dream's actual nucleus, distorted by an admixture of other material (Freud, 1901, p. 667).[28]

Thus the extremities of the dream, and the two forms of fantasy which are found there, seem, if not to link up, at least to communicate from within and, as it were, to be symbolic of each other.

We have spoken of a progression in Freud's thought with regard to the metapsychological status of fantasy. It does, of course, move towards differentiation, but we believe we have already shown that this goes without suppression of the homology between different levels of fantasy, and above all there is no attempt to make the line of major differentiation coincide with the topographical barrier (censorship), which separates the conscious and preconscious systems from the unconscious. The difference occurs within the unconscious:

> Unconscious fantasies have either been unconscious all along or—as is more often the case—they were once conscious fantasies, daydreams, and have since been purposely forgotten and have become unconscious through "repression" (Freud, 1908, p. 161).

This distinction is later, in Freudian terminology, to coincide with that between original fantasies and others, those that one might call secondary, whether conscious or unconscious.[29]

Apart from this fundamental difference, the unity of the fantasy whole depends however on their mixed nature, in which both the structural and the imaginary can be found, although to different degrees. It is with this in mind that Freud always held the model fantasy to be the reverie, that form of novelette, both stereotyped and infinitely variable, which the subject composes and relates to himself in a waking state.

The daydream is a shadow play, utilizing its kaleidoscopic material drawn from all quarters of human experience, but also involving the original fantasy, whose dramatis personae, the court cards, receive their notation from a family legend which is mutilated, disordered and misunderstood. Its structure is the primal fantasy in which the Oedipus configuration can be easily distinguished, but also the daydream—if we accept that analysis discovers typical and repetitive scenarios beneath the varying clusters of fable.

However, we cannot classify or differentiate different forms of fantasy[30] as they shift between the poles of reverie or primal fantasy, simply, or even essentially, by the variability or inversion of the ratios between imaginary ingredient and structural link. Even the structure seems variable. In terms of daydream, the scenario is basically in the first person, and the subject's place clear and invariable. The organization is stabilized by the secondary process, weighted by the ego: the subject, it is said, lives out his reverie. But the original fantasy, on the other hand, is characterized by the absence of subjectivization, and the subject is present in the scene: the child, for instance, is one character amongst many in the fantasy "a child is beaten." Freud insisted on this visualization of the subject on the same level as the other protagonists, and in this sense the screen memory would have a profound structural relationship with original fantasies.[31]

"A father seduces a daughter" might perhaps be the summarized version of the seduction fantasy. The indication here of the primary process is not the absence of organization, as is sometimes suggested, but the peculiar character of the structure, in that it is a scenario with multiple entries, in which nothing shows whether the subject will be immediately located as daughter; it can as well be fixed as father, or even in the term seduces.

When Freud asked himself whether there was anything in man

comparable to the "instinct in animals" (Freud, 1915, p. 195), he found the equivalent, not in the drives (Triebe) but in primal fantasies (Freud, 1918, p. 120, note). It is a valuable clue, since it demonstrates indirectly his unwillingness to explain fantasy on biological grounds: far from deriving fantasy from the drives, he preferred to make them dependent on earlier fantasy structures. It is also valuable in clarifying the position of certain contemporary concepts. Finally, it leads us to investigate the close relationship between desire and fantasy involved in the term Wunschphantasie (wish-fantasy).

Isaacs, for instance, considered unconscious fantasies to be "an activity parallel to the drives from which they emerge." She sees them as the "psychological expression" of experience, which is itself defined by the field of force set up by libidinal and aggressive drives and the defences they arouse. Finally she is concerned to establish a close link between the specific forms of fantasy life and the bodily zones which are the seat of the drives, though this leads her to underestimate one part of the Freudian contribution to the theory both of fantasy and drives. In her view, fantasy is only the imagined transcription of the first objective of any drive, which is a specific object: the "instinctual urge" is necessarily experienced as a fantasy which, whatever its content (desire to suck, in a baby), will be expressed, as soon as verbalization is possible,[32] by a phrase consisting of three parts: subject (I), verb (swallow, bite, reject), object (breast, mother).[33] Of course, in so far as the drives are, for the Kleinians, in the first place in the nature of relationships, Isaacs shows how such a fantasy of incorporation is also experienced in the other sense, the active becoming passive. Furthermore, this fear of a return to sender is a constituent element of the fantasy itself. But it is hardly enough to recognize the equivalence of eating and being eaten in the fantasy of incorporation. So long as there is some idea of a subject, even if playing a passive role, are we sure to reach the structure of deepest fantasy?

For Isaacs, fantasy is the direct expression of a drive, and almost consubstantial with it, and can, in the last resort, be reduced to the relationship which links subject to object by a verb of action (in the sense of the omnipotent wish). This is because, for her, the structure of the drive is that of a subjective intentionality and inseparable from its object: the drive "intuits" or "knows" the object which will satisfy it. As the fantasy, which at first expresses libidinal and destuctive drives, quickly transforms itself into a form of defence, so finally it is the whole of the subject's internal dynamic which is deployed in accordance with this unique type of organization. Such a concept postulates, in agreement with certain Freudian formulations, that "all that is conscious has passed through a preliminary unconscious stage," and that the ego is "a differentiated part of the id." One is therefore obliged to provide every mental operation with an underlying fantasy which can itself be reduced on principle to an instinctual aim. The biological subject is in a direct line of continuity with the subject of fantasy, the sexual, human subject, in accordance with the series: soma ® id ® fantasy (of desire, of defence) ® ego mechanism: the action of repression is difficult to grasp, since "fantasy life" is more implicit than repressed, and contains its own conflicts by virtue of the co-existence within the psyche of contradictory aims. There is, in fact, a profusion of fantasy, in which it is impossible to recognize the special type of structure which Freud tried to distinguish and where the elusive but elective relationship which he established between fantasy and sexuality also dissolves.

It is a little surprising that Freud, at a time when he fully recognized the existence and extent of sexuality and fantasy in the child, should have continued, as for instance in a footnote to the Three Essays in 1920 (1905, p. 226), to consider the period of maximum fantasying activity to occur in the period of pubertal and pre-pubertal masturbation.[34] It is perhaps because to him there was a close correlation between fantasy and auto-erotism, which was not sufficiently accounted for by the belief that the second is camouflaged by the first. In fact he seems to be sharing the common belief that in the absence of real objects the subjects seeks and creates for himself an imaginary satisfaction.

Freud himself did much to authorize this viewpoint when he tried to establish a theoretical model of desire, both in its object and purpose.[35] The origin of fantasy would lie in the hallucinatory satisfaction of desire; in the absence of a real object, the infant reproduces the experience of the original satisfaction in a hallucinated form. In this view the most fundamental fantasies would be those which tend to recover the hallucinated objects linked with the very earliest experiences of the rise and the resolution of desire.[36]

But before we try to discover what the Freudian fiction (Fiktion) is really intended to cover, we must be clear about its meaning, more particularly since it is rarely formulated in detail, but always presupposed in Freud's concept of the primary process. One might consider it a myth of origin: by this figurative expression Freud claims to have recovered the very first upsurgings of desire. It is an analytic "construction", or fantasy, which tries to cover the moment of separation between before and after, whilst still containing both: a mythical moment of disjunction between the pacification of need (Befriedigung) and the fulfilment of desire (Wunscherfüllung), between the two stages represented by real experience and its hallucinatory revival, between the object that satisfies and the sign[37] which describes both the object and its absence: a mythical moment at which hunger and sexuality meet in a common origin.

If, caught in our own turn by the fantasy of origins, we were to claim to have located the emergence of fantasy, we should start from the standpoint of the real course of infantile history, and the development of infantile sexuality (see from the viewpoint of Chap. 2 of Three Essays), and we should relate it to the appearance of auto-erotism, to the moment of what Freud calls the "pleasure premium." This is not a pleasure in the fulfilment of function, or the resolution of tension created by needs, but a marginal product, emerging from the world of needs, these vitally important functions whose aims and mechanisms are assured and whose objects are pre-formed.

But in speaking of the appearance of auto-erotism, even when taking care not to transform it into a stage of libidinal development, and even stressing its permanence and presence in all adult sexual behaviour, one is liable to lose sight of all that gives the notion its true meaning, and all that can illuminate the function as well as the structure of fantasy.

If the notion of auto-erotism is frequently criticized in psycho-analysis, this is because it is incorrectly understood, in the object-directed sense, as a first stage, enclosed within itself, from which the subject has to rejoin the world of objects. It is then easy to demonstrate, with much clinical detail, the variety and complexity of the links which, from the beginning, relate the infant to the outer world and, particularly, to its mother. But when Freud, principally in the Three Essays, speaks of auto-erotism, he has no intention of denying the existence of a primary object relationship. On the contrary, he shows that the drive becomes auto-erotic, only after the loss of the object.[38] If it can be said of auto-erotism that it is objectless, it is in no sense because it may appear before any object relationship,[39] nor because on its arrival no object will remain in the search for satisfaction, but simply because the natural method of apprehending an object is split in two: the sexual drive separated from the non-sexual functions, such as feeding, which are its support (Anlehnung[40]) and which indicate its aim and object.

The "origin" of auto-erotism would therefore be the moment when sexuality, disengaged from any natural object, moves into the field of fantasy and by that very fact becomes sexuality. The moment is more abstract than definable in time, since it is always renewed, and must have been preceded by erotic excitation, otherwise it would be impossible for such excitation to be sought out. But one could equally state the inverse proposition, that it is the breaking in of fantasy which occasions the disjunction of sexuality and need.[41] The answer to the question of whether this is a case of circular causality or simultaneous appearance is that however far back one may go they originate from the same point.

Auto-erotic satisfaction, in so far as it can be found in an autonomous state, is defined by one very precise characteristic: it is the product of the anarchic activity of partial drives, closely linked with the excitation of specific erogenous zones, an excitation which arises and is stilled on the spot. It is not a global, functional pleasure, but a fragmented pleasure, an organ pleasure (Organlust) and strictly localized.

It is known that erogeneity can be attached to predestined zones of the body (thus, in the activity of sucking, the oral zone is destined by its very physiology to acquire an erogenous value), but it is also available to any organ (even internal organs), and to any region or function of the body. In every case the function serves only as support, the taking of food serving, for instance, as a model for fantasies of incorporation. Though modelled on the function, sexuality lies in its difference from the function: in this sense its prototype is not the act of sucking, but the enjoyment of going through the motions of sucking (Ludeln), the moment when the external object is abandoned, when the aim and the source assume an autonomous existence with regard to feeding and the digestive system. The ideal, one might say, of auto-erotism is "lips that kiss themselves."[42] Here, in this apparently self-centred enjoyment, as in the deepest fantasy, in this discourse no longer addressed to anyone, all distinction between subject and object has been lost.

If we add that Freud constantly insisted on the seductive role of the mother (or of others), when she washes, dresses or caresses her child,[43] and if we note also that the naturally erogenous zones (oral, anal, uro-genital, skin), are not only those which most attract the mother's attention, but also those which have an obvious exchange value (orifices or skin covering) we can understand how certain chosen parts of the body itself may not only serve to sustain a local pleasure, but also be a meeting place with maternal desire and fantasy, and thus with one form of original fantasy.

By locating the origin of fantasy in the auto-erotism, we have shown the connection between fantasy and desire. Fantasy, however, is not the object of desire, but its setting. In fantasy the subject does not pursue the object or its sign: he appears caught up himself in the sequence of images. He forms no representation of the desired object, but is himself represented as participating in the scene although, in the earliest forms of fantasy, he cannot be assigned any fixed place in it (hence the danger, in treatment, of interpretations which claim to do so). As a result, the subject, although always present in the fantasy, may be so in a desubjectivized form, that is to say, in the very syntax of the sequence in question. On the other hand, to the extent that desire is not purely an upsurge of the drives, but is articulated into the fantasy, the latter is a favoured spot for the most primitive defensive reactions, such as turning against oneself, or into an opposite, projection, negation: these defences are even indissolubly linked with the primary function of fantasy, to be a setting for desire, insofar as desire itself originates as prohibition, and the conflict may be an original conflict.

But as for knowing who is responsible for the setting, it is not enough for the psychoanalyst to rely on the resources of his science, nor on the support of myth. He must also become a philosopher.

Summary

1. The status of fantasy cannot be found within the framework of the opposition reality-illusion (imaginary). The notion of

psychical reality introduces a third category, that of structure.

2. Freud's theory of seduction (1895–97) is re-examined from the point of view of its pioneering and demonstrative value: it permits the analysis of the dialectic relationship between fantasy productions, the underlying structures, and the reality of the scene. This "reality" is to be sought in an ever more remote or hypothetical past (of the individual or of the species), which is postulated on the horizon of the imaginary, and implied in the very structure of the fantasy.

3. Freud's so-called abandonment of the reality of infantile traumatic memories, in favour of fantasies which would be based only on a biological, quasi-endogenous evolution of sexuality, is only a transitional stage in the search for the foundation of neurosis. On the one hand seduction will continue to appear as one of the data of the relationship between child and adult (Freud, Ferenczi); on the other hand, the notion of primal (or original) fantasies (Urphantasien), of "inherited memory traces" of prehistoric events, will in turn provide support for individual fantasies.

   The authors propose an interpretation of this notion: such a pre-history, located by Freud in phylogenesis, can be understood as a prestructure which is actualized and transmitted by the parental fantasies.

4. Original fantasies are limited in their thematic scope. They relate to problems of origin which present themselves to all human beings (Menschenkinder): the origin of the individual (primal scene), the origin of sexuality (seduction), and the origin of the difference between the sexes (castration).

5. The origin of fantasy cannot be isolated from the origin of the drive (Trieb) iself. The authors, reinterpreting the Freudian concept of the experience of satisfaction, locate this origin in the auto-erotism, which they define not as a stage of evolution but as the moment of a repeated disjunction of sexual desire and non-sexual functions: sexuality is detached from any natural object, and is handed over to fantasy, and, by this very fact, starts existing as sexuality.

6. The metapsychological status of this mixed entity, the fantasy, is finally established. The authors refuse to accept the main line of separation between conscious and unconscious fantasies

(Isaacs). They place this division between the original and the secondary fantasies (whether repressed or conscious) and demonstrate the relationship and the profound continuity between the various fantasy scenarios—the stage-setting of desire—ranging from the daydream to the fantasies recovered or reconstructed by analytic investigation.

Notes

1. Translated from the French, "Fantasme originaire, fantasmes des origines, origine du fantasme", in Les Temps Modernes (1964) 19, no. 215.

2. "Good" and "bad" objects are "imagos which are a phantastically distorted picture of the real objects upon which they are based" (Klein, 1934).

3. It is fascinating to observe how Melanie Klein, who provides an uninterrupted interpretation of the transference relationship, never brings in any "in reality", or even an "as if."

4. However, we have found in the case of actual adoption to which we are referring clinical manifestations quite obviously different from those encountered in adoption fantasies: an actualization, quickly blurred, of fantasies of the recovery of the mother, episodes where the attempts to rejoin the true mother, are worked out symbolically in a kind of secondary state, etc. Even in treatment, from the very beginning, many elements such as dream contents, the repeated occurrence of sleep during the session, showing a massive working out of a far-reaching tendency, demonstrated the disjunction between crude reality and verbalization.

5. S.E., 4–5. p. 620. The successive reformulations of this principle in the various editions of the Traumdeutung show both Freud's concern to define accurately the concept of psychical reality, and the difficulties he experienced in so doing—Cf. Strachey's note to this passage.

6. One further word about the suspension of judgment in the analytic rule: "Verbalize everything, but do no more than verbalize." This is not suspension of the reality of external events for the benefit of subjective reality. It creates a new field, that of verbalization, where the difference between the real and the imaginary may retain its value (cf. the case of the patient referred to above). The homology between the analytic and the unconscious field, whose emergence it stimulates, is not due to their common subjectivity, but to the deep kinship between the unconscious

and the field of speech. So it is not: "It is you who say so," but "It is you who say so."

7. Especially the section entitled "Infantile Sexuality and Self-Analysis".

8. In Studies on Hysteria we already find the idea that psychological trauma cannot be reduced to the once and for all effect on an organism of some external event. "The causal relation between the determining psychical trauma and the hysterical phenomenon is not of a kind implying that the trauma merely acts like an agent drovocateur, in releasing the symptom which thereafter leads an independent existence. We must presume rather that the psychical trauma—or more precisely the memory of the trauma—acts like a foreign body which long after its entry must be regarded as an agent that is still at work" (S.E., 2, p. 6).

9. The problem is constantly present in these terms in such works as Freud's Beyond the Pleasure Principle, Inhibitions, Symptoms and Anxiety, and Rank's Trauma of Birth.

10. "It seems to me more and more that the essential point of hysteria is that it results from perversion on the part of the seducer, and more and more that heredity is seduction by the father" (Letter 52).

11. He never ceased to assert this relationship, (cf. Outline of Psychoanalysis, S.E., 23 pp. 185–6) but without stating the theory.

12. From the beginning Freud rejected the banal thesis which attributed the unpleasure provoked by sexuality to a purely external prohibition. Whether they are of internal or external origin, desire and prohibition go hand in hand. "We shall be plunged deep into the riddles of psychology if we enquire into the origin of the unpleasure which is released by premature sexual stimulation and without which the occurrence of a repression cannot be explained. The most plausible answer will recall the fact that shame and morality are the repressing forces and that the neighbourhood in which nature has placed the sexual organs must inevitably arouse disgust at the same time as sexual experiences. ... I cannot think that the release of unpleasure during sexual experiences is the consequence of a chance admixture of certain unpleasurable factors. ... In my opinion there must be some independent source for the release of unpleasure in sexual life: if that source is present, it can activate sensations of disgust, lend force to morality, and so on' (Draft K).

13. It would be easy to demonstrate that Freud, throughout his life, continued to insist on the reality of the fact of seduction.

14. And no longer the expression of the child's spontaneous, biological sexual activity.

15. "I have learned to explain a number of fantasies of seduction as attempts at fending off memories of the subject's own sexual activity (infantile masturbation)" (Freud, 1906, p. 274).

16. There is an obvious similarity between the Freudian schema of Nachträglichkeit and the psychotic mechanism of "repudiation" (forclusion) described by Lacan: that which has not been admitted to symbolic expression ("repudiated") reappears in reality in the form of hallucination. This non-symbolization corresponds precisely to the earliest time described by Freud. As Lacan and Freud illustrate their theory by the case of the Wolf Man, it may be asked whether Lacan may not have treated as specifically psychotic what is really a very general process, or whether Freud has not taken the exception to be the rule, when basing his demonstration on case of psychosis.

Freud's demonstration is strengthened by the fact that in this particular case the primal scene is very probably authentic. But one might conceive of such absence of subjective elaboration or of symbolization, normally characteristic of the first stage, as not a prerogative of a truly experienced scene. This "foreign body", which is to be internally excluded, is usually brought to the subject, not by the perception of a scene, but by parental desire and its supporting fantasy. Such would be the typically neurotic case: in the first stage (not locatable in time, since it is fragmented into the series of transitions to autoerotism (Cf. pp. 15–16 below)), a pre-symbolic symbolic, to paraphrase Freud, is isolated within the subject who will, at a later stage, recover and symbolize it. In psychosis the first stage would consist of naked reality, and is evidently not symbolized by the subject, but will offer an irreducible nucleus for any later attempt at symbolization. Hence, in such cases, the failure, even the catastrophy, of the second stage.

This offers an approach to a distinction between repression (original) and the psychotic mechanism which Freud tried to delimit throughout his work (more particularly by describing it as Verleugnung: denial), and which Lacan called "forclusion".

17. We might be accused of exaggeration in speaking of concept. "Original fantasy" does not, of course, form part of the classical psychoanalytic concepts. Freud uses it marginally in his very precise study of the question whose development we have traced. The phrase therefore has the value of an "index" and requires clarification.

18. An ever present concern of Freud's (Cf. Draft M): "One of our brightest hopes is that we may be able to define the number and species of fantasies as well as we can those of the 'scenes'."

19. "Wherever experiences fail to fit in with the hereditary schema, they become remodelled in the imagination. ... It is precisely such cases that are calculated to convince us of the independent existence of the schema. We are often able to see the schema triumphing over the

experience of the individual; as when in our present case, the boy's father became the castrator and the menace of his infantile sexuality in spite of what was in other respects an inverted Oedipus complex. ... The contradictions between experience and the schema seem to supply the conflicts of childhood with an abundance of material" (Freud, 1918, pp. 119–20).

20. We are not here trying to develop a coherent psychoanalytic theory which would involve the relationship between the level of the Oedipus structure and that of the original fantasies. One would first have to define what was meant by the Oedipus structure. Indeed the structural aspect of the Oedipus complex—considered both in its basic function and in its triangular form—was worked out much later by Freud: it does not appear at all, for instance, in the Three Essays (1905). The so-called generalized formulation of the complex appeared first in The Ego and the Id (1923), and the generalization in question cannot be taken in any formal sense: it describes a limited series of concrete positions within the interpsychological field created by the father-mother-child triangle. From the point of view of structural anthropology, one might see this as one of the forms of the law governing human interchanges, a law which in other cultures might be incarnated in other persons and in other forms. The prohibitory function of the law might, for instance, be expressed by an agency other than the father. By adopting this solution the analyst would feel he had lost an essential dimension of his experience: the subject is, admittedly, located in a structure of inter-relationship, but the latter is transmitted by the parental unconscious. It is therefore less easy to assimilate it to a language system than to the complexities of a particular speech.

   Freud's concept of the Oedipus complex is, in fact, remarkable for its realism: whether it is represented as an inner conflict (nuclear complex) or as a social institution, the complex remains a given fact; the subject is confronted by it: "every new arrival on this planet is faced by the task of mastering it" (Three Essays, S.E., 7, p. 226, footnote).

   Perhaps it was the realism of the concept which led Freud to allow the notion of original fantasy to co-exist alongside the Oedipus complex, without being concerned to articulate them: here the subject does not encounter the structure, but is carried along by it.

21. According to Freud it is, incidentally, a projection, the projection of a beat in her clitoris, in the form of a noise. There would be a new, circular, relationship between the pulsation which actualizes the fantasy, and the drive which arouses it.

22. "Built up out of things that have been heard about and then subsequently turned to account, they combine things that have been

experienced and things that have been heard about past events (from the history of parents and ancestors) and things seen by the subject himself. They are related to things heard in the same way as dreams are related to things seen" (Draft L). And again: "Fantasies arise from an unconscious combination of things experienced and heard" (Draft M).

23. If we ask what these fantasies mean to us, we are embarking on a different level of interpretation. We then see that they are not only symbolic, but represent the insertion, mediated by an imagined scenario, of the most radically formative symbolism, into corporeal reality. The primal scene represents for us the conjunction of the biological fact of conception and birth with the symbolic fact of filiation: it unites the "savage act" of coitus and the existence of a mother-child-father triad. In the fantasies of castration the conjunction of real and symbolic is even more apparent. With regard to seduction, we should add that it was not only, as we believe we have shown, because Freud had come across numerous actual cases, that he was able to use a fantasy as a scientific theory, and thus, by a roundabout way, hit on the true function of fantasy. It was also because he was trying to account, in terms of origins, for the advent of sexuality to human beings.

24. The proposal to eliminate the unfortunate confusion by the graphological device (using "ph" for unconscious fantasies and "f" for the daydream type) has been declared at times to be real progress, the result of half a century of psychoanalysis. Whether or not this distinction is in fact justified, it seems undesirable to use it in translations of Freud's work. It betrays little respect for the text to render words such as Phantasie or Phantasieren, which Freud invariably employed, by different terms according to the context. Our opposition to this terminological and conceptual innovation rests on three grounds: (i) the distinction should not be introduced into translations of Freud's work, even if the interpretation of his thought were correct; (ii) this interpretation of Freud's thought is incorrect; (iii) this distinction contributes less to the study of the problem than Freud's concept.

25. "In favourable circumstances, the subject can still capture an unconscious fantasy of this sort in consciousness. After I had drawn the attention of one of my patients to her fantasies, she told me that on one occasion she had suddenly found herself in tears in the street and that, rapidly considering what it was she was actually crying about, she had got hold of a fantasy to the following effect. In her imagination she had formed a tender attachment to a pianist who was well known in the town (though she was not personally acquainted with him); she had had a child by him (she was in fact childless); and he had then deserted her and her child and left them in poverty. It was at this point in her

romance that she had burst into tears" (Freud, 1908).

26. "They draw near to consciousness and remain undisturbed so long as they do not have an intense cathexis, but as soon as they exceed a certain height of cathexis they are thrust back." (Freud, 1915, p. 191.)

27. There must of course be a dismantling of the secondary elaboration in order to be able to take the dream element by element. But Freud does not forget that by setting everything on the same level, which is one of the aspects of psychoanalytic listening, the structure, the scenario, becomes itself an element, just as much, for instance, as the global reaction of the subject to his own dream.

28. Freud seems also to have indicated that, generally speaking, desire can be more readily discovered in the structure of the fantasy than in the dream, unless the dream has been much restructured by the fantasy, as is particularly the case in "typical dreams". "If we examine the structure [of fantasies] we shall perceive the way in which the wishful purpose that is at work in their production, has mixed up the material of which they are built, has re-arranged it and has formed it into a new whole" (S.E., 5, p. 492).

29. We suggest the following schema:–

> The repression which returns secondary fantasies to the unconscious would be that described by Freud as "secondary repression" or "after-pressure". A further type of repression, more mythical and obscure, which Freud called "primal repression" (Urverdrängung) corresponds to the constitution of the primal fantasies or their reception by the individual. We attempt later to indicate an approach to this subject. Cf. also Laplanche and Leclaire, "L'inconscient, une étude psychanalytique," Les Temps Modernes, July 1961.

30. Amongst which we should obviously include screen memories and infantile sexual theories.

31. Freud saw in this characteristic of screen-memories that they were not true memories, yet of all conscious fantasies, they are the only ones to claim reality. They are true scenes, the screens of primal fantasies or scenes.

32. According to Isaacs, "primary phantasies are ... dealt with by mental processes far removed from words." It is only through practical necessity that we express them in words, but we thereby introduce a "foreign element". Isaacs, using one of Freud's expressions, speaks of "the language of drives", and it is true that it is not its verbal or non-verbal character which defines the nature of language. But if Isaacs confuses language and the power of expression, perhaps this leads here to a failure to appreciate the originality of Melanie Klein's concepts: her attempt to describe a language which is non-verbal, but nonetheless

structured, on the basis of pairs of opposites (good-bad, inner-outer). The audacity of the technique does at least assume a reference, not to the mobile expression of instinctual life, but to some fundamental oppositions.

33. Cf. the variants formulated by Isaacs: "I want to eat her all up," "I want to keep her inside me," "I want to tear her to bits," "I want to throw her out of me," "I want to bring her back," "I must have her now," etc.

34. More often than not masturbation implies, of course, an imaginary relationship with an object: thus it can only be described as auto-erotic from an external standpoint, to the extent that the subject obtains satisfaction by resorting solely to his own body. But an infantile auto-erotic activity, such as sucking the thumb, in no sense implies the absence of any object. What makes it eventually auto-erotic is, as we shall show later, a special mode of satisfaction, specific to the "birth" of sexuality, which lingers on into pubertal masturbation.

35. "The first wishing (Wünschen) seems to have been a hallucinatory cathecting of the memory of satisfaction" (Freud, 1900, p. 598).

36. Cf. for instance Isaacs's interpretation of Freud's hypothesis of the first hallucination: "It seems probable that hallucination works best at times of less instinctual tension, perhaps when the infant half-awakes and first begins to be hungry. ... The pain of frustration then stirs up a still stronger desire, viz. the wish to take the whole breast into himself and keep it there as a source of satisfaction; and this in its turn will for a time omnipotently fulfil itself in belief, in hallucination. ... This hallucination of the internal satisfying breast may, however, break down altogether if frustration continues, and hunger is not satisfied, the instinct-tension proving too strong to be denied."

It is obvious that the author is in difficulty about reconciling a hallucinated satisfaction with the demands of a frustrated instinct. How indeed can an infant feed itself on wind alone? The Freudian model is incomprehensible unless one understands that it is not the real object, but the lost object; not the milk, but the breast as a signifier, which is the object of the primal hallucination.

37. The breast, wrongly named "object of desire" by psychoanalysts.

38. "At a time at which the first beginnings of sexual satisfaction are still linked with the taking of nourishment, the sexual instinct has a sexual object outside the infant's own body in the shape of his mother's breast. It is only later that the instinct loses that object, just at the time, perhaps, when the child is able to form a total idea of the person to whom the organ that is giving him satisfaction belongs" (Freud, 1905, p. 222). The passage is also invaluable as a further indication that the very constitution of the auto-erotic fantasy implies not only the partial object

142   UNCONSCIOUS PHANTASY

(breast, thumb or substitute), but the mother as a total person, withdrawing as she becomes total. This "totalization" is not to be understood as in the nature of a Gestalt, but by reference to the child's demand, which may be granted or refused by the mother.

39. Described by some psychoanalysts as an "objectless" stage, on a genetic basis, which one might call totalitarian, since it confuses the constitution of the libidinal object with that of objectivity in the external world, and claims to establish stages in the development of the ego as "organ of reality", stages which they also hold to be correlative with those of the libido.

40. Elsewhere (in our Vocabulaire de psychanalyse, Presses Universitaires de France, Paris, 1967), we are developing this notion which is fundamental to the Freudian theory of instincts.

41. In one of his first reflections on fantasy Freud notes that the Impulse could perhaps emanate from fantasy (Draft N).

42. Cf. also in Instincts and their Vicissitudes, the analysis of the pairs of opposites, sadism-masochism, voyeurism-exhibitionism. Beneath the active or passive form of the phrase (seeing, being seen, for instance), we must assume a reflexive form (seeing oneself) which, according to Freud, would be primordial. No doubt this primordial degree is to be found when the subject no longer places himself in one of the different terms of the fantasy.

43. "... A child's intercourse with anyone responsible for his care affords him an unending source of sexual excitation and satisfaction from his erotogenic zones. This is especially so since the person in charge of him, who, after all, is as a rule his mother, herself regards him with feelings that are derived from her own sexual life, and quite clearly treats him as a substitute for a complete sexual object" (1905, p. 223). It is however customary to say that Freud took a long time to recognize the link with the mother.

References

Breuer, J., & Freud, S. (1895). *Studies on Hysteria. S.E., 1.*

Ferenczi, S. (1933). Confusion of tongues between the adult and the child. In: *Final Contributions to the Problems and Methods of Psycho-Analysis.* London: Hogarth, 1955.

Freud, S. (1900). *The Interpretations of Dreams. S.E., 4–5.*

Freud, S. (1901). On dreams. *S.E., 5.*

Freud, S. (1905). *Three Essays on the Theory of Sexuality. S.E., 7.*

Freud, S. (1906) My views on the part played by sexuality in the neuroses. *S.E., 7.*

Freud, S. (1908). Hysterical phantasies and their relation to bisexuality. *S.E., 9.*

Freud, S. (1911). Formulations on the two principles of mental functioning. *S.E., 12.*

Freud, S. (1914). On the history of the psycho-analytic movement. *S.E., 14.*

Freud, S. (1915). The unconscious. *S.E., 14.*

Freud, S. (1915). A case of paranoia running counter to the psycho-analytic theory of the disease. *S.E., 14.*

Freud, S. (1915). Instincts and their vicissitudes. *S.E., 14.*

Freud, S. (1916–1917). *Introductory Lectures. S.E., 15–16.*

Freud, S. (1916). The paths to the formation of symptoms. *S.E., 16.*

Freud, S. (1918). From the history of an infantile neurosis. *S.E., 17.*

Freud, S. (1925). An autobiographical study. *S.E., 20.*

Freud, S. (1933). Femininity. *S.E., 22.*

Freud, S. (1940). *An Outline of Psycho-Analysis. S.E., 23.*

Freud, S. (1950). *The Origins of Psycho-Analysis*. London: Imago, 1954.

Isaacs, S. (1948). The nature and function of phantasy. *Int. J. Psychoanal., 29.*

Klein, M. (1934). A contribution to the psychogenesis of manic-depressive states. *Contributions to Psycho-Analysis*. London: Hogarth, 1949.

Klein, M. (1960). *Narrative of a Child Psycho-Analysis*. London: Hogarth.

CHAPTER FIVE

The nature and function of phantasy

Susan Isaacs

Introduction

A survey of contributions to psycho-analytical theory would show that the term "phantasy" has been used in varying senses by different authors and at different times. Its current usages have widened considerably from its earliest meanings.

Much of this widening of the concept has so far been left implicit. The time is ripe to consider the meaning and definition of the term more explicitly. (Ch.N.1.)

When the meaning of a technical term does become extended in this way, whether deliberately or insensibly, it is usually for a good reason—because the facts and the theoretical formulations they necessitate require it. *It is the relationships between the facts* which need to be looked at more closely and clarified in our thoughts. This chapter is mostly concerned with the definition of "phantasy"; that is to say, with describing the *series of facts* which the use of the term helps us to identify, to organise and to relate to other significant series of facts. Most of what follows will consist of this more careful study of the relationships between different mental processes.

As the work of psycho-analysis, in particular the analysis of young children, has gone on and our knowledge of early mental life has developed, the relationships which we have come to discern between the earliest mental processes and the later more specialised types of mental functioning commonly called "phantasies" have led many of us to extend the connotation of the term "phantasy" in the sense which is now to be developed. (A tendency to widen the significance of the term is already apparent in many of Freud's own writings, including a discussion of unconscious phantasy.[1])

It is to be shown that certain mental phenomena which have been generally described by various authors, not usually in reference to the term "phantasy", to in fact imply the activity of unconscious phantasies. By correlating these phenomena with the unconscious phantasies with which they are bound up, their true relationships to other mental processes can be better understood, and their function and full importance in the mental life appreciated.

This chapter is not primarily concerned to establish any particular content of phantasy. It will deal with the nature and function of phantasy as a whole, and its place in the mental life. Actual examples of phantasy will be used for illustrative purposes, but it is not suggested that these examples cover the field; nor are they chosen systematically. It is true that the very same evidence which establishes the existence of phantasies even at the earliest ages gives us some indication of their specific character; yet to accept the general evidence for the activity of phantasy from the beginning of life and the place of phantasy in the mental life as a whole does not automatically imply accepting any particular phantasy content at any given age. The relation of content to age may appear to some extent in succeeding chapters, for which this chapter is intended to pave the way by general considerations.

To understand the nature and function of phantasy in the mental life involves the study of the earliest phases of mental development, i.e. during the first three years of life. Scepticism is sometimes expressed as to the possibility of understanding psychic life at all in the earliest years—as distinct from observing the sequence and development of behaviour. In fact we are far from having to rely upon mere imagination or blind guesswork, even as regards the first year of life. When all the observable facts of behaviour are considered in the light of *analytic* knowledge gained from adults and from children over two years of age, and are brought into relation with analytic principles, we arrive at many hypotheses carrying a high degree of probability and some certainties regarding early mental processes.

Our views about phantasy in these earliest years are based almost wholly upon inference, but then this is true at any age. Unconscious phantasies are always inferred, not observed as such; the technique of psycho-analysis as a while is largely based upon inferred knowledge. As has often been pointed out regarding the adult patient too, he does not tell us his unconscious phantasies directly, nor, for that matter, his preconscious resistances. We can often observe quite directly emotions and attitudes of which the patient himself is unaware; these and many other observed data (such as those instanced later, on pp. 150–153) make it possible and necessary for us to infer that such and such resistances or phantasies are operating. This is true of the young child as well as of the adult.

The data to be drawn upon here are of three main sorts, and the conclusions to be put forward are based upon a *convergence* of these lines of evidence.

(a) Considerations regarding the relationships between certain established facts and theories, many of which facts and theories, although quite familiar in psycho-analytic thought, have hitherto been dealt with in a relatively isolated way. When considered fully, these relationships require the postulates which will be put forward, and by means of these postulates become better integrated and more adequately understood.

(b) Clinical evidence gained by analysts from the actual analysis of adults and children of all ages.

(c) Observational data (non-analytic observations and experimental studies) of the infant and young child, by the various means at the disposal of the science of child development.

Methods of Study

(a) Observational Methods

Before considering our main thesis, it may be useful to survey briefly certain fundamental principles of method which provide us with the material for conclusions as to the nature and function of

phantasy, and which are exemplified both in clinical (psychoanalytic) studies and in many of the most fruitful recent researches
into the development of behaviour.

A variety of techniques for the study of particular aspects of
child development has been evolved in recent years. It is a notable
fact that observational researches into the development of personality and social relationships, and especially those which attempt to
reach understanding of motives and of mental process generally,
tend to pay more and more regard to certain methodological
principles, now to be discussed. These principles bring them into
closer line with clinical studies and thus form a valuable link between
observational methods and analytic technique. They are (a) attention
to details; (b) observation of context; (c) study of genetic continuity.

(a) All serious contributions to child psychology in recent years
could be instanced as illustrations of the growing appreciation of
the need to attend to *the precise details* of the child's behaviour,
whatever the field of enquiry may be: emotional, social, intellectual,
locomotor or manipulative skills, perception and language. The
researches of Gesell, Shirley, Bayley and many others into early
mental development exemplify this principle. So do the experimental and observational studies of social development, or the
researches into infant behaviour by D.W. Winnicott and M.P.
Middlemore. (Ch.N.2.) Middlemore's research on the behaviour of
infants in the feeding situation, for example, demonstrated how
varied and complex even the earliest responses of infants turn out to
be when noted and compared in close detail, and how intimately
the child's experiences, for example, the way he is handled and
suckled, influence succeeding phases of feeling and phantasy and
his mental processes generally.

Most advances in observational and experimental technique
have been devised to facilitate the precise observation and
recording of details of behaviour. We shall later refer to the great
importance of this principle in psycho-analytic work and the way in
which it helps us to discern the content of early phantasies.

(b) The principle of noting and recording *the context of observed data*
is of the greatest importance, whether in the case of a particular
instance or sort of social behaviour, of particular examples of play,

questions asked by the child, stages in the development of speech—whatever the data may be. By "context" is meant, not merely earlier and later examples of the same sort of behaviour, but the whole immediate setting of the behaviour being studied, in its social and emotional situation. With regard to phantasy, for example, we have to note *when* the child says this or that, plays this or that game, performs this or that ritual, masters (or loses) this or that skill, demands or refuses a particular gratification, shows signs of anxiety, distress, triumph, glee, affection or other emotions; who is present—or absent—at the time; what is his general emotional attitude or immediate feeling towards these adults or playmates; what losses, strains, satisfactions have been recently experienced or are being now anticipated? And so on and so forth.

The importance of this principle of studying the psychological context of particular data in the mental life has become increasingly recognised amongst students of children's behaviour, whatever mental process or function of behaviour happens to be the subject of study. Many examples could be given: e.g. the study of temper tantrums, by Florence Goodenough; of the innate bases of fear, by C.W. Valentine; of the development of speech in infancy, by M.M. Lewis; of the development of sympathy in young children, by L.B. Murphy. (Ch.N.2.)

Murphy's work, in especial, has shown how indispensable is this principle in the study of social relationships, and how far more fruitful it proves than any purely quantitative or statistical treatment of types of behaviour or traits of personality, made without reference to context.

One of the outstanding examples of the way in which attention to precise details in their total context may reveal the significance of a piece of behaviour in the inner psychic life of the child is Freud's observation of the play of a boy of eighteen months of age. This boy was a normal child, of average intellectual development, and generally well behaved. Freud writes:

> He did not disturb his parents at night; he scrupulously obeyed orders about not touching various objects and not going into certain rooms; and above all he never cried when his mother went out and left him for hours together, although the tie to his mother was a very close one: she had not only nourished him herself, but had cared for him and brought him up without any outside help. Occasionally,

however, this well-behaved child evinced the troublesome habit of flinging into the corner of the room or under the bed all the little things he could lay his hands on, so that to gather up his toys was often no light task. He accompanied this by an expression of interest and gratification, emitting a loud long drawn out "o-o-o-oh" which in the judgement of the mother (one that coincided with my own) was not an interjection but meant "gone away" (*fort*). I saw at last that this was a game, and that the child used all his toys only to play "being gone" (*fortsein*) with them. One day I made an observation that confirmed my view. The child had a wooden reel with a piece of string wound round it ... he kept throwing it with considerable skill, held by the string, over the side of his little draped cot, so that the reel disappeared into it, then said his significant "o-o-o-oh" and drew the reel by the string out of the cot again, greeting its reappearance with a joyful "Da" (there). This was therefore the complete game, disappearance and return, the first act being the only one generally observed by the onlookers, and the one untiringly repeated by the child as a game for its own sake, although the greater pleasure unquestionably attached to the second act.

The meaning of the game was then not far to seek. It was connected with the child's great cultural achievement—the forgoing of the satisfaction of an instinct—as the result of which he could let his mother go away without making any fuss. He compensated himself for this, as it were, by himself enacting the same disappearance and return with the objects within his reach.

Later on, Freud also noted a further detail in the boy's behaviour:

One day when the mother had been out for some hours she was greeted on her return by the information "Baby o-o-o-oh" which at first remained unintelligible. It soon proved that during his long lonely hours he had found a method of bringing about his own disappearance. He had discovered his reflection in the long mirror which nearly reached to the ground and had then crouched down in front of it, so that the reflection was "*fort*".

The observation of this detail of the sounds with which the boy greeted his mother's return called attention to the further link of the child's delight in making his own image appear and disappear in the mirror, with its confirmatory evidence of his triumph in controlling feelings of loss, by his play, as a consolation for his mother's absence.

Freud also brought to bear upon the boy's play with the wooden reel other and more remote facts which many observers would not have thought had any relation to it, such as the child's general relationship to his mother, his affection and obedience, his capacity to refrain from disturbing her and to allow her to absent herself for hours together without grumbling or protest. Freud thus came to understand much of the significance of the child's play in his social and emotional life, concluding that in the boy's delight in throwing away material objects and then retrieving them, he enjoyed the phantasied satisfaction of controlling his mother's comings and goings. On this basis he could tolerate her leaving him in actuality, and remain loving and obedient.

The principle of observing context, like that of attention to detail, is an essential element in the technique of psycho-analysis, whether with adults or children.

(c) The third fundamental principle, of value both in observational and in analytic studies, is that of *genetic continuity*.[2]

Experience has already proved that throughout every aspect of mental (no less than of physical) development, whether in posture, locomotor and manipulative skill, in perception, imagination, language or early logic, any given phase develops by degrees out of preceding phases in a way which can be ascertained both in general outline and in specific detail. This established general truth serves as a guide and pointer in further observations. All studies of developmental status (such as those of Gesell and Shirley) rest upon this principle.

It does not mean that development proceeds at an even pace throughout. There are definite crises in growth, integrations which from their nature bring radical changes in experience and further achievement, e.g. learning to walk is such a crisis; but dramatic though it be in the changes it introduces into the child's world, actual walking is but the end phase of a long series of developing co-ordinations. Learning to talk is another such crisis; but again, one prepared for and foreshadowed in every detail before it is achieved. So true is this that the definition of talking is purely a matter of convention. Commonly it is taken to mean the use of two words, an arbitrary standard useful for purposes of comparison, but not intended to blur the continuous course of development. Speech development *begins*, as has often been shown, with the sounds made by the infant when hungry or feeding in the first few weeks of life; and on the other hand, the changes occurring *after* the mastery of the first words are as continuous and as varied and complex as those occurring before this moment.

One aspect of speech development having a special bearing upon our present problems is the fact that *comprehension of words long antedates their use.* The actual length of time during which the child shows that he understands much that is said to him, or spoken in his presence, yet has not come to the point of using any words himself, varies much from child to child. In some highly intelligent children, the interval between comprehension and use of words may be as much as one year. This time-lag of use behind comprehension is found generally throughout childhood. Many other intellectual processes, also, are expressed in action long before they can be put into words. (Ch. N.2.)

Examples of rudimentary thought emerging in action and in speech from the second year of life are given in the studies of speech development by M.M. Lewis. The experimental studies of the development of logical thinking, by Hazlitt and others, show the same principle at work in later years (Ch. N.2.)

This general fact of genetic continuity, and its particular exemplifications in speech development, have a specific bearing upon one important question: are phantasies active in the child at the time when the relevant impulses first dominate his behaviour and his experience, or do these become so only in retrospect, when later on he can put his experience into words? The evidence clearly suggests that phantasies are active along with the impulses from which they arise.[3]

Genetic continuity thus characterises every aspect of development at all ages. There is no reason to doubt that it holds true of phantasy as well as of overt behaviour and of logical thinking. Is it not, indeed, one of the major achievements of psycho-analysis to have shown that the development of the instinctual life, for instance, had a continuity never understood before Freud's work? The essence of Freud's theory of sexuality lies in just this fact of detailed continuity of development.

Probably no psycho-analyst would question the abstract

principle, but it is not always appreciated that it is far more than this. *The established principle of genetic continuity is a concrete instrument of knowledge.* It enjoins upon us to accept no particular facts of behaviour or mental processes as *sui generis*, ready-made, or suddenly emerging, but to regard them as items in a developing series. We seek to trace them backwards through earlier and more rudimentary stages to their most germinal forms; similarly, we are required to regard the facts as manifestations of a process of growth, which has to be followed forward to later and more developed forms. Not only is it necessary to study the acorn in order to understand the oak, but also to know about the oak in order to understand the acorn. (Ch. N.2.)

(b) The Method of Psycho-Analysis

These three ways of obtaining evidence of mental process from observation of behaviour—that of noting the context, observing details and approaching any particular data as a part of a developmental process—are essential aspects of the work of psycho-analysis, and most fully exemplified there. They are indeed its breath of life. They serve to elucidate the nature and function of phantasy, as well as of other mental phenomena.

The observation of detail and of context are so intimately bound up in analytic work that they may be briefly dealt with together. With adult patients, as well as children, the analyst not only listens to all the details of the actual content of the patient's remarks and associations, including what is not said as well as what is, but notes also where emphasis is put, and whether it seems appropriate. Repetition of what has already been told or remarked, in its immediate affective and associative context; changes occurring in the patient's account of events in his earlier life, and in the picture he presents of people in his environment, as the work goes on; changes in his ways of referring to circumstances and to people (including the names he gives them), from time to time, all serve to indicate the character and activity of the phantasies operating in his mind. So do idiosyncrasies of speech, or phrases and forms of description, metaphors and verbal style generally. Further data are the patient's selection of facts from a total incident, and his denials (e.g. of things he has previously said, of states of mind which would be appropriate to the content of what he is saying, of real objects seen or incidents occurring in the analytic room, of facts in his own life which can certainly be inferred from the other known content of his life or family history, of facts known by the patient about the analyst or of happenings in public affairs, such as war and bombs). The analyst notes the patient's manner and behaviour as he enters and leaves the room, as he greets the analyst or parts from him, and while he is on the couch; including every detail of gesture or tone of voice, pace of speaking and variations in this, idiosyncratic routine or particular changes in mode of expression, changes of mood, every sign of affect or denial of affect, in their particular nature and intensity and their precise associative context. These, and many other such kinds of detail, taken as a context to the patient's dreams and associations, help to reveal his unconscious phantasies (among other mental facts). The particular situation in the internal life of the patient at the moment gradually becomes clear, and the relation of his immediate problem to earlier situations and actual experiences in his history is gradually made plain.

The third principle, that of genetic continuity, is inherent in the whole approach and the moment-by-moment work of psycho-analysis.

Freud's discovery of the successive phases of libidinal develop-ment, and the continuity of the various manifestations of the sexual wishes from infancy to maturity, has not only been fully confirmed with every patient analysed, but, as in the case of every sound generalisation of observed facts, has proved to be a reliable instrument for further understanding of new data.

Observations in the analytic field of the development of phantasy and of the continuous and developing interplay between psychic reality and knowledge of the external world, are fully in accordance with the data and generalisations regarding develop-ment arrived at in other fields, such as bodily skills, perceptions, speech and logical thinking. As with the external facts of behaviour, so with the development of phantasy, we have to regard each manifestation at any given time and in any given situation as a member of a developing series whose rudimentary beginnings can be traced backwards and whose further, more mature, forms can be followed forwards. Awareness of the way in which the content and form of phantasy at any given time are bound up with the successive phases of instinctual development, and of the growth of the ego, is always operating in the analyst's mind. To make this plain (in concrete detail) to the patient is an inherent part of the work.

It was by attending to the details and the context of the patient's speech and manner, as well as of his dreams and associations, that Freud laid bare both the fundamental instinctual drives in the mental life, and the varied processes—the so-called *"mental mechanisms"*—by which impulses and feelings are controlled and expressed, internal equilibrium is maintained and adaptation to the external world achieved. These "mechanisms" are very varied in type and many of them have received close attention. In the view of the present writers, all these various mechanisms are intimately related to particular sorts of phantasy, and at a later point the character of this relationship will be gone into.

Freud's discoveries were made almost entirely from the analysis of adults, supplemented by certain observations of children. Melanie Klein, in her direct analytic work with children of two years onwards, developed the full resources of analytic technique by using the children's play with material objects, their games and their bodily activities towards the analyst, as well as their talk about what they were doing and feeling, or what had been happening in their external lives. The make-believe and manipulative play of young children exemplify those various mental processes (and therefore, as we shall see, the phantasies) first noted by Freud in the dream-life of adults and in their neurotic symptoms. In the child's relationship to the analyst, as with the adult's, the phantasies arising in the earliest situations of life are repeated and acted out in the clearest and most dramatic manner, with a wealth of vivid detail.

Transference Situation
It is especially in the patient's emotional relation to the analyst that the study of context, of details and of continuity of development proves fruitful for the understanding of phantasy. As is well know, Freud early discovered that patients repeat towards their analyst situations of feeling and impulse, and mental processes generally, which have been experienced earlier on in their relationships to people in their external lives and personal histories. This transference on to the analyst of early wishes, aggressive impulses, fears and other emotions, is confirmed by every analyst.

The personality, the attitudes and intentions, even the external characteristics and the sex of the analyst, *as seen and felt in the patient's mind*, change from day to day (even from moment to moment) according to changes in the inner life of the patient (whether these are brought about by the analyst's comments or by outside happenings). That is to say, *the patient's relation to his analyst is almost entirely one of unconscious phantasy*. Not only is the phenomenon of "transference" as a whole evidence of the existence and activity of phantasy in every analysand, whether child or adult, ill or healthy; observed in detail, its changes also enable us to decipher the particular character of the phantasies at work in particular situations and their influence upon other mental processes. The "transference" has turned out to be the chief instrument of learning what is going on in the patient's mind, as well as of discovering or reconstructing his early history; the unfolding of his transference phantasies, and the tracing of their relation to early experiences and present-day situations form the chief agency of the "cure".

Repetition of early situations and "acting-out" in the transference carry us back far beyond the earliest conscious memories; the patient (whether child or adult) often shows us, with the most vivid and dramatic detail, feelings, impulses and attitudes appropriate not only to the situations of childhood but also to those of the earliest months of infancy. In his phantasy towards the analyst, the patient is back in his earliest days, and to follow these phantasies in their context and understand them in detail is to gain solid knowledge of what actually went on in his mind as an infant.

Mental Life Under Two Years of Age
For the understanding of phantasy and other mental processes in children from the end of the second year onwards, we thus have not only all the evidence of observed behaviour in ordinary life, but also the full resources of the analytic method used directly.

When we turn to children under two years, we bring certain proved instruments of understanding to the study of their responses to stimuli, their spontaneous activities, their signs of affect, their play with people and with material objects, and all the varied aspects of their behaviour. First, we have those principles of observation already outlined—the value of observing context, of noting precise details, and of regarding the data observed at any one moment as being members of a series which can be traced backwards to their rudimentary beginnings and forwards to their more mature forms. Secondly, we have the insight gained from direct analytic experience into the mental processes so clearly expressed in similar types of behaviour (continuous with these earlier forms) in children of more than two years; above all, the evidence yielded by the repetition of situations, emotions, attitudes and phantasies in the "transference", during analyses of older children and of adults.

Using these various instruments, it becomes possible to formulate certain hypotheses about the earliest phases of phantasy and of learning, of mental development generally, which can be credited with a considerable degree of probability. There are gaps in our understanding, and from the nature of the case these may take time to remove. Nor are our inferences as certain as those regarding later development. But there is much which is definitely clear, and much more that only awaits further detailed observations, or more patient correlating of the observable facts, to yield a high degree of understanding.

II The Nature and Function of Phantasy

To turn now to our main theses:

As has been said, it is on the basis of the convergence of these various lines of evidence that the present-day significance of the concept of phantasy is to be discussed. A consideration of all these sorts of fact and theory calls for a revision of the usages of the term.

Common Usages of the Term "Phantasy"

Among psycho-analytic writers, the term has sometimes referred (in line with everyday language) only to *conscious* "fantasies", of the nature of day-dreams. But Freud's discoveries soon led him to recognise the existence of *unconscious* phantasies. This reference of the word is indispensable. The English translators of Freud adopted a special spelling of the word "phantasy", with the *ph*, in order to differentiate the psycho-analytical significance of the term (i.e. predominantly or entirely unconscious phantasies from the popular word "fantasy", meaning conscious day-dreams, fictions and so on. The psycho-analytical term "phantasy" essentially connotes *unconscious* mental content, which may or may not become conscious.

This meaning of the word has assumed a growing significance, particularly in consequence of the work of Melanie Klein on the early stages of development.

Again, the word "phantasy" has often been used to mark a contrast to "reality", the latter word being taken as identical with "external" or "material" or "objective" facts. But when external reality is thus called "objective" reality, this makes an implicit assumption which denies to psychical reality its *own objectivity as a mental fact*. Some analysts tend to contrast "phantasy" with "reality" in such a way as to undervalue the dynamic importance of phantasy. A related usage is to think of "phantasy" as something "merely" or "only" imagined, as something unreal, in contrast with what is actual, what *happens* to one. This kind of attitude tends towards a depreciation of psychical reality and of the significance of mental processes *as such*.[4]

Psycho-analysis has shown that the quality of being "merely" or "only" imagined is not the most important criterion for the understanding of the human mind. When and under what conditions "psychical reality" is in harmony with external reality is one special part of the total problem of understanding mental life as a whole: a very important part indeed; but, still, "only" one part. This will be discussed more fully later.

Freud's discovery of *dynamic psychical reality* initiated a new epoch of psychological understanding.

He showed that the inner world of the mind has a continuous living reality of its own, with its own dynamic laws and characteristics, different from those of the external world. In order to understand the dream and the dreamer, his psychological history, his neurotic symptoms or his normal interests and character, we have to give up that prejudice in favour of external reality, and of our conscious orientations to it, that under-valuation of internal reality, which is the attitude of the ego in ordinary civilised life today.[5]

A further point, of importance in our general thesis, is that unconscious phantasy is fully active in the normal, no less than in the neurotic mind. It seems sometimes to be assumed that only in the "neurotic" is psychical reality (i.e. unconscious phantasy) of paramount importance, and that with "normal" people its significance is reduced to vanishing point. This view is not in accordance with the facts, as they are seen in the behaviour of ordinary people in daily life, or as observed through the medium of psycho-analytic work, notably in the transference. The difference between normal and abnormal lies in the way in which the unconscious phantasies are dealt with, the particular mental processes by means of which they are worked over and modified; and the degree of direct or indirect gratification in the real world and adaptation to it, which these favoured mechanisms allow.

Phantasy as the Primary Content of Unconscious Mental Processes
Thus far, we have been upon familiar ground. If, however, we bring recent clinical data into closer relation with certain formulations of Freud's, we take a definite step forward in understanding the function of phantasy.

A study of the conclusions arising from the analysis of young children leads to the view that phantasies are the primary content of unconscious mental processes. Freud did not formulate his views on this point in terms of phantasy, but it can be seen that such a formulation is in essential alignment with his contributions.

Freud has said that "... everything conscious has a preliminary unconscious stage ..."[6]. All mental processes originate in the unconscious and only under certain conditions become conscious. They arise either from instinctual needs or in response to external stimuli acting upon instinctual impulses. "We suppose that it [the id] is somewhere in direct contact with somatic processes and take over from the instinctual needs and give them *mental expression*."[7]

Now in the view of the present writers, this "mental expression" of instinct *is* unconscious phantasy. Phantasy is (in the first instance) the mental corollary, the psychic representative, of instinct. There is no impulse, no instinctual urge or response which is not experienced as unconscious phantasy.

In the beginning of his researches, Freud was concerned particularly with libidinal desires, and his "mental expression of instinctual needs" would refer primarily to libidinal aims. His later studies, however, and those of many other workers, have required us to include destructive impulses as well.

The first mental processes, the psychic representatives of

libidinal and destructive instincts, are to be regarded as the earliest beginning of phantasies. In the mental development of the infant, however, phantasy soon becomes also a means of defence against anxieties, a means of inhibiting and controlling instinctual urges and an expression of reparative wishes as well. The relation between phantasy and wish-fulfilment has always been emphasised; but our experience has shown, too, that most phantasies (like symptoms) also serve various other purposes as well as wish-fulfilment; e.g. denial, reassurance, omnipotent control, reparation, etc. It is, of course, true that, in a wider sense, all these mental processes which aim at diminishing instinctual tension, anxiety and guilt, also serve the aim of wish-fulfilment; but it is useful to discriminate the specific modes of these different processes and their particular aims.

All impulses, all feelings, all modes of defence are experienced in phantasies which give them *mental* life and show their direction and purpose.

A phantasy represents the particular content of the urges or feelings (for example, wishes, fears, anxieties, triumphs, love or sorrow) dominating the mind at the moment. In early life, there is indeed a wealth of unconscious phantasies which take specific form in conjunction with the cathexis of particular bodily zones. Moreover, they rise and fall in complicated patterns according to the rise and fall and modulation of the primary instinct-impulses which they express. The world of phantasy shows the same protean and kaleidoscopic changes as the contents of a dream. These changes occur partly in response to external stimulation and partly as a result of the interplay between the primary instinctual urges themselves.

It may be useful at this point to give some examples of specific phantasies, without, however, discussing the particular age or time relations between these actual examples.

In attempting to give such examples of specific phantasies we are naturally obliged to put them into words; we cannot describe or discuss them without doing so. This is clearly not their original character and inevitably introduces a foreign element, one belonging to later phases of development, and to the pre-conscious mind. (Later on we shall discuss more fully the relation between phantasies and their verbal expression.)

On the basis of those principles of observation and interpretation which have already been described and are well established by psycho-analytic work, we are able to conclude that when the child shows his desire for his mother's breast, he *experiences* this desire as a specific phantasy—"I want to suck the nipple". If desire is very intense (perhaps on account of anxiety), he is likely to feel: "I want to eat her all up." Perhaps to avert the repetition of loss of her, or for his pleasure, he may feel: "I want to keep her inside me." If he is feeling fond, he may have the phantasy: "I want to stroke her face, to pat and cuddle her." At other times, when he is frustrated or provoked, his impulses may be of an aggressive character; he will experience these as, e.g.: "I want to bite the breast; I want to tear her to bits." Or if, e.g. urinary impulses are dominant, he may feel: "I want to drown and burn her." If anxiety is stirred by such aggressive wishes, he may phantasy: "I myself shall be cut or bitten up by mother"; and when his anxiety refers to his internal object, the breast which has been eaten up and kept inside, he may want to eject her and feel: "I want to throw her out of me." When he feels loss and grief, he experiences, as Freud described: "My mother has gone for ever." He may feel: "I want to bring her back, I must have her *now*", and then try to overcome his sense of loss and grief and helplessness by the phantasies expressed in auto-erotic satisfactions, such as thumb-sucking and genital play: "If I suck my thumb, I feel she *is* back here as part of me, belonging to me and giving me pleasure." If, after having in his phantasy attacked his mother and hurt and damaged her, libidinal wishes come up again, he may feel he wants to restore his mother and will then phantasy: "I want to put the bits together again", "I want to make her better", "I want to feed her as she has fed me"; and so on and so forth.

Not merely do these phantasies appear and disappear according to changes in the instinctual urges stirred up by outer circumstance, they also exist together, side by side in the mind, even though they be contradictory; just as in a dream, mutually exclusive wishes may exist and be expressed together.

Not only so: these early mental processes have an omnipotent character. Under the pressure of instinct tension, the child in his earliest days not only feels: "I want to", but implicitly phantasies: "I am doing" this and that to his mother; "I *have* her inside me", when he wants to. The wish and impulse, whether it be love or hate, libidinal or destructive, tends to be felt as actually fulfilling itself, whether with an external or an internal object. This is partly because of the overwhelmingness of his desires and feelings. In his earliest days, his own wishes and impulses fill the whole world at the time when they are felt. It is only slowly that he learns to distinguish between the wish and the deed, between external facts and his feelings about them. The degree of differentiation partly depends upon the stage of development reached at the time, and partly upon the momentary intensity of the desire or emotion. This omnipotent character of early wishes and feelings links with Freud's views about hallucinatory satisfaction in the infant.

Hallucination and Primary Introjection
Freud had been led (by his study of unconscious processes in the minds of adults) to assume that, in the beginning of mental life, "... whatever was thought of (desired) was simply imagined in an hallucinatory form, as still happens with our dream-thoughts every night". This he calls the child's "attempts at satisfaction by hallucination".[8]

What, then, does the infant hallucinate? We may assume, since it is the oral impulse which is at work, first, the nipple, then the breast, and later, his mother as a whole person; and he hallucinates the nipple or the breast in order to enjoy it. As we can see from his behaviour (sucking movements, sucking his own lip or a little later his fingers, and so on), hallucination does not stop at the mere picture, but carries him on to what he is, in detail, going to do with the desired object which he imagines (phantasies) he has obtained. It seems probable that hallucination works best at times of less intense instinctual tension, perhaps when the infant half awakes and first begins to be hungry, but still lies quiet. As tension increases, hunger and the wish to suck the breast becoming stronger, hallucination is liable to break down. The pain of frustration then stirs up a still stronger desire, *viz.* the wish to take the whole breast into himself and keep it there, as a source of satisfaction; and this in its turn will for a time omnipotently fulfil itself in belief, in hallucination. We must assume that the incorporation of the breast is bound up with the earliest forms of the phantasy-life. This hallucination of the internal satisfying breast may, however, break down altogether if frustration continues and hunger is not satisfied, instinct tension proving too strong to be denied. Rage and violently aggressive feelings and phantasies will then dominate the mind, and necessitate some adaptation.

Let us consider further what Freud has to say about this situation. He goes on:

> In so far as it is auto-erotic, the ego has no need of the outside world, but ... it cannot but for a time perceive instinctual stimuli as painful. Under the sway of the pleasure principle, there now takes place a further development. The objects presenting themselves, in so far as they are sources of pleasure, are absorbed by the ego into itself, "introjected" (according to an expression coined by Ferenczi): while, on the other hand, the ego thrusts forth upon the external world whatever within itself gives rise to pain (*v. infra*: the mechanism of projection.[9]

Although in describing introjection, Freud does not use the phrase "unconscious phantasy", it is clear that his concept accords with our assumption of the activity of unconscious phantasy in the earliest phase of life.

Difficulties in Early Development Arising from Phantasy
Many of the familiar difficulties of the young infant (e.g. in feeding and excreting, or his phobias of strangers and anxiety at being left alone, etc.) can best be integrated with well-established analytic views, and their significance more fully understood, if they are seen as manifestations of early phantasy.

Freud commented on some of these difficulties, e.g. he referred to "... the situation of the infant when he is presented with a stranger instead of his mother"; and after speaking of the child's anxiety, added: "... the expression of his face and his reaction of crying indicate that he is feeling pain as well ... As soon as he misses his mother he behaves as if he were never going to see her again".[10] Freud also referred to "the infant's misunderstanding of the facts ..."

Now, by "pain" Freud obviously does not here mean bodily, but *mental* pain; and mental pain has a content, a meaning, and implies phantasy. On the view presented here, "he behaves as if he were never going to see her again" means his phantasy is that his mother has been destroyed by his own hate or greed and altogether lost. His awareness of her absence is profoundly coloured by his feelings towards her—his longing and intolerance of frustration, his hate and consequent anxieties. His "misunderstanding of the facts" is that same "subjective interpretation" of his perception of her absence which, as Joan Riviere points out,[11] is a characteristic of phantasy.

On another occasion, when speaking of oral frustrations, Freud says: "It looks far more as if the desire of the child for its first form of nourishment is altogether insatiable, and as if it never got over the pain of losing the mother's breast ... It is probable, too, that the fear of poisoning is connected with weaning. Poison is the nourishment that makes one ill. Perhaps, moreover, the child traces his early illnesses back to this frustration."[12]

How would it be possible for the child to "trace his early illnesses back to this frustration" unless at the time of the frustration he experienced it *in his mind*, retained it and later on remembered it unconsciously? At the time when he experiences the frustration, there is not merely a bodily happening but also a mental process, i.e. a phantasy—the phantasy of having a bad mother who inflicts pain and loss upon him. Freud says the fear of poisoning is probably connected with weaning. He does not discuss this connection further; but it implies the existence of phantasies about a poisoning breast, such as Melanie Klein's work has shown.

Again, when Freud speaks of the feelings the little girl has about her mother, he refers to the child's "dread of being killed by the mother".[13]

Now to speak of a "dread of being killed by the mother" is obviously a way of describing the child's phantasy of a murderous mother. In our analytic work, we find that the phantasy of the "murderous" mother supervenes upon that of the mother who is attacked with murderous intent by the child. Sometimes the phantasy of the vengeful mother may come to conscious expression in words later on, as in the small boy, reported by Dr Ernest Jones, who said of his mother's nipple when he saw her feeding a younger child: "That's what you bit me with." As we can confirm by analysis of the transference in every patient, what has happened here is that the child has projected his own oral aggressive wishes on to the object of those wishes, his mother's breast. In his phantasy which accompanies this projection, she (the mother or her breast) is now going to bite him to bits as he wanted to do to her.

Phantasies and Words

We must now consider very briefly the relation between phantasies and words.

The primary phantasies, the representatives of the earliest impulses of desire and aggressiveness, are expressed in and dealt with by mental processes far removed from words and conscious relational thinking, and determined by the logic of emotion. At a later period they may under certain conditions (sometimes in children's spontaneous play, sometimes only in analysis) become capable of being expressed in words.

There is a wealth of evidence to show that phantasies are active in the mind long before language has developed, and that even in the adult they continue to operate alongside and independently of words. Meanings, like feelings, are far older than speech, alike in racial and in childhood experience.

In childhood and in adult life, we live and feel, we phantasy and act far beyond our verbal meanings. E.g. some of our dreams show us what worlds of drama we can live through in visual terms alone. We know from drawing, painting and sculpture and the whole world of art, what a wealth of implicit meaning can reside even in a shape, a colour, a line, a movement, a mass, a composition of form or colour, or of melody and harmony in music. In social life, too, we know from our own ready and intuitive response to other people's facial expression, tones of voice, gestures,[14] etc., how much we appreciate directly without words, how much meaning is implicit in what we perceive, sometimes with never a word uttered, or even in spite of words uttered. These things, perceived and imagined and felt about, are the stuff of experience. Words are a means of *referring* to experience, actual or phantasied, but are not identical with it, not a substitute for it. Words may evoke feelings and images and actions, and point to situations; they do so by virtue of being signs of experience, not of being themselves the main material of experience.

Freud made quite clear, in more than one passage, his own view that words belong to the conscious mind only and not to the realm of unconscious feelings and phantasies. He spoke, e.g., of the fact that it is real objects and persons which we invest with love and interest, not their names (Ch. N.3.)

And of visual memory he wrote: "... it approximates more

closely to unconscious processes than does thinking in words, and it is unquestionably older than the latter, both ontogenetically and phylogenetically".[15]

Perhaps the most convincing evidence of the activity of phantasy without words is that of hysterical *conversion-symptoms*.[16] In these familiar neurotic symptoms, ill people revert to a primitive pre-verbal language, and make use of sensations, postures, gestures and visceral processes to express emotions and unconscious wishes or beliefs, i.e. phantasies. The psychogenic character of such bodily symptoms, first discovered by Freud and followed up by Ferenczi, has been confirmed by every analyst; their elucidation is a commonplace in the work with many types of patient. Each detail of the symptoms turns out to have a specific meaning, i.e. to express a specific phantasy; and the various shifts of form and intensity and bodily part affected reflect changes in phantasy, occurring in response to outer events or to inner pressures.

We are not, however, left to depend upon even such convincing general considerations from adults and older children, but can occasionally gather quite direct evidence from a young child that a particular phantasy may dominate his mind long before its content can be put into words.

As an example: a little girl of one year and eight months, with poor speech development, saw a shoe of her mother's from which the sole had come loose and was flapping about. The child was horrified, and screamed with terror. For about a week she would shrink away and scream if she saw her mother wearing any shoes at all, and for some time could only tolerate her mother's wearing a pair of brightly coloured house shoes. The particular offending pair was not worn for several months. The child gradually forgot about the terror, and let her mother wear any sort of shoes. At two years and eleven months, however (fifteen months later), she suddenly said to her mother in a frightened voice, "Where are Mummy's broken shoes?" Her mother hastily said, fearing another screaming attack, that she had sent them away, and the child then commented, "They might have eaten me right up".

The flapping shoe was thus *seen* by the child as a threatening mouth, and responded to as such, at one year and eight months, even though the phantasy could not be put into words till more than a year later. Here, then, we have the clearest possible evidence that a phantasy can be felt, and felt as real, long before it can be expressed in words.

Phantasies and Sensory Experience

Words, then, are a late development in our means of expressing the inner world of our phantasy. By the time a child can use words— even primitive words such as "Baby o-o-o-oh"—he has already gone through a long and complicated history of psychic experience.

The first phantasied wish-fulfilment, the first "hallucination", is bound up with *sensation*. Some pleasurable sensation (organ-pleasure) there must be, very early, if the baby is to survive. For instance, if, for one reason or another, the first sucking impulse does not lead to pleasurable satisfaction, acute anxiety is aroused in the infant. The sucking impulse itself may then tend to be inhibited or to be less well co-ordinated than it should. In extreme cases, there may be complete inhibition of feeding, in less marked instances "pining" and poor development. If, on the other hand, through a natural unity of rhythm between mother and child, or the skilful handling of any difficulties that may arise, the infant is soon able to receive pleasurable satisfaction at the breast, good co-ordination of sucking and a positive attitude to the suckling process is set up which goes on automatically thereafter, and fosters life and health.[17] Changes of contact and temperature, the inrush of sound and light stimulation, etc. are manifestly felt as painful. The inner stimuli of hunger and desire for contact with the mother's body are painful, too. But sensations of warmth, the desired contact, satisfaction in sucking, freedom from outer stimuli, etc. soon bring actual experience of pleasurable sensation. At first, the whole weight of wish and phantasy is borne by sensation and affect. The hungry or longing of distressed infant feels actual sensations in his mouth or his limbs or his viscera, which *mean to him* that certain things are being done to him or that he is doing such and such a thing as he wishes, or fears. He *feels as if* he were doing so and so, e.g. touching or sucking or biting the breast which is actually out of reach. Or he feels as if he were being forcibly and painfully deprived of the breast, or as if *it* were biting *him*; and this, at first, probably without visual or other plastic images.

Interesting material bearing upon this point is offered by M.P. Middlemore,[18] from the analysis of a girl of two years nine months, who was treated for severe feeding difficulties. In her play, both at home and during her analysis, she was continually biting. "Among other things she pretended to be a biting dog, a crocodile, a lion, a pair of scissors that could cut up cups, a mincing machine and a machine for grinding cement." Her unconscious phantasies and conscious imaginative play were thus of an intensely destructive nature. In actuality, she had from birth refused to suck the breast, and her mother had had to give up the attempt to breast-feed her because of the infant's complete lack of interest and response. When she came to analysis, she was eating very little and never without persuasion. She had thus had no experience of actually "attacking" the breast, not even in sucking, let alone in biting as the animals did whose fierce attacks she played out. Middlemore suggests that the bodily sensations, i.e. the pangs of hunger, which disturbed the infant were the source of these fierce phantasies of biting and being bitten.[19] (Ch. N.4.)

The earliest phantasies, then, spring from bodily impulses and are interwoven with bodily sensations and affects. They express primarily an internal and subjective reality, yet from the beginning they are bound up with an actual, however limited and narrow, experience of objective reality.

The first bodily experiences begin to build up the first memories, and external realities are progressively woven into the texture of phantasy. Before long, the child's phantasies are able to draw upon plastic images as well as sensations—visual, auditory, kinaesthetic, touch, taste, smell images, etc. And these plastic images and dramatic representations of phantasy are progressively elaborated along with articulated perceptions of the external world.

Phantasies do not, however, take *origin* in articulated knowledge of the external world; their source is internal, in the instinctual impulses. E.g. the inhibitions of feeding sometimes appearing in quite young infants, and very commonly in children after weaning and in the second year, turn out (in later analysis) to arise from the anxieties connected with the primary oral wishes of intense greedy love and hate: the dread of destroying (by tearing to bits and devouring) the very object of love, the breast that is so much valued and desired.[20]

It has sometimes been suggested that unconscious phantasies such as that of "tearing to bits" would not arise in the child's mind before he had gained the conscious knowledge that tearing a person to bits would mean killing him or her. Such a view does not meet the case. It overlooks the fact that such knowledge is *inherent* in bodily impulses as a vehicle of instinct, in the *aim* of instinct, in the excitation of the organ, i.e. in this case, the mouth.

The phantasy that his passionate impulses will destroy the breast does not require the infant to have actually seen objects eaten up and destroyed, and then to have come to the conclusion that he could do it too. This aim, this relation to the object, is inherent in the character and direction of the impulse itself, and in its related affects.

To take another example: the difficulties of children in the control of urination are very familiar. Persistent enuresis is a common symptom even in the middle years of childhood. In the analysis of children and adults it is found that such difficulties arise from particularly powerful phantasies regarding the destructive effect of urine and the dangers connected with the act of urinating. (These phantasies are found in normal people as well, but for particular reasons they have become specially active in incontinent children.) Now the child's difficulty in controlling his urine is connected with phantasies that it is very potent for evil. These anxieties in their turn spring from destructive impulses. It is primarily because he *wants* his urine to be so very harmful that he comes to believe that it is so, not primarily because his mother gets cross when he wets the bed, and certainly not because he has ever observed that his urine is as harmful as in his phantasies he really believes it to be; nor because he has conscious awareness that people may be drowned and burned in external reality.

The situation goes back to early infancy. In the phantasy: "I want to drown and burn mother with my urine", we have an expression of the infant's fury and aggression, the wish to attack and annihilate mother by means of his urine, partly because of her frustrating him. He wishes to flood her with urine in burning anger. The "burning" is an expression both of his own bodily sensations and of the intensity of his rage. The "drowning", too, expresses the *feeling* of his intense hate and of his omnipotence, when he floods his mother's lap. The infant feels: "I *must* annihilate the bad mother." He overcomes his feeling of helplessness by the omnipotent phantasy: "I can and *will* abolish her"—by whatever means he possesses;[21] and when urinary sadism is at its height, what he feels he can do is to flood and burn her with his urine. Doubtless the "flooding" and "burning" also refer to the way in which he feels *he* is overcome, flooded, by his helpless rate, and burnt up by it. The whole world is full of his anger, and he will himself be destroyed by it if he cannot vent it on his mother, discharging it on her with his urine. The rush of water from the tap, the roaring fire, the flooding river or stormy sea, when these are seen or known about as external realities, link up in his mind with his early bodily experiences, instinctual aims and phantasies. And when he is given names for these things, he can *then* sometimes put these phantasies into words.

Similarly with the infant's feelings about his excretions as good things which he wishes to give to his mother. In certain moods and moments he does feel his urine and faeces to be something mother wants and the gift of them is his means of expressing his love and gratitude towards her. Such phantasies of faeces and urine as beneficent are certainly strengthened by the fact that mother is pleased when he gives them at the proper time and place; but his observation of his mother's pleasure is not the primary origin of his feeling of them as good. The source of this lies in his *wish* to give them as good—e.g. to feed his mother as she has fed him, to please her and do what she wants; and in his feeling of the goodness of his organs and of his body as a whole, when he is loving her and feeling her good to him. His urine and faeces are then instruments of his potency in love, just as his voice and smile can also be. Since the infant has so few resources at his command for expressing either love or hate, he has to use all his bodily products and activities as means of expressing his profound and overwhelming wishes and emotions. His urine and faeces may be either good or bad in his phantasy, according to his intentions at the moment of voiding and the way (including at a later period the time and place) in which they are produced.

These feelings and fears about his own bodily products link with the so-called "infantile sexual theories". Freud first drew attention to the fact, since then very widely observed, that young children, consciously as well as unconsciously, form their own spontaneous theories about the origin of babies and the nature of parental sexual intercourse, based upon their own bodily capacities, e.g. babies are made from food, and parental intercourse consists in mutual feeding or eating. Father puts the good food into mother, he feeds her with his genital in return for her feeding him with her breast, and then she has the babies inside her. Or they are made from faeces. Father puts faeces into mother and in so far as the child is loving and able to tolerate the parents' love for each other, he may feel this is good and gives mother life inside her. At other times, when he is feeling full of hate and jealousy and completely intolerant of his parents' intercourse, he wishes father to put bad faeces into mother— dangerous, explosive substances which will destroy her inside, or to urinate into her in a way that will harm her. These infantile sexual theories are obviously not drawn from observation of external events. The infant has never observed that babies are made from food and faeces, nor seen father urinate into mother. His notions of parental intercourse are derived from his own bodily impulses under the pressure of intense feeling. His phantasies express his wishes and his passions, using his bodily impulses, sensations and processes as their material of expression. (Ch. N.5.)

These and other specific contents of early phantasies, no less than the ways in which they are experienced by the child and their modes of expression, are in accordance with his bodily development and his capacities for feeling and knowing at any given age. The are a *part* of his development, and are expanded and elaborated along with his bodily and mental powers, influencing and being influenced by his slowly maturing ego.

The Relation of Early Phantasy to the Primary Process

The earliest and most rudimentary phantasies, bound up with sensory experience and being affective interpretations of bodily sensations, are naturally characterised by those qualities which Freud described as belonging to the "primary process": lack of co-ordination of impulse, lack of sense of time, of contradiction and of negation. Furthermore, at this level, there is no discrimination of external reality. Experience is governed by "all or none" responses and the absence of satisfaction is felt as a positive evil. Loss, dissatisfaction or deprivation are felt in sensation to be positive, painful experiences.

We are all familiar with the feeling of being "full of emptiness". Emptiness *is* positive, in sensation; just as darkness is an actual thing, not the mere absence of light, whatever we may know.

Darkness falls, like a curtain or blanket. When the light comes it drives away the darkness; and so on.

Thus, when we say (justifiably) that the infant feels a mother who does not remove a source of pain to be a "bad" mother, we do not mean that he has a clear notion of the negative fact of his mother's not removing the source of pain. That is a later realisation. The pain itself is positive; the "bad" mother is a positive experience, undistinguished at first from the pain. When at six months or so, the infant sits up and *sees* that his mother, as an external object, does not come when he wants her, he may then make the link between what he sees, *viz.* her not coming, and the pain or dissatisfaction he feels.[22]

When the infant misses his mother and behaves "as if he were never going to see her again", it does not mean that he then has discriminative notions of time, but that the pain of loss is an absolute experience, with a quality of sheer "neverness" about it—until mental development of reality have brought discriminative perceptions and images.

The "primary process" is, however, not to be regarded as governing the *whole* of mental life of the child during any measurable period of development. It might conceivably occupy the main field for the first few days, but we must not overlook the first adaptations of the infant to his external environment, and the fact that both gratification and frustration are experienced from birth onwards. The progressive alterations in the infant's responses during the first weeks and onwards show that even by the second month there is a very considerable degree of integration in perception and behaviour, with signs of memory and anticipation.

From this time on, the infant spends an increasing amount of time in experimentative play, which is, at one and the same time, an attempt to adapt to reality and an active means of expressing phantasy (a wish-enactment and a defence against pain and anxiety).

The "primary process" is in fact a limiting concept only. As Freud said, "So far as we know, a psychic apparatus possessing only the primary process does not exist, and is to that extent a theoretical fiction." (Ch. N.6.) Later on he speaks of the "belated arrival" of the secondary processes, which seem at first sight somewhat contradictory. The contradiction is resolved if we take the "belated arrival" to refer not so much to the *onset* of the secondary processes, their rudimentary beginnings, but rather to their full development. (Such a view would best accord with what we can see of the infant's actual development, in adaptation to reality, in control and integration.

Instinct, Phantasy and Mechanism

We must now consider another important aspect of our problem, that of the relation between instincts, phantasies and mechanisms. A good deal of difficulty and certain confusions on this matter have appeared in various discussions; one of the aims of this section is to clarify the relations between these different concepts.

The distinction between, e.g., the phantasy of incorporation and the mechanism of introjection has not always been clearly observed. For example, in discussions about specific oral phantasies of devouring or otherwise *incorporating* a concrete object, we often meet with the expression: "The *introjected* object". Or people have sometimes spoken of the "introjected breast", again mixing up the concrete bodily phantasy with the general mental process. It is especially with regard to the mechanisms of introjection and projection that these difficulties seem to have arisen, although the problem of the relation between instincts, phantasies and mechanisms can be considered in a more general way with regard to every variety of mental mechanism.

To consider "introjection" and "projection", in particular: these are abstract terms, the names of certain fundamental mechanisms or methods of functioning in the mental life. They refer to such facts as that ideas, impressions and influences are taken into the self and become part of it; or that aspects or elements of the self are often disowned and attributed to some person or group of persons, or some part of the external world. These common mental processes, plainly seen in both children and adults, in ordinary social life as well as in the consulting room, are "mechanisms", i.e. particular ways in which mental life operates, as a means of dealing with internal tensions and conflicts.

Now these mental mechanisms are intimately related to certain pervasive phantasies. The phantasies of incorporating (devouring, absorbing, etc.) loved and hated objects, persons or parts of persons, into ourselves are amongst the earliest and most deeply unconscious phantasies, fundamentally oral in character since they are the psychic representatives of the oral impulses. Some of these oral phantasies have been described above, for example: "I want to take and I am taking her (mother or breast) into me." The distinction should be kept clear between a specific phantasy of incorporating an object and the general mental mechanism of introjection. The latter has a far wider reference than the former, although so intimately related to it. To understand the relationship between phantasies and mechanisms, we must look more closely at the relation of both to instinct. In our view, phantasy is the operative link between instinct and ego-mechanism.

An instinct is conceived as a borderline psychosomatic process. It has a bodily aim, directed to concrete external objects. It has a representative in the mind which we call a "phantasy". Human activities derive from instinctual urges; it is only through the phantasy of what would fulfil our instinctual needs that we are enabled to attempt to realise them in external reality. (Ch. N.7.)

Although themselves psychic phenomena, phantasies are primarily about bodily aims, pains and pleasures, directed to objects of some kind. When contrasted with external and bodily realities, the phantasy, like other mental activities, is a figment, since it cannot be touched or handled or seen; yet it is real in the experience of the subject. It is a true mental function and it has real effects, not only in the inner world of the mind but also in the external world of the subject's bodily development and behaviour, and hence of other people's minds and bodies.

We have already touched incidentally upon many examples of the outcome of particular phantasies; for example, in young children, such difficulties as feeding and excretory troubles and phobias; to these could be added so-called "bad habits", ticks, tantrums, defiance of authority, lying and thieving, etc. We have spoken also of hysterical conversion-symptoms in people of all ages as being the expression of phantasy.[23] Examples are alimentary disturbances, headaches, susceptibility to catarrh, dysmenorrhoea, and many other psychosomatic changes. But ordinary bodily characteristics, other than illnesses, such as manner and tone of voice in speaking, bodily posture, gait of walking, mode of handshake, facial expression, handwriting and mannerisms generally, also turn out to be determined directly or indirectly by specific phantasies. These are usually highly complex, related both to the internal and the external worlds, and bound up with the psychical history of the individual.

It is noteworthy how often and to what a degree such bodily

expressions of individual phantasies may change, whether temporarily or permanently, during the process of analysis. In moments of depression, for instance, the manner of walking and holding the body, the facial expression and voice, the patient's whole bodily response to the physical world as well as to people, will be different from what it is at times of elation, of defiance, of surrender, of determined control of anxiety, etc. These changes during analysis are sometimes quite dramatic.

In outside life, people may have phases of dropping and breaking or losing things, of stumbling and falling, of a tendency to bodily accidents.[24] One has only to look round at people in ordinary life, in the tube train, the bus or restaurant or family life, to see the endless differentiations of bodily characteristics, e.g. mannerisms, individualities and idiosyncrasies in dress and speech, etc., through which dominant phantasies and the emotional states bound up with them are expressed.

Analytic work brings the opportunity to understand what these varied details signify, what particular changing sets of phantasies are at work in the patient's mind—about his own body and its contents, and about other people and his bodily or social relation to them now or in the past. Many such bodily traits become modified and sometimes considerably altered after the analysis of the underlying phantasies.

Similarly, the broader social expressions of character and personality show the potency of phantasies. E.g. people's attitudes to such matters as time and money and possessions, to being late or punctual, to giving or receiving, to leading or following, to being "in the limelight" or content to work among others, and so on and so forth, are always found in analysis to be related to specific sets of varied phantasies. The development of these can be followed out through their various functions of defence in relation to specific situations, back to their origins in primary instinctual sources.

Freud drew attention to a striking example in his study of the "Exceptions",[25] where he discussed the interesting character trait exhibited by quite a number of people, that of regarding or even proclaiming themselves as exceptions and behaving as such— exceptions from any demands made by particular persons, such as members of the patient's family or the physician, or by the external world in general. Freud refers to Shakespeare's Richard III as a supreme example of this, and in his discussion he penetrated to some of the phantasies lying behind the apparently simple defiance of Richard on account of his deformity. Freud suggests that Richard's soliloquy[26] is by no means mere defiance, but signifies an unconscious argument (which we should call a phantasy) as follows: " 'Nature has done me a grievous wrong in denying me that beauty of form which wins human love. Life owes me reparation for this, and I will see that I get it. I have a right to be an exception, to overstep those bounds by which others let themselves be circumscribed. I may do wrong myself, since wrong has been done to me.' "

An example which may be quoted from the writer's analytic experience is that of an adolescent boy who came for treatment because of serious difficulties in his home and public school life— e.g. very obvious lying of a sort that was certain to be found out, aggressive behaviour, and a wild untidiness in dress. In general the conduct and attitude of this boy of sixteen years of age were entirely out of keeping with his family traditions; they were those of a social outcast. Even when the analysis had brought sufficient improvement for him to join the Air Force, soon after the outbreak of war, he could not follow the normal course of events for those in his social circumstances. He did brilliant work in the Air Force and built up an excellent reputation, but always refused to accept a commission. At the beginning of the analysis he had been lonely and miserable, and entirely without friends. Later he was able to maintain steady friendships, and was very much liked in the Sergeants' Mess, but was quite unable to live up to the social traditions of his family, in which there were distinguished officers.

This boy's illness, as always, was determined by many complex causes of external circumstances and internal response. He had a rich phantasy-life, but dominant amongst all other of his phantasies was that the only way of overcoming his aggressiveness towards his younger brother (ultimately, his father) was to renounce all ambition in their favour. He felt it impossible for both himself and his younger brother (a normal, gifted and happy person) to be loved and admired by his mother and father. In bodily terms, it was impossible for them both, himself and his younger brother (ultimately himself and his father), to be potent; this notion arose in the depths of his mind from the early phantasies of incorporating his father's genital; he felt that if he himself sucked out father's genital from his mother, swallowed it up and possessed it, then the good genital would be destroyed, his younger brother could not have it, would never grow up, never become potent or loving or wise, indeed, never exist! By electing to renounce everything in favour of his younger brother (ultimately, of his father) the boy modified and controlled his aggressive impulses towards both his parents, and his fears of them.

In this boy, many subsidiary internal processes and external circumstances had served to make this particular phantasy dominate his life—the notion that there is only one good thing of a kind—*the* good breast, *the* good mother, *the* good father's penis; and if one person has this ideal object, another must suffer its loss, and thus become dangerous to the possessor. This phantasy is widely found, although inmost people it becomes modified and counterbalanced during development, so that it plays a far less dominant part in life.

Similarly, Freud brings out that Richard's claim to be an exception is one which we all of us feel, although in most people it becomes corrected and modified or covered up. Freud remarks: "Richard is an enormously magnified representation of something we may all discover in ourselves." (Ch. N.8.) Our view that phantasy plays a fundamental and continuous part, not only in neurotic symptoms but also in normal character and personality, is thus in agreement with Freud's comments.

To return to the particular problem of the phantasy of incorporation; the mental process or unconscious phantasy of incorporating is described in abstract terms as the process of introjection. As we have seen, whichever it be called, its real psychic effects follow. It is not an actual bodily eating up and swallowing, yet it leads to actual alterations in the ego. These "mere" beliefs about internal objects, such as, "I have got a good breast inside me", or, it may be, "I have got a bitten-up, torturing bad breast inside me—I must kill it and get rid of it", and the like, lead to real effects: deep emotions, actual behaviour towards external people, profound changes in the ego, character and personality, symptoms, inhibitions and capacities.

Now the relation between such oral phantasies of incorporation and the earliest processes of introjection has been discussed by Freud in his essay on "Negation". Here he not only states that even the intellectual functions of judgement and reality-testing "are derived from the interplay of the *primary instinctual impulses*" [my italics], and rest upon the *mechanism* of introjection (a point to which we shall return shortly): he also shows us the part played in this derivation by *phantasy*. Referring to that aspect of judgement which asserts or denies that a thing has a particular property, Freud says: "Expressed in the language of the oldest, that is, of the oral instinctual impulses, the alternative runs thus: 'I should like to take this into me and keep that out of me.' That is to say, it is to be either *inside me* or outside me."[27] The wish thus formulated is the same thing as a phantasy.

What Freud picturesquely calls here "the language of the oral impulse", he elsewhere calls the "mental expression" of an instinct, i.e. the phantasies which are the psychic representatives of a bodily aim. In this actual example, Freud is showing us the phantasy that is the mental equivalent of an *instinct*. But he is at one and the same time formulating the subjective aspect of the *mechanism* of introjection (or projection). Thus *phantasy is the link between the id-impulse and the ego-mechanism*, the means by which the one is transmuted into the other. "I want to eat that and therefore I have eaten it" is a phantasy which represents the id impulse in the psychic life; it is at the same time the subjective experiencing of the mechanism or function of introjection.

The problem of how best to describe the process of introjection related to the phantasy of incorporation is often dealt with by saying that what *is* introjected is an image or "*imago*". This is surely quite correct; but it is too formal and meagre a statement of a complex phenomenon to do justice to the facts. For one thing, this describes only the preconscious processes, not the unconscious.

How does anyone—whether psychologist or other person—come to know this distinction, to realise that what he has actually "taken inside", his internal object, is an image and not a bodily concrete object? By a long and complex process of development. This, in broad outline, must include the following steps, among others:

(a) The earliest phantasies are built mainly upon oral impulses, bound up with taste, smell, touch (of the lips and mouth), kinaesthetic, visceral, and other somatic sensations; these are at first more closely linked with the experience of "taking things in" (sucking and swallowing) than with anything else. The visual elements are relatively small.

(b) These sensations (and images) are a bodily experience, at first scarcely capable of being related to an external, spatial object. (The kinaesthetic, genital and visceral elements are not usually so referred.) They give the phantasy a concrete bodily quality, a "me-ness", experienced *in* the body. On this level, images are scarcely if at all distinguishable from actual sensations and external perceptions. The skin is not yet felt to be a boundary between inner and outer reality.

(c) The visual element in perception slowly increases, becoming suffused with tactile experience and spatially differentiated. The early visual images remain largely "eidetic" in quality— probably up to three of four years of age. They are intensely vivid, concrete and often confused with perceptions. Moreover, they remain for long intimately associated with somatic responses: they are very closely linked with emotions and tend to immediate action. (Many of the details referred to here so summarily have been well worked out by psychologists.)

(d) During the period of development when the visual elements in perception (and in corresponding images) begin to predominate over the somatic, becoming differentiated and spatially inte- grated, and thus making clearer the distinction between the inner and the outer worlds, the concrete bodily elements in the total experience of perceiving (and phantasying) largely under- go *repression*. The visual, externally referred elements in phantasy become relatively de-emotionalised, de-sexualised, independent, in consciousness, of bodily ties. They become "images" in the narrower sense, representations "in the mind" (but not, consciously, incorporations in the body) of external objects recognised to be such. It is "realised" that the external objects are outside the mind, but their images are "in the mind".

(e) Such images, however, draw their power to affect the mind by being "in it", i.e. their influence upon feelings, behaviour, character and personality upon the mind as a whole, *from their repressed unconscious somatic associates* in the unconscious world of desire and emotions, which *form the link with the id*; and which do mean, in unconscious phantasy, that the objects to which they refer are believed to be inside the body, to be incorporated.

In psycho-analytic thought, we have heard more of *"imago"* than of "image". The distinctions between an *"imago"* and an "image" might be summarised as: (a) *"imago"* refers to an *unconscious* image; (b) *"imago"* usually refers to a person or part of a person, the earliest objects, whilst "image" may be of any object or situation, human or otherwise; and (c) *"imago"* includes all the somatic and emotional elements in the subject's relation to the imaged person, the bodily links in unconscious phantasy with the id, the phantasy of incorporation which underlies the process of introjection; whereas in the "image" the somatic and much of the emotional elements are largely repressed.

If we pay enough attention to the details of the way in which other mental mechanisms operate in the minds of our patients, every variety of mechanism can be seen to be related to specific phantasies or sorts of phantasy. They are always *experienced* as phantasy. For example, the mechanism of *denial* is expressed in the mind of the subject in some such way as: "If I don't admit it [i.e. a painful fact] it isn't true." Or: "If I don't admit it, no-one else will know that it is true." And in the last resort this argument can be traced to bodily impulses and phantasies, such as; "If it doesn't come out of my mouth, that shows it isn't inside me"; or "I can prevent anyone else *knowing* it is inside me". Or: "It is all right if it comes out of my anus as flatus or faeces, but it mustn't come out of my mouth as words." The mechanism of *scotomisation* is experienced in such terms as: "What I don't see I need not believe"; or "What I don't see, other people don't, and indeed doesn't exist".

Again, the mechanism of compulsive confession (which many patients indulge in) also implies such unconscious argument as the following: "If I say it, no-one else will", or "I can triumph over them by saying it first, or win their love by at least appearing to be a good boy."[28]

In general it can be said that ego-mechanisms are all derived ultimately from instincts and innate bodily reactions. "The ego is a differentiated part of the id." (Ch. N.9.)

Phantasy, Memory Images and Reality
In quoting just now from Freud's essay on "Negation" we noted his view that the intellectual functions of judgement and reality-testing "are derived from the interplay of the primary instinctual impulses". If, then, phantasy be the "language" of these primary instinctual impulses, it can be assumed that phantasy enters into the

earliest development of the ego in its relation to reality, and supports the testing of reality and the development of knowledge of the external world.

We have already seen that the earliest phantasies are bound up with sensations and affects. These sensations, no matter how selectively over-emphasised they may be under the pressure of affect, bring the experiencing mind into contact with external reality, as well as expressing impulses and wishes.[29]

The external world forces itself upon the attention of the child, in one way or another, early and continuously. The first psychical experiences result from the massive and varied stimuli of birth and the first intake and expulsion of breath—followed presently by the first feed. These considerable experiences during the first twenty-four hours must already evoke the first mental activity, and provide material for both phantasy and memory. Phantasy and reality-testing are both in fact present from the earliest days.[30]

External perceptions begin to influence mental processes at a certain point (actually from birth on, though initially they are not appreciated as external). At first the psyche deals with most external stimuli, as with the instinctual ones, by means of the primitive mechanisms of introjection and projection. Observation of the infant during the first few weeks shows that in so far as the external world does not satisfy our wishes, or frustrates or interferes with us, it is at once hated and rejected. We may then fear it and watch it and attend to it, in order to defend ourselves against it; but not until it is in some degree libidinised through its connections with oral satisfaction, and thus receives some measure of love, can it be played with and learnt about and understood.

We conclude with Freud that the disappointingness of hallucinatory satisfaction is the first spur to some degree of adaptation to reality. Hunger is not satisfied by hallucinating the breast, whether as an external or an internal object, although waiting for satisfaction may be made more tolerable by the phantasy. Sooner or later, hallucination breaks down, and a measure of adaptation to real external conditions (e.g. making demands on the external world by crying, seeking movements, restlessness, etc., and by adopting the appropriate posture and movements when the nipple arrives) is turned to instead. Here is the beginning of adjustment to reality and of the development of appropriate skills and of perception of the external world. Disappointment may be the first stimulus to adaptive acceptance of reality, but the postponement of satisfaction and the suspense involved in the complicated learning and thinking about external reality which the child presently accomplishes—and for increasingly remote ends—can only be endured and sustained when it also satisfies instinctual urges, represented in phantasies, as well. Learning depends upon interest, and interest is derived from desire, curiosity and fear—especially desire and curiosity.

In their developed forms, phantasy-thinking and reality-thinking are distinct mental processes, different modes of obtaining satisfaction. The fact that they have a distinct character when fully developed, however, does not necessarily imply that reality-thinking *operates* quite independently of unconscious phantasy. It is not merely that they "blend and interweave";[31] their relationship is something less adventitious than this. In our view, *reality-thinking cannot operate without concurrent and supporting unconscious phantasies;*[32] e.g. we continue to "take things in" with our ears, to "devour" with our eyes, to "read, mark, learn and inwardly digest" throughout life.

These conscious metaphors represent unconscious psychic reality. It is a familiar fact that all early learning is based upon the oral impulses. The first seeking and mouthing and grasping of the breast is gradually shifted on to other objects, the hand and eye only slowly attaining independence of the mouth, as instruments of exploration and of knowing the outer world.

All through the middle part of his first year, the infant's hand reaches out to everything he sees in order to put it into his mouth, first, to try and eat it, then at least to suck and chew it, and later to feel and explore it. (Only later do his hand and eye become independent of his mouth.) This means that the objects which the infant touches and manipulates and looks at and explores are invested with oral libido. He could not be interested in them if this were not so. If at any stage he were entirely auto-erotic, he could never learn. The instinctual drive towards taking things into his mind through eyes and fingers (and ears, too), towards looking and touching and exploring, satisfies some of the oral wishes frustrated by his original object. Perception and intelligence draw upon this source of libido for their life and growth. Hand and eye retain an oral significance throughout life, in unconscious phantasy and often, as we have seen, in conscious metaphor.

In her papers "Infant Analysis" and "The Importance of Symbol Formation in the Development of the Ego" Melanie Klein took up Ferenczi's view that (primary) identification, which is the fore-runner of symbolism, "arises out of the baby's endeavour to rediscover in every object his own organs and their functioning", and also Ernest Jones's[33] view that the pleasure-principle makes it possible for two separate objects to be equated because of an affective bond of interest. She showed, by means of illuminating clinical material, how the primary symbolic function of external objects enables phantasy to be elaborated by the ego, allows sublimations to develop in play and manipulation and builds a bridge from the inner world to interest in the outer world and knowledge of physical objects and events. His pleasurable interest in his body, his discoveries and experiments in this direction, are clearly shown in the play of an infant of three or four months. In this play he manifests (among other mechanisms) this process of symbol formation, bound up with those phantasies which we later discover in analysis to have been operating at the time. *The external physical world is in fact libidinised largely through the process of symbol formation.*

Almost every hour of free association in analytic work reveals to us something of the phantasies which have promoted (mainly through symbol formation) and sustained the development of interest in the external world and the process of learning about it, and from which the power to seek out and organise knowledge about it is drawn. It is a familiar fact that, from one point of view, every instance of concern with reality, whether practical or theoretical, is also a sublimation.[34]

This, in its turn, means that *pari passu* some measure of "synthetic function" is exercised upon instinctual urges from the beginning. The child could not learn, could not adapt to the external world (human or not) without some sort and degree of control and inhibition, as well as satisfaction, of instinctual urges, progressively developed from birth onwards.

If, then, the intellectual functions are derived from the interplay of the primary instinctual impulses, we need, in order to understand either phantasy or reality-testing and "intelligence", to look at mental life as a whole and to see the relation between these various functions during the whole process of development. To keep them apart and say "this is perception and knowledge, but *that* is something quite different and unrelated, that is mere phantasy", would be to miss the *developmental* significance of both functions. (Ch. N.10.)

Certain aspects of the nexus between thought and phantasy were discussed in the writer's *Intellectual Growth in Young Children*.[35] From direct records of spontaneous make-believe play among a group of children between two and seven years of age, it was possible to show the various ways in which such imaginative play, arising ultimately from unconscious phantasies, wishes and anxieties, creates practical situations which call for knowledge of the external world. These situations may then often be pursued for their own sake, as problems of learning and understanding, and thus lead on to actual discoveries of external fact or to verbal judgement and reasoning. This does not always happen—the play may for periods be purely repetitive; but at any moment a new line of inquiry or argument may flash out, and a new step in understanding be taken by any or all of the children taking part in the play.

In particular, observation made it clear that spontaneous make-believe play creates and fosters the first forms of "as if" thinking. In such play, the child recreates selectively those elements in past situations which can embody his emotional or intellectual need of the present, and adapts the details, moment by moment, to the present play situation. This ability to evoke the *past* in imaginative play seems to be closely connected with the growth of the power to evoke *the future* in constructive hypothesis, and to develop the consequences of "ifs". The child's make-believe play is thus significant not only for the adaptive and creative intentions which when fully developed mark out the artist, the novelist and the poet, but also for the sense of reality, the scientific attitude and the growth of hypothetical reasoning.

Summary
The argument of this paper may now be summarised:

(1) *The concept of phantasy* has gradually widened in psycho-analytic thought. It now requires clarification and explicit expansion to integrate all the relevant facts.
(2) On the views here developed:
  (a) Phantasies are the primary content of unconscious mental processes.

(b) Unconscious phantasies are primarily about bodies, and represent instinctual aims towards objects.

(c) These phantasies are, in the first instance, the psychic representatives of libidinal and destructive instincts; early in development they also become elaborated into defences, as well as wish-fulfilments and anxiety-contents.

(d) Freud's postulated "hallucinatory wish-fulfilment" and his "primary identification", "introjection" and "projection" are the basis of the phantasy life.

(e) Through external experience, phantasies become elaborated and capable of expression, but they do not depend upon such experience for their existence.

(f) Phantasies are not dependent upon words, although they may under certain conditions be capable of expression in words.

(g) The earliest phantasies are experienced in sensations; later, they take the form of plastic images and dramatic representations.

(h) Phantasies have both psychic and bodily effects, e.g. in conversion symptoms, bodily qualities, character and personality, neurotic symptoms, inhibitions and sublimations.

(i) Unconscious phantasies form the operative link between *instincts* and *mechanisms*. When studied in detail, every variety of ego-mechanism can be seen to arise from specific sorts of phantasy, which in the last resort have their origin in instinctual impulses. "The ego is a differentiated part of the id." A mechanism is an abstract general term describing certain mental processes which are experienced by the subject as unconscious phantasies.

(j) Adaptation to reality and reality-thinking require the support of concurrent unconscious phantasies. Observation of the ways in which knowledge of the external world develops shows how the child's phantasy contributes to his learning.

(k) Unconscious phantasies exert a continuous influence throughout life, both in normal and neurotic people, the differences lying in the specific character of the dominant phantasies, the desire or anxiety associated with them and their interplay with each other and with external reality.

Chapter Notes

Ch. N.1 (p. 145)

As has often been pointed out, exact definition, urgent though it may be, is only possible in the later phases of a science. It cannot be done in the initial stages. "The view is often defended that sciences should be built up on clear and sharply defined basal concepts. In actual fact no science, not even the most exact, begins with such definitions. The true beginning of scientific activity consists rather in describing phenomena and then in proceeding to group, classify and correlate them. Even at the stage of description it is not possible to avoid applying certain abstract ideas to the material in hand, ideas derived from various sources and certainly not the fruit of the new experience only. Still more indispensable are such ideas— which will later become the basal concepts of the science—as the material is further elaborated. They must at first necessarily possess some measure of uncertainty; there can be no question of any clear delimitation of their content. So long as they remain in this condition, we come to an understanding about their meaning by repeated references to the material of observation, from which we seem to have deduced our abstract ideas, but which is in point of fact subject to them. Thus, strictly speaking, they are in the nature of conventions; although everything depends on their being chosen in no arbitrary manner, but determined by the important relations they have to the empirical material—relations we seem to divine before we can clearly recognise and demonstrate them. It is only after more searching investigations of the field in question that we are able to formulate with increased clarity the scientific concepts underlying it ... The progress of science, however, demands a certain elasticity, even in these definitions. The science of physics furnishes an excellent illustration of the way in which even those "basal concepts" that are firmly established in the form of definitions are constantly being altered in their content." (Freud, 1915, "Instincts and Their Vicissitudes", *S.E.*, 14, pp. 117–118.)

Ch. N.2 (p. 148)

In this chapter note are included all my references to the literature of early mental development, and to observational studies of infant behaviour, etc., together with comments on some of it, and also some discussion of certain instances of children's behaviour known or reported to me.

A. Gesell, (1) *Infancy and Human Growth*, Macmillan, 1928; *Biographies of Child Development*. Hamish Hamilton, 1939; (3) *The First Five Years of Life*. Methuen, 1940.

M. Shirley, *The First Two Years*, Vols. I, II and III, University of Minnesota Press, 1933. (A study of the development of twenty-five normal children.)

N. Bayley, *The California Infant Scale of Motor Development*. University of California Press, 1936.

D.W. Winnicott, 'The Observation of Infants in a Set Situation", *International Journal of Psycho-Analysis*, XXII, 1941, pp. 229–49.

Merell P. Middlemore, *The Nursing Couple*. Hamish Hamilton, 1941.

Florence Goodenough, *Anger in Young Children*. University of Minnesota Press, 1931. Goodenough trained her observers to record not merely the frequency and time distribution of temper tantrums, but also the context of social and emotional situations and physiological conditions in which they occurred. In this way, she was able to elucidate, to a degree which had not been done before, the nature of the situations which give rise to temper tantrums in young children.

C.W. Valentine, "The Innate Bases of Fear". *Journal of Genetic Psychology*, Vol. XXXVII. Repeating Watson's work on the subject of innate fears, Valentine paid attention to the total situation in which the child was placed as well as to the precise nature of the stimuli applied. He concluded that the setting is always a highly important factor in determining the particular response of the child to a particular stimulus. It is a *whole situation* which affects the child, not a single stimulus. The presence or absence of the mother, for example, may make all the difference to the child's actual response.

M.M. Lewis, *Infant Speech*. Kegan Paul, 1936. Lewis not only made a complete phonetic record of the development of speech in an infant from birth onwards, but also noted the social and emotional situations in which particular speech sounds and speech forms occurred, enabling us to infer some of the emotional sources of the drive to speech development.

Lois Barclay Murphy has made a considerable contribution to problems of social development in a series of careful studies of the personalities of young children and their social relationships. *Social Behavior and Child Personality*, Columbia University Press, 1937, p. 191. She showed that it is useless to attempt either ratings of personality as a whole, or of particular traits such as sympathy, without having constant regard to the context of the behaviour studied. The social behaviour and personal characteristics of young children vary according to the specific social context. For example, one boy is excited and aggressive when another particular boy is present, but not so when that boy is absent. Murphy's work gives us many such glimpses of the feelings and motives which enter into the development of the child's traits of personality. She sums up her study of "sympathetic behaviour" in young children playing in a group … "the behavior which constitutes this trait is dependent upon the functional relation of the child to each situation, and when shifts in status give a basis for a changed interpretation of the situation in which the child finds himself, changed behavior occurs. A significant proportion of the variations in a child's behavior which we have discussed are related to the child's security, as affected by competitive situations with other children, disapproval by adults, or guilt and self-accusation in relation to injury to another child, …" thus emphasising that sympathetic behaviour (as one aspect of personality) cannot be understood apart from the variations in the context in which it is shown.

An example of the value of observing the context of behaviour has been reported to the writer by a Nursery School Superintendent (Miss D E May). She observed in many cases that when a two-year-old child was left in the nursery school for the first time and was feeling lonely and anxious because of the parting with his mother and being in a strange world, the plaything which most readily comforted him was the "posting box", a box into which he could drop through appropriate holes in the lid a number of small bricks, the lid then being taken off and the lost objects rediscovered inside. The child thus seemed to be able to overcome his feelings of loss about his mother by means of this play, in which he lost and rediscovered objects at his own will—a play on similar lines to that described by Freud.

Another example from the same nursery school is that of a boy of two years and four months, who was terrified and utterly miserable on his second day in the school. He stood by the observer, holding her hand and at first sobbing, occasionally asking, "Mummy coming, Mummy coming?" A tower of small bricks was placed on a chair near him. At first he ignored the bricks, then when another child had a box of bricks nearby, he quickly carried to this box all but two of the bricks on the chair. The remaining two, a small cube and a larger triangular brick, he placed together on the chair, touching each other, in a position similar to that of himself and the observer who was seated beside him. He then came back and again held the adult's hand. Now he was able to stop crying, and seemed much calmer. When another child came up and removed the bricks, he fetched them back again and put them in position once more, patting the small brick against the triangular one in a gentle and contented way, and then once again held the observer's hand and looked round at the other children quietly.

Here again we see a child comforting himself and overcoming feelings of loss and terror by a symbolic act with the two material objects. He showed that if he were allowed to put two objects (the two bricks) close together, as he wished to be close to his mother, he could control his distress and feel contented and trustful with another adult, believing she would enable him to find his mother again.

These instances illustrate the fact that some degree of insight into the child's feelings and phantasies can be gained from observation in ordinary life, provided we pay attention to details and to the social and emotional context of the particular data.

Hazlitt, in her chapter on "Retention, Continuity, Recognition and Memory", in *The Psychology of Infancy* (p. 78), says: "The favourite game of 'peep-bo' which the child may enjoy in an appropriate form from about the third month gives proof of the continuity and retentiveness of the mind of the very young child. If impressions died away immediately and the child's conscious life were made up of a number of totally disconnected moments this game could have no charm for him. But we have ample evidence that at one moment he is conscious of the change in experience, and we can see him looking for what has just been present and is now gone."

Hazlitt's whole treatment of those problems takes the line that explicit memory grows out of early recognition, i.e. "any process of perceiving which gives rise to a feeling of familiarity". She goes one: "In speaking of the month-old child's sucking reaction to the sound of the human voice it has not been assumed that the child recognises the voices, that there is a conscious experience corresponding to the idea 'voices again'. There may or may not be such conscious experience ... As the weeks go by, however, numberless instances of recognition occur in which the child's expression and general behaviour form a picture so like that which accompanies conscious experience of recognition at the later stages that it is difficult to resist the inference that the child is recognising in the true sense of the word. Records tell of children from eight weeks onwards appearing to be distressed by strange and reassured by familiar faces."

Hazlitt also takes the view that even judgement is present from a very early time, e.g. in the child's adaptive responses, in the third and fourth months. Hazlitt has no doubt that the very earliest responses of the infant show the rudimentary qualities from which memory, imagination, thinking, etc. develop. She says: "Another argument for the view here taken that judgement is present from a very early time is that the expression of surprise at stimuli which are not surprising through their intensity, but from being changed in some way from their usual appearance, is quite common by six months and shows itself every now and then much earlier than this."

Another important field in which this law of genetic continuity operates is that of logical relations. The experimental studies of Hazlitt ("Children's Thinking", (1930)) and others have shown that the child can understand and act upon certain logical relations (such as identity, exception, generalisation, etc.) long before he can express these relations in words. And he can understand them in simple concrete terms before he can appreciate them in a more abstract form. E.g. he can act upon the words "all ... but not ..." when he cannot yet understand the word "except"; again, he can comprehend and act upon "except" before he can use the word himself.

M.M. Lewis, "The Beginning of Reference to Past and Future in a Child's Speech", *British Journal of Educational Psychology*, VII, 1937, and "The Beginning and Early Functions of Questions in a Child's Speech", ibid., VIII, 1938.

Baldwin, "Canons of Genetic Logic", *Thought and Things, or Genetic Logic*.

Ch. N.3. (p. 165)

"The system Ucs contains the thing-cathexes of the object, the first and true object-cathexes; the system Pcs originates in a hyper-cathexis of this concrete idea by a linking up of it with the verbal ideas of the words corresponding to it. It is such hyper-cathexes, we may suppose, that bring about higher organisation in the mind and make it possible for the primary process to be succeeded by the secondary process which dominates Pcs." ("The Unconscious" (1915), *Collected Papers*, IV, pp. 133–4.)

Ch. No.4 (p. 168)

"A girl of two years and nine months was treated for feeding difficulties. She ate very little—never without being persuaded by her parents—but in her games and fantasies during analysis and at home she was continually biting. Among other things she pretended to be a biting dog, a crocodile, a lion, a pair of scissors that could cut up cups, a mincing machine and a machine for grinding cement. The history of her feeding was peculiar. She was weaned during the first fortnight because she showed no interest in the breast and would not feed. She slept during sucking and refused the nipple repeatedly, not with much ado, but by quietly turning the head away. The difficulty in feeding seemed to have originated entirely in the child, for the mother secreted a fair amount of milk to begin with; moreover she had suckled an elder child successfully and wanted to feed this one. As I did not watch the attempts at breast-feeding I cannot say whether the inertia was a simple one or whether, as I presume, it masked irritability. What was clear was that the baby was unwilling to suck, while difficulties which began at the breast continued steadily through all kinds of feeding from bottle, spoon and cup. Until she came for treatment she had never put a spoonful of food into her own mouth. The point is that although she had never sucked the breast properly, still less 'attacked' it, she entertained very fierce fantasies of biting. What was their physical foundation, unless it was the feelings which disturbed her during hunger?" (M.P. Middlemore, *The Nursing Couple*, pp. 189–90, Hamish Hamilton, 1941.)

Ch. N.5 (p. 171)

Scupin records an instance (of his own boy of eleven-and-a-half months) which illustrates the interpretation of an observed reality in terms of phantasy arising from the infant's own primary instinctual life. "When we [his parents] were fighting in fun, he suddenly uttered a wild scream. To try if it was the noise we made that had frightened him, we repeated the scene in silence; the child looked at his father in horror, then stretched his arms out longingly to his mother and snuggled affectionately up against her. It quite gave the impression that the boy believed his mother was being hurt, and his scream was only an expression of sympathetic fear." (Quoted by W. Stern in *Psychology of Early Childhood*, p. 138.)

An example of a child in the second year being comforted by ocular proof that his parents were not fighting was noted by a colleague of the writer's. His boy suffered from frequent attacks of anxiety, the cause of which was not understood, and he could take comfort from neither parent. But they found, at first by accident, that when he was in these moods, if they kissed *each other* (not him) in his presence, his anxiety was immediately relieved. It is thus to be inferred that the anxiety was connected with his fear of his parents quarrelling, and his phantasy of their intercourse being mutually destructive, the anxiety being relieved and the child reassured by the visible demonstration that they could love each other and be gentle together in his presence.

Ch. N.6 (p. 172)

More fully Freud writes: "When I termed one of the psychic processes in the psychic apparatus the *primary* process, I did so not only in consideration of its status and functions, but was also able to take account of the temporal relationship actually involved. So far as we know, a psychic apparatus possessing only the primary process does not exist, and is to that extent a theoretical fiction; but this at least is a fact: that the primary processes are present in the apparatus from the beginning, while the secondary processes only take shape gradually during the course of life, inhibiting and overlaying the primary, whilst gaining complete control over them perhaps only in the prime of life. Owing to this belated arrival of the secondary processes, the essence of our being, consisting of unconscious wish-impulses, remains something which cannot be grasped or inhibited by the preconscious; and its part is once and for all restricted to indicating the most appropriate paths for the wish-impulses originating in the unconscious ...'' (Freud, 1900, *The Interpretation of Dreams*, S.E., 5, p. 596.)

Ch. N.7. (p. 174)

As Dr Adrian Stephen said in the Discussion on this paper in the British Psycho-Analytical Society, 1943:

> To go back to Freud's writings: at the very beginning of his *Three Essays on the Theory of Sexuality* he describes instincts as having aims and objects. Aim is the word for the behaviour which an instinct impels us to take, for instance sexual intercourse, and object is the word for the person with whom the intercourse is to take place; or eating, I take it, may be the aim of an instinct and food the object. Freud in this passage was obviously thinking of cases in which the object is a concrete object, but he would certainly have agreed, as I suppose we all should, that the object may be imaginary or, if you like, phantastic ...

> Of course we all know that phantasies are built up on the basis of memories, memories of satisfaction and frustration and so on, and as we grow older and as our instincts evolve and our store of memories becomes greater and more varied no doubt our phantasies change considerably in the complexity and variety of their content; but it is difficult to suppose that instinctual impulses, even in a small baby, are not accompanied by some sort of phantasies of their fulfilment. To suppose this would be really to suppose that a baby can have a wish without wishing for anything—and to my thinking wishing for something implies phantasying the fulfilment of that wish ...

> We all of us know what it is to be thirsty. In this condition we mostly try to get hold of something to drink and we probably have

conscious and unconscious phantasies both about the drink we want and about how to obtain it. We can then describe our psychic processes in two ways. We can say that we want a drink or that we want to quench our thirst. In the one case we are describing a phantasy about the object, in the other we are describing our aim of reducing instinctual tension. In actual fact though we are employing different words and different concepts the facts we are trying to describe are really the same. What we want is not merely the drink and not merely the satisfaction of quenching our thirst. What we want is the thirst-satisfying drink—and our phantasy is that we get this drink and to say this is certainly not to deny the importance of the pleasure.

The phantasy and the impulse to get pleasure are not two separate psychic entities, though it may be useful sometimes to separate them conceptually; they are two aspects of one psychic process ...

Ch. N.8 (p. 177)

Freud writes: "... now we feel that we ourselves could be like Richard, nay, that we are already a little like him. Richard is an enormously magnified representation of something we can all discover in ourselves. We all think we have reason to reproach nature and our destiny for congenital and infantile disadvantages; we all demand reparation for early wounds to our narcissism, our self-love. Why did not nature give us the golden curls of Balder or the strength of Siegfried or the lofty brow of genius or the noble profile of aristocracy? Why were we born in a middle-class dwelling instead of in a royal palace? We could as well carry off beauty and distinction as any of those whom now we cannot but envy." (S. Freud, 1916, "Some Character-Types met with in Psycho-Analytic Work", S.E., XIV, p. 315.)

Ch. N.9. (p. 180)

"... one must not take the difference between ego and id in too hard-and-fast a sense, nor forget that the ego is a part of the id which has been specially modified." (S. Freud, 1923, The Ego and the Id, S.E., XIX, p. 38.) Again, "... Originally, of course, everything was id; the ego was developed out of the id by the continual influence of the external world. In the course of this slow development certain material in the id was transformed into the preconscious state and was thus taken into the ego." (S. Freud, 1940, *Outline of Psycho-Analysis, S.E.*, XXIII, p. 117.)

Ch. N.10 (p. 184)

M. Brierley has also written:

> ... the existence of "internalised object" phantasies would not contravene the memory-trace hypothesis since memories and phantasies have a common trace origin. All images are memory-images, re-activations of past experience. It was suggested that, artificially simplified, the concept of an "internalised good object" is the concept of an unconscious phantasy gratifying the wish for the constant presence of the mother in the form of a belief that she is literally inside the child. Such an unconscious phantasy would help the child to retain conscious memory of its mother during temporary absences though it might fail to bridge a prolonged absence. A two-year-old child's memory of its mother will not be a simple system but the resultant of two years of life with her. The conscious memory will be the accessible part of a far more extensive unconscious mother-system having its roots in earliest infancy. ("Notes on Metapsychology as Process Theory", pp. 103–4.)

Notes

1. In the Discussion on this paper in the British Psycho-Analytic Society in 1943, Dr Ernest Jones commented with regard to this extension of the meaning of "phantasy": "I am reminded of a similar situation years ago with the word 'sexuality'. The critics complained that Freud was changing the meaning of this word, and Freud himself once or twice seemed to asset to this way of putting it, but I always protested that he made no change in the meaning of the word itself: what he did was to extend the conception and, by giving it a fuller content, to make it more comprehensive. This process would seem to be inevitable in psycho-analytical work, since many conceptions, e.g. that of conscience, which were previously known only in their conscious sense, must be widened when we add to this their unconscious significance."
2. Cf. Chapter 11, p. 40
3. This question is bound up with the problem of *regression*, which is discussed in Chapter V.

4. Cf. Freud, "There is a most surprising characteristic of unconscious (repressed) processes to which every investigator accustoms himself only by exercising great self-control; it results from their entire disregard of the reality-test; thought-reality is placed on an equality with external actuality, wishes with fulfilment and occurrences ... One must, however, never allow oneself to be misled into applying to the repressed creations of the mind the standards of reality; this might result in undervaluing the importance of phantasies in symptom-formation on the ground that they are not actualities; or in deriving a neurotic sense of guilt from another source because there is no proof of actual committal of any crime." (S. Freud, 1911, "Formulations Regarding the Two Principles in Mental Functioning", S.E., XII, p. 225.)

5. "An abandonment of the overestimation of the property of conscious-ness is the indispensable preliminary to any genuine insight into the course of psychic events ..." (S. Freud, 1900, *The Interpretation of Dreams*, S.E., V, p. 567.)

6. *Loc. cit*, p. 362.

7. S. Freud (1932) *New Introductory Lectures*, S.E., XXII, p. 98.

8. S. Freud (1911) "Formulations Regarding the two Principles in Mental Functioning", S.E., XII.

9. S. Freud (1915) "Instincts and Their Vicissitudes", S.E., 14, p. 108.

10. S. Freud (1926) *Inhibitions, Symptoms and Anxiety*, S.E., XX, p. 172.

11. Chapter 11, p. 41.

12. S. Freud (1932) *New Introductory Lectures*, S.E., XXII, p. 122.

13. S. Freud (1931) "Female Sexuality", S.E., XXI, p. 226. These occasional references by Freud to phantasies in young children, quoted above, are examples of the way in which the intuitive insight of his genius, perforce scientifically unsupported and unexplained at the time, is being confirmed and made intelligible both by the work of certain of his followers, notably Melanie Klein, and by observations of behaviour.

14. "When the lady drank to the gentleman only with her eyes, and he pledged with his, was there no conversation because there was neither noun nor verb?" (Samuel Butler).

15. S. Freud (1923) *The Ego and the Id*, S.E., XIX, p. 21.

16. Dr Sylvia Payne pointed out this connection in the Discussion on this paper in the British Psycho-Analytical Society, 1943.

17. M.P. Middlemore, *The Nursing Couple* (1941).

18. *Loc.cit.*, pp. 189–90.

19. It was said by Dr W.C.M. Scott, in the Discussion at the British Psycho-Analytical Society, 1943, that the adult way of regarding the body and the mind as two separate sorts of experience can certainly not hold true of the infant's world. It is easier for adults to observe actual sucking

than to remember or understand what the experience of sucking is to the infant, for whom there is no dichotomy of body and mind, but a single, undifferentiated experience of sucking and phantasying. Even those aspects of psychological experience which we later on distinguish as "sensation", "feeling", etc. cannot in the early days be distinguished and separated. Sensations, feelings, as such, emerge through development from the primary whole of experience, which is that of sucking-sensing-feeling-phantasying. This total experience becomes gradually differentiated into its various aspects of experience: bodily movements, sensations, imaginings, knowings and so on.

20. We recall that according to Freud, "The ego is first and foremost a body-ego" (S. Freud, 1923, *The Ego and the Id*, *S.E.*, XIX, p. 26). As Dr Scott said, we need to know more about what "the body" means in unconscious phantasy, and to consider the various studies made by neurologists and general psychologists of the "body-scheme". On this view, the unconscious body-scheme or "phantasy of the body" plays a great part in many neuroses and in all psychoses, particularly in all forms of hypochondriasis.

21. Very often grasping, touching, looking and other activities are felt to be disastrously harmful, as well.

22. This is a highly simplified account of a very complex process, dealt with more fully by Paula Heimann and Melanie Klein, in later chapters.

23. S. Freud (1932) *New Introductory Lectures*, *S.E.*, XXII, p. 119. "Hysterical symptoms spring from phantasies and not from real events."

24. "Accident proneness" has long been recognised among industrial psychologists. The well-known superstition that "if you break one thing you're sure to break three before you've finished", is a strong confirmation of the view that such tendencies spring from phantasies.

25. "Some Character-Types met with in Psycho-Analytic Work" *S.E.* (1916).

26. "But I, that am not shaped for sportive tricks,
    Nor made to court an amorous looking-glass;
    I, that am rudely stamp'd, and want love's majesty
    To strut before a wanton ambling nymph;
    I, that am curtail'd of this fair proportion,
    Cheated of feature by dissembling Nature,
    Deform'd, unfinish'd, sent before my time
    Into this breathing world, scarce half made up,
    And that so lamely and unfashionable,
    That dogs bark at me as I halt by them;

    "And therefore, since I cannot prove a lover,
    To entertain these fair well-spoken days,
    I am determined to prove a villain,
    And hate the idle pleasure of these days."

27. S. Freud (1925) "Negation", *S.E.*, XIX, p. 238.
28. In the analysis, a great deal of mocking and triumph and intention to defeat the analyst can often be discerned behind the "goodness" of such compulsive confessions.
    "He put in his thumb
    And pulled out a plum,
    And said, 'What a good boy am I'."
29. Cf. Chapter 11.
30. An appreciation of what external facts, e.g. the way he is fed and handled in the very beginning, and later the emotional attitudes and conduct of both his parents, or his actual experience of loss or change, *mean* to the child in terms of his phantasy-life gives a greater weight to real experiences than would usually be accorded by those who have no understanding of their phantasy value to the child. Such actual experiences in early life have a profound effect upon the character of his phantasies as they develop, and therefore upon their ultimate outcome in his personality, social relationships, intellectual gifts or inhibitions, neurotic symptoms, etc.
31. As M. Brierley once put it: "phantasy-thinking ... and reality-thinking constantly blend and interweave in the patterns of current mental activity"—in adults as well as children.
    W. Stern, too, has written at length (although in reference to the child's conscious fantasies) of "this mutual, intimate intermingling of reality and imagination", which he says is "a fundamental fact" (*Psychology of Early Childhood*, p. 277).
32. Cf. Chapter IV.
33. "The Theory of Symbolism" (1916).
34. See, e.g. E.F. Sharpe, "Similar and Divergent Unconscious Determinants Underlying the Sublimations of Pure Art and Pure Science" (1935).
35. Pp. 99–106.

CHAPTER SIX

Phantasy and reality

Hanna Segal

T
he interplay between phantasy and reality moulds our view of the world and our personalities. I have discussed this subject in earlier papers (Segal, 1957, 1978), and in this short paper to commemorate the Controversial Discussions of fifty years ago I will address myself to only two of its aspects: how the interplay of phantasy and reality affects perception (much written about in psychoanalytical literature) and action, a subject rather neglected in the literature.

In an unpublished paper which he gave to the British Society towards the end of his life, Money-Kyrle described his own psychoanalytical development in three stages. When he was in his first analyses, with Jones and Freud, he thought pathology was due to the repression of the libido. After his third analysis, with Melanie Klein, his focus shifted to the conflict between love and hate. Finally, he came to think that the roots of pathology were in misconceptions, and his attention turned increasingly to cognitive development.

The recognition of misconceptions has, in fact, been the crucial task of analysis ever since Freud discovered transference. In the here-and-now relationship with the analyst an image is formed of the analyst, and a gradual analysis of this image leads the patient to recognise his misconceptions: for instance, at its simplest, the patient reacts to the analyst as though he were a figure of the past and gradually comes to see how this is the case. In this process, not only are misconceptions of the current relationship corrected, but the past is revised.

The misconceptions in relation to the original figures can also be corrected, because, as we have discovered, transference is not a simple phenomenon of projecting onto the analyst the figures of the parents. In the transference it is internal figures, sometimes part-objects, which are projected, and it is these internal objects which are distorted by phantasies. Through analysis we discover that the internal models on which we base our attitudes to one another do not correspond to a current reality; nor, to a large extent, even to a past reality.

The basic function of phantasy, according to Freud is to fulfil an unfulfilled desire when it is unacceptable to consciousness, the desire and the wish fulfilling phantasy become unconscious.

With the introduction of the reality principle one mode of thought activity was split off; it was kept free from reality testing and remained subordinated to the pleasure principle alone. This activity is phantasying, which begins already in children's play and later continues as day dreaming, abandoning dependence on real objects.

This dates the beginnings of phantasy as quite late in development.

Strachey (1967), in his editorial notes to Freud's paper "Instincts and their vicissitudes", drew attention to the fact that Freud wavered between two definitions of instincts: in some papers he described the instinct as "a concept on the frontier between the mental and the somatic ... the psychical representative or the stimuli originating within the organism and reaching the mind", in another paper as "the concept on the frontier between the somatic and the mental ... the psychical representative of organic forces". Strachey said "These accounts seem to make it plain that Freud was drawing no distinction between the instinct and its psychical representative". He was apparently regarding the instinct itself as the psychical representative of somatic forces. If now, however we turn to later papers in the series, we seem to find him drawing a very sharp distinction between the instinct and its "psychical representative". And Strachey went on to give several references, for instance quoting from the paper on "The unconscious" (1915): An instinct can never become an object of consciousness—only the idea that represents the instinct can. Even in the unconscious, moreover, an instinct cannot be represented otherwise than by an idea. In his paper "Formulations on the two principles of mental functioning" (1911) Freud postulates that the infant fills the gap between desire and satisfaction by a hallucinatory wish fulfilment—an omnipotent hallucination of satisfaction.

Klein extended Freud's concept of phantasy to include that of the early hallucinatory wish fulfilment. This allowed her (Klein, 1933), contrary to what Freud, his daughter Anna and others thought or are still thinking to postulate that phantasy life is present in the baby since birth. Together with Isaac's further clarifications of the concept of unconscious phantasy, this allowed Klein and her followers to bridge the gap between the two ways in which Freud viewed the instincts.

Ideas representing the instincts would be the original primitive phantasies. The operation of an instinct in this view is expressed and represented in mental life by the phantasy of the satisfaction of that instinct by an appropriate object since instincts operate from birth, some crude phantasy as I have already mentioned, can be assumed to exist from birth. The first hunger and the instinctual striving to satisfy that hunger are accompanied by the phantasy of an object capable of satisfying that hunger. As phantasies derive directly from instincts on the borderline between the somatic and psychical activity, these original phantasies are experienced as somatic as well as mental phenomena. So long as the pleasure pain principle is in the ascendant, phantasies are omnipotent and no differentiation between phantasy and reality experience exists. The phantasised objects and the satisfaction derived from them are experienced as physical happenings.

As Klein wrote, after Freud had described the duality of the life and the death instinct, in her view, the early phantasies are the expression of both instincts and therefore the hallucinations could be persecutory as well as blissful.

Freud suggested that at some point the infant discovers that omnipotence does not satisfy his needs, and that a picture of reality has to be formed. The pleasure principle gives way to reality principle as a significant organiser of psychic life. I think the central point of Freud's analysis is as true now as it was eighty-one years ago, but at what point, how, and by what mechanisms is this transition achieved? "And why does it sometimes fail?"

Because according to Klein phantasy life exists and interacts with the external reality from the beginning of life, there is never a total primacy of the pleasure principle in the newborn baby (see also Isaacs, 1948). The omnipotence of the phantasy is therefore never complete. The phantasy of an ideal breast breaks down if the frustration is too prolonged or intense. Equally, the persecutory phantasies can be alleviated or overcome by the reality of a good experience. At the same time, however, the infant perceives reality in terms of his omnipotent phantasies, good experiences merging with ideal phantasies, and frustration and deprivation being experienced as a persecution of bad objects.

The ascendance of the reality principle nevertheless does not mean that phantasy is abandoned. It continues, but in the unconscious, and is expressed symbolically. Even our most primitive desires find symbolic forms of expressions. But how they express themselves is crucial. Freud has said that every man marries his mother; yet he expressed shock and horror at a colleague marrying a woman old enough to be his mother (communication by Joan Riviere in an obituary). Why, then is it true that all men marry their mothers, and yet this universal phantasy can also be at the root of disastrous marriages and deep pathology?

In 1957, I suggested that the solution to the question may hinge on the nature of symbolism. I indicated that there is a distinction between concrete symbolism, in which the symbol is equated with what is symbolised, and a more evolved form, in which the symbol represents the object but is not confused and identified with it, and does not lose its own characteristics. Concrete symbolism leads to misperception and false beliefs.

Philosophers of mind have also considered the relation between desires and beliefs. Wollheim, in his papers and his book *The Thread of Life* (1984), makes the point that when desire is confused with belief, belief becomes incorrigible and irrational. Much of recent psychoanalytic work is now focused on this area of perception and misperception. I think this may be due to the fact that the processes of perception are particularly subject to the vagaries of projective identification, as described by Klein.

I have connected the concretisation of the symbol with the predominance of projective identification in the paranoid-schizoid position. Excessive projective identification equates the object with the projected part of the subject, leading to a concrete identificate (Sohn, 1985): treating the symbol not only as though it were the original object, but also, and predominantly, as part of oneself. When desire is projected into an object it becomes confused with belief. This view was later refined by others.

For instance, Bion (1957) drew attention to the fact that it is the pathology of projective identification rather than the intensity which gives rise to concretisation. In particular, he thought, the projection and fragmentation of one's own perceptual apparatus leads not only to a misperception of the object, but also to the mutilation of one's own perceptual apparatus. I would add to this that in such situations what is also projected is the cognitive capacity itself and the judgmental capacity, so that the objects are experienced as all-knowing and judgmental—the bad objects created often have a powerful superego quality. I shall not describe here the evolution of Bion's ideas about the container and the contained and the formation of beta and alpha elements, as these are well known.

The failure of symbolic processes is clearly seen in pathological mourning. You can retain a mourned object in your mind in an alive way while being aware of its real absence. It can be brought alive in one's mind. But if the mourning is felt as the concrete presence inside one's body of a corpse, then no mourning processes can happen. You cannot bring a real corpse to life, any more than you can change faeces back into milk. Such an object can only bring you down into melancholia or be expelled in mania, as described by Abraham (1924).

A central debating point in 1943–4 during the Freud-Klein controversies was whether those early processes are analysable. I think they are, because they are unavoidably relived and repeated in the transference and so subject to interpretation.

Let me give an example from a supervised case. For a long time the patient had been on the waiting-list of the London Clinic of Psychoanalysis, having originally come with an anxiety of being homosexual. Unbeknown to my candidate, he had become very disturbed during the waiting period. When, after a short preliminary interview, he came to his first session, he glared at the couch and said, "I will not lie down for you. I lay down and submitted to men often enough". His looks and his demeanour, as well as the communication, clearly conveyed that he was in a completely deluded state. The candidate responded by saying, "You are afraid that I shall not be able to distinguish between psychoanalytic treatment and buggery". This communication made the patient relax almost immediately, and the psychoanalytic process had started.

The candidate picked up immediately not only that the patient made a concrete identification between lying on the couch and analysis and a homosexual experience; he also understood that the confusion was projected by the patient into him; not only was the homosexuality projected into him, but also the psychotic functioning itself. Later in the treatment it appeared that in the waiting period, unable to tolerate the waiting, the patient had had his first homosexual experience and became very paranoid after it. He obviously equated the first session of analysis with that experience. Here the candidate interpreted a most primitive phantasy of a concrete projective identification, alive in the very first session.

The fluctuations between more or less concrete methods of functioning are most clearly shown by psychotic patients, and are, I think, amenable to analysis. For instance, a patient of mine, with severe psychotic episodes, who is a computer theoretician, had a hallucination of being attacked by thousands of little computers taking possession of his brain. My first interpretation was that the computers were my soulless interpretations invading him. Later he could relate it to the fact, which we knew about, that he had for weeks been having grandiose phantasies of installing a new kind of computer in all the schools throughout England, which would enable him to control all the education in the country. Fragments of himself were to be lodged everywhere. And as we were familiar with his constant attempts at controlling my mind, and fragmenting it, I could gradually relate it in a more dynamic way to what he felt he had done to my mind and what my mind, fragmented into thousands of interpretations, was felt to do to him. The psychotic situation was defused, and normal functioning, in and out of the session, restored.

I have cited these examples from a borderline and a psychotic patient, but the same processes underlie severe neurotic pathology. Klein considered that neurosis is a way of containing underlying psychotic anxieties (1932).

In *The Thread of Life*, after discussing false beliefs, Wollheim makes a link between phantasy and action. He differentiates between what he calls acting on desire, which is rational, and acting on phantasy (false belief), which is irrational, and makes an added point that acting on phantasy is compulsive, while desire is a powerful incentive but it does not lead to compulsive action. I agree with Wollheim's distinction, except in one respect. I think that acting on desire is also acting on phantasy. What he calls "acting on phantasy" I would call "acting on delusion". Rational action also involves phantasy. But the difference is in the way phantasy functions. Or, to put it another way, the difference is in the level of phantasy.

Acting on delusion is characterised by certain conjoint phenomena: a misperception of external reality; a misperception of internal reality, for instance, the reality of one's desire; and a compulsion to act, rather than a choice of action.

Why is it that living on the pleasure-pain principle in a hallucinated world should lead to compulsive action? It can lead to no action, living in an hallucinated world, and complete withdrawal. But is also produces compulsive action. Phantasy always contains a wish to act; we all want to fulfil our dreams. But in the case of acting on delusion the wish becomes a compulsion, sometimes a compulsion which goes counter to all conscious wishes and intentions. Why this compulsion? It is, I think, due to the fact that those misperceptions arise in relation to projective identification, and that there is an unbreakable tie between the self and the object of such projections.

A study of criminal cases shows in crude ways the nature of the tie. Often the wish to murder is an attempt to expel and get rid of the wish to kill oneself or to die. The murderer of the "Babes in the Wood" tried to kill himself at the age of 3. Killing those other children was an attempt to externalise a part of himself that had to be annihilated, and thereby get rid of the suicidal impulse. Projections into internal objects often deal with guilt—as in a murderer of prostitutes who claimed that he killed them because God had told him to.

I saw a similar mechanism of projection into an internal object, leading to compulsion, early in the analysis of a psychotic I had in treatment. He told me, rather sadly, that he did not like killing, but there was nothing he could do now: all his voices (he used to have eight of them) now combined into one voice to tell him that he must kill me because I was all bad. I knew what the stimulus was in this situation. He had seen a man's hat in the hall. The patient was quite unaware either of his sexual desires or of his sexual jealousy in relation to me. The perception of the real situation, and of his own desire to kill, were replaced by an hallucinatory voice telling him that he must kill me because I was bad.

These, as I have said, are very gross examples, but this kind of delusion underlies irrational behaviour of a neurotic type as well as in the case of my obsessional patient. There are, of course, many differences between criminal acts and symptoms neurosis, two major ones being that in the neurotic and the borderline patient the delusion does not invade the whole of the personality, but is encapsulated in a symptom. Also, the ambivalence is more in evidence, as in the Rat Man case and in my patient.

When more libidinal parts of the self are projected there is also a tie between the subject and object that cannot be broken. Wollheim says that phantasy exercises a lure. It lures one into action. With projective identification, the desires are vested in the objects, and the objects exercise a lure. There is a link that cannot be broken or denied if the object is felt to be possessed by a part of oneself and becomes it, because reciprocally the self is then tied and, as it were, pulled by the object in which a part of him is invested—pulled into compulsive action.

In the Clarembaud Syndrome a person forms the delusion that another is in love with him or her, and pursues them to the point of destruction and self-destruction. This we can observe in analysis in the erotic transference.

Compulsive actions also tend to be repeated. The compulsion to repeat acting on delusion comes from many sources. Partly it is because, as Bion (1963) has described, concrete beta elements can only be expelled, and action is often a mode of expelling. It is also because the action never accomplishes its objects. It is a delusion to think that we can get rid of impulses or parts of the self by getting rid of them into an object.

Thus, acting on misperception is both compulsive and repetitive, since it always misses its objective. But what is acting on desire? What is the reality principle? Freud (1920) says that the reality principle is the pleasure-pain principle tested in reality. But what is being tested? An hypothesis can be tested. I think that it is implicit in desire that it gives rise to a phantasy of its fulfilment. A phantasy is like a wishful hypothesis which is constantly matched with reality (Segal, 1964, 1978). If the phantasy is omnipotent, desire disappears and phantasy becomes a delusion. But in the more normal infant there is a capacity to perceive a reality different from the phantasy. The phantasy is tested.

Forming a picture of the real object and differentiating it from the hallucinated object, noting its real characteristics, both good and bad, can lead to a wish for the action to obtain the most satisfaction from the object. A rational action must be based on recognition of realities.

Freud also emphasises the importance of the recognition of an external reality. This is, however, inextricably linked with the recognition of the internal reality of one's own desires and phantasies. This recognition necessitates tolerance of gaps in satisfaction, and therefore of one's own ambivalence towards the desired object.

In "Formulations on the two principles of mental functioning", Freud (1911) speaks of two ways of dealing with gaps in satisfaction. One is the omnipotent hallucinatory phantasy—the other leads to the development of thought. He describes thought as "experimental action". I think the original experimental action is already alive in preverbal phantasy. Phantasies can be tested by perception; some by action: crying when hungry, biting in anger, attracting attention and love with a smile, etc. But there is also experimental testing of the phantasy without an action. If phantasy is, as I suggest, a set of primitive hypotheses about the nature of an object and the world, one can experiment in phantasy with, "What would happen if ...?"

It differs from the delusional phantasy, which creates an "as-if" world, and it introduces a consideration of a "what-if?", a consideration of probabilities of "what would happen if?" It is the basis of imagination as distinct from delusion or daydreams based on a delusion. It is a basis of flexible thought and rational action, since rational action takes into consideration the consequences of the action. Rationality necessitates imagination. I see the infant experimenting in preverbal phantasy and testing in external reality as a budding scientist, and a successful one. We are often amazed at the speed with which the infant learns about the nature of the world.

I spoke of the nature and function of phantasy. But I think these are interlinked. When the phantasy is predominantly of a fragmentation and projection then it leads to a functioning on a concrete level—a psychotic mode of functioning. When phantasies allow at least some perception of a separate object and one's feelings towards it, there is in the phantasies an inbuilt attitude to the world which allows for repeated reality-testing. Wollheim introduces a concept which I think is germane to the Sandlers' (1994) concept of the present unconscious. Wollheim differentiates between dispositional phantasies and occurrent phantasies. The dispositional phantasies define our personality, character, aims, behaviour, etc. and are based on archaic projections and introjections. Occurrent phantasies, on the other hand, are mental states: they are stirred by occurrent events. According to Wollheim, the occurrent phantasies may be more or less under the domination of the dispositional ones.

I think the differentiation corresponds to Sandler's differentiation between the past unconscious and the present unconscious. Where I differ from Sandler is on whether dispositional phantasies are analysable. I think dispositional phantasies or the past unconscious permeate to a greater or lesser extent the occurrent phantasies, and I think that not only are they analysable but that the analysis of the occurrent ones only will never fundamentally alter them.

A shift must be achieved to some extent from an archaic phantasy organisations, which distorts perception and leads to compulsive action, to one based more on a depressive-position organisation, with its in-built capacity for reality-testing, which is then reflected in the nature and function of the occurrent phantasies as well.

References

Abraham, K. (1924). Mania. In: *Selected Papers on Psychoanalysis* (pp. 470–476). London: Hogarth Press and The Institute of Psycho-Analysis, 1927.

Bion, W. R. (1957). Differentiation of the psychotic from the non-psychotic personalities. *Int. J. Psychoanal.*, *38*: 266–275 [also in *Second Thoughts* (pp. 43–44). London: Heinemann, 1967].

Bion, W. R. (1963). *Elements of Psycho-Analysis*. London: Heinemann.

Freud, S. (1911). Formulations on the two principles of mental functioning. *S.E., 12*.

Freud, S. (1920). *Beyond the Pleasure Principle. S.E., 18*.

Klein, M. (1932). *The Psychoanalysis of Children*. London: Hogarth Press, 1975.

Sandler, J., & Sandler, A.-M. (1994). Phantasy and its transformations: a contemporary Freudian view. *Int. J. Psychoanal.*, *75*: 387–394.

Segal, H. (1957). Notes on symbol formation. *Int. J. Psychoanal.*, *38*: 391–397 [also in *Delusion and Creativity*. London: Free Association Books].

Segal, H. (1978). On symbolism. *Int. J. Psychoanal.*, *59*: 315–319 [also in *Delusion and Creativity*. London: Free Association Books].

Segal, H. (1991). Imagination, play and art. In: *Dream, Phantasy and Art* (pp. 101–109). London/New York: Tavistock Routledge.

Sohn, L. (1985). Narcissistic organisation, projective identification and the formulation of the identificate. *Int. J. Psychoanal.*, *66*: 201–213.

Strachey, J. (1967) Editorial note to Freud, S. (1915) Instincts and their vicissitudes. *S.E., 1*.

Wollheim, R. (1984). *The Thread of Life*. Cambridge Univ. Press.

CHAPTER SEVEN

Imagination, play and art

Hanna Segal

U nconscious phantasy underlies and colours all our activities however realistic. But certain phenomena and activities aim more directly at the expression, elaboration, and symbolization of unconscious phantasies. Not only night dreams, but also day-dreams, play, and art, fall under this heading. They have many elements in common. Freud showed the closeness between day-dream and dream, and day-dream and art. Klein at times compared play with free associations and dreams, and emphasized the crucial role of play in the whole development of the child, including sublimation, and considered inhibitions in play as a most serious symptom. Art and play, however, differ from dream and day-dream because, unlike those, they are also an attempt at translating phantasy into reality.

Play is a way both of exploring reality and of mastering it; it is a way of learning the potential of the material played with, and of its limitations, and also the child's own capabilities and limitations. It is also learning to distinguish between the symbolic and the real. The child is aware that to play is to "pretend". The little child who makes pies out of sand sometimes tries to eat them or feed them to others. But it soon learns that pies made of sand are not for eating or feeding: they are "make-believe" pies. In the normal child this will not inhibit his play. He will enjoy the satisfaction of expressing his phantasy of being mother or father cook, and the pleasure of having in reality made a new, attractive object. His play can then become increasingly imaginative: exploring what else can be done with, and be represented by the sand, sand which is not in fact a pie and which therefore can be used in many different ways.

A child's normal play is a major way of working through a conflict. I remember watching a boy of just under three, when his mother was away for a day giving birth to his first sibling. First he made a complex rail track for his wooden toy train. He filled it with little toy people and they had several crashes. Then he brought in ambulances. Soon he delineated some fields with his little bricks and filled them with toy animals. A complicated play resulted in shifting male, female, and baby animals in and out of the fields and train. There were fights and crashes; ambulances came to the rescue. Throughout, he was telling himself stories. He introduced bigger toy men to regulate the traffic, and so on. In other words, he presented the birth of new babies and his conflicts about it in very many different ways. For an interested observer it was fascinating to watch.

The capacity to play freely depends on the capacity for symbolization. When the symbolic function is disturbed it may lead to inhibition. In the case of an autistic child the inhibition is almost total. A disturbance of symbolization can also lead to forms of play which preclude learning by experience and freedom to vary play. When symbolization is dominated by primitive projective identification and the toy is symbolically equated too concretely with the object symbolized, it cannot be used imaginatively.

The little psychotic girl described by Geissman-Chambon (1990) could, to begin with, only "play" with pebbles. The "play" was restricted to sucking them, spitting them out, or using them as weapons. Geissman-Chambon describes the evolution of the child's capacity to play with objects and to draw. Dick (Klein 1930), like that little girl, had an interest in only a few objects, particularly door-handles. In his material one can see that objects which for other children could be play material are too terrifying, too identified with phantasy persecutors, to be suitable for pleasurable play.

Play has roots in common with those of the night dream.

Playing, like dreaming, is a way of working through an unconscious phantasy and it is subject to similar disturbances. The contrast between the play of the little boy described above and that of autistic children corresponds to the contrast I describe between the neurotic and psychotic use of dreams. Children who are not psychotic may express their psychotic phantasies in play, thereby mastering them and subjecting them to reality-testing. But the boundaries between psychotic and neurotic are fluid; often the psychotic content breaks through the play.

For instance, a little girl of two and a half, at the beginning of her analysis, would get into a complete panic if, rummaging in her toy drawer, she came across a little toy lion. A small boy who used a little red car to represent himself one day accidentally broke the car. He became terrified, tried to hide under the analyst's skirt, clinging to her legs, shivering. It seemed that the car was felt to *be* him at that moment, rather than to *represent* him, and the breakdown of the little car was experienced as himself breaking down.

Play in such circumstances can become a life-and-death matter. Obsessional defences against such psychotic fears may lead to rigidity in play, close to obsessional ceremonials. When psychotic content breaks through, play may have to be abandoned. Or when excessive defences against such anxieties are used it may become compulsive, rigid, and repetitive.

Like dreams, play is not primarily meant for communication; though, unlike dreams, it often becomes so. It is often a link between children playing together. In a psychoanalytic session, play, like dreams, quickly becomes a major means of communication. There is, however, an important difference between night dreams and play: it is a difference in relation to reality.

Night dream, the "royal road", is concerned only with achieving a phantasy resolution to a phantasy problem: "It's only a dream." Not so play, which makes an important connection with reality. In Klein's view, children's play is a most important way of making a symbolic connection between phantasy and reality; and playing together is an important step in socialization. Two cannot dream together, but two or more can play together.

Day-dreaming is probably the activity closest to Freud's original idea of a libidinal wish-fulfilment. It largely ignores reality. In a day-dream one can be a hero, an accomplished lover, a genius, or whatever one chooses. Aggressive phantasies can find their fulfilment, in being a great warrior, commanding armies, leading brigands, and so on—though usually the day-dreamer wants to see himself as good too. Commonly, the robber would be a Robin Hood kind of hero. Day-dreaming always involves splitting. Unlike the night dream, the day-dream ignores internal reality and deeper conflict. It is an omnipotent wish-fulfilment. It is indeed much closer to the original "wish-fulfilment" as described by Freud than the night dream. Therefore it is often repetitive and shallow, and always egocentric. Characters other than oneself in the day-dream are usually cardboard ones. This kind of naïve day-dreaming is characteristic of latency and early adolescence. But adults day-dream too. It is only the most defended, restricted, and rigid individual who is bereft of day-dreams. Lack of day-dreams makes a very poor and dull personality. And one may well suspect that the unconscious phantasy is too horrifying to be allowed any access to the waking life and a day-dream. Our day-dreams often include our plans for the future, but in a more normal adult they are then subjected to reality-testing and abandoned or modified if they conflict with reality. However, day-dreams which continue unabated and intense into adulthood, and play an important role in mental life are usually a hallmark of schizoid borderline states, if not of psychosis.

A patient of mine, subject to psychotic breakdowns, when not in a state of breakdown spends hours fantasying in this way. He imagines himself as a great politician, or writer, or sometimes a Mafia leader, an only slightly updated version of his early-puberty day-dreams. His other "day-dreams" are more overtly sexual. But even if they are not overtly sexual, when he is day-dreaming he is in a masturbatory state of mind, completely cut off from reality. This leads to a permanent vicious circle: the more he day-dreams the less he achieves in reality; and the less he achieves the more he is driven into his day-dreams. At times of acute stress the day-dreams take over, become his reality, and the outcome is a psychotic breakdown.

Day-dreams of this kind are very defensive and based on severe splitting in which reality perceptions and unwanted parts of the personality have been completely split off. Projective identification plays a large part: in latency and adolescence, various heroes are identified with. In more pathological day-dreaming projective identification may completely take over the subject's personality. A person living his day-dream is not, in fact, himself.

Day-dreams, understandably, have a bad press in psychoanalysis. And yet they are not far from something highly valued, that is, imagination. Day-dreams can be the beginning of story-telling. A patient of mine was very preoccupied in latency with day-dreams of the Robin Hood kind, but he would also tell stores based on these day-dreams to entertain his siblings and at times they became quite imaginative. It could have led to his becoming a writer. When Proust's Elstir, the painter, says, "If a little dream is dangerous the cure for it is not less dreaming but more dreaming, the whole dream", he speaks not of night dreams but of day-dreams. It is his response to the narrator saying that his family complained of his spending too much time day-dreaming. I like to think that Elstir's "more dreaming", "the whole dream", refers to the move from day-dreaming to imagination. The whole dream, to my mind, means less splitting, more integration, and reaching deeper layers of the mind.

Freud has said that the artist's phantasy must lose its egocentric character to become compatible with art. "Losing the egocentric character", I think involves a modification of the pleasure principle. It necessitates integrating one's perceptions of external reality that includes others and the perception of one's own relation to them. It also includes perception of the relations between them. In other words, imagination, unlike the typical day-dream, necessitates some abandonment of omnipotence and some facing of the depressive position. This makes imagination richer and more complex than a wish-fulfilling day-dream. The deeper the layers of the mind which can thus be mobilized, the richer, denser, and more flexible is imagination.

I shall illustrate the kind of shift between day-dreaming and imagination I have in mind by the material of a patient, L. L tends to get lost in a dream state in which the analyst, representing his mother, becomes erotized. As a child he oscillated between states of great over-activity and dreamy withdrawal. During the week preceding a holiday he was very inaccessible, but very comfortable and dreamy on the couch. Towards the end of the week he brought the following dream. *He was arranging some pink serviettes on a table and a woman disturbed him. He was absolutely furious and woke up with the strength of his fury.*

He associated the pink serviettes with an au pair he found attractive, and also with the "pink brothels" which we had talked about before a previous holiday. (On that occasion he dreamed several versions of rooms with pink wallpaper which he associated to luxury brothels and to which we referred later as "pink brothels". They represented a phantasy of his being inside a very erotized maternal womb. At that time he was often in the daytime in a kind of dreamy, erotic haze.) He thought the woman in the dream who kept interrupting him must be the analyst interpreting. Suddenly he shifted to an apparently quite different theme. He said he went to see a Hogarth exhibition and was tremendously impressed. He liked Hogarth and had a book of photographic reproductions. But the reproductions were very different from the original lithographs. They were blurred, made smaller, and because they were photographs they were reversed—so different from the lithographs, which were precise, very deeply etched and gave an impression of depth. Knowing that he could well afford to buy what he pleased, I asked him, if the photographic reproductions were so unsatisfactory, why he bought them rather than some lithographs.

He laughed, and said I would find it hard to believe but he was very attracted by the fact that the pictures in the book were reversed. And then he added, "I rather feel now like the adolescent I told you about who was completely mad and terribly proud of it. I thought the reverse pictures were something rather original and exciting." He said that looking at the lithographs, he was also impressed to rediscover that they had a perspective and that they were very deeply etched, a feature not conveyed at all by the photographic reproduction. He then went on to say how much he admired Hogarth. Hogarth had such a precise vision. He could express fun, humour, sexuality, but never shirk the perception of degradation or horror as well. And he repeated, "It is all so deeply etched."

I think that in these associations he was showing the difference between a wish-fulfilling day-dream based on splitting, reversal, idealization, self-idealization and complete egocentricity, his object being a pink brothel, de-humanized and only there to serve his needs, and Hogarth's imagination that is based on perception of reality which has perspective and which is "deeply etched". But at the moment when his associations shifted he was also showing a shift in himself from a masturbatory, day-dreaming state to one of feeling and imagination, since his own imagination was functioning when he was describing his reaction to the lithographs.

The next day he had a dream of *waiting for an elevator*. (He had lived for some time in the USA and occasionally used American expressions.) He did not associate directly to the dream but spoke with some pain and envy of a man, X, whom he had met the previous day. He had always been envious of X, whom he considered more intelligent and productive than he was himself. He remembered that some time ago X invited him to dinner and he could not go because his wife was ill. He, the patient, was furious with his wife, and he thought X would be annoyed with them too. But when he telephoned X he was surprised that X was very concerned about his wife's illness and asked him a lot about it. The patient was ashamed that he himself was so little interested in his wife's illness that he could not even adequately answer the concerned questions of his friend. He said he now realized that X functioned on some level quite different from that on which he himself functioned at the time. At that point I drew his attention to the fact that, unusually for him, he had called the lift an "elevator", and suggested that his taking the elevator represented maybe his own wish to function on a more elevated level. He agreed with that, and added that there was a lift to the consulting-room which he never took. He always walked the two flights of stairs. Also, he wondered whether in the dream he wanted to wait for the life because, when he walked up the stairs, he was usually alone on the staircase, and he thought of the lift as shared. I thought of the previous session and agreed that the higher level of mental functioning he was talking about involved the existence of others. I think his day-dream was losing its "egocentric character" and coming closer to imagination. The "higher level" involved admission of his rivalries and jealousy—for instance, of X. It also involved the recognition of pain in himself and in others, including a capacity for concern shown by the admired and envied X. In other words, it involved facing the conflicts of the depressive position. All those feelings were missing in his dreams of pink brothels and associated day-dreams, in which, paradoxically, he always saw himself alone.

I mentioned the patient who told stories to his siblings as one who might have become a writer. His analysis revealed why he could not become one; and indeed he never thought of writing as a possible profession for himself. He was a very defended, well-organized person, who sought treatment partly because of incomprehensible attacks of anxiety and depression. He always came to his sessions with "a good story", not boring, nor necessarily shallow or repetitive, but always logical and consistent. Psycho-analytical insight itself was often used to make a connected coherent story about himself and others. Gradually a deep split was revealed. Behind the stores there was a feeling of chaos and dread—a horror which, unlike Hogarth, he could never integrate enough to be able to express and symbolize. His stories were still a defensive structure against a deeper and more anxious reality, just like the stories he told himself and his siblings to ward off nightmares.

It occurred to me, when reading science fiction, that the difference between day-dream and imagination could be seen as a difference between "as-if" and "what-if". The bulk of pulp science fiction, known also as space opera, is an "as-if" world: a martial hero or heroine conquers stars, roams space, and defeats villains. This kind of science fiction is pure escapism, making even day-dreaming easy, since someone else has made the effort to plot it. But not all science fiction is like that. There are science-fiction stories squarely rooted in reality. They are usually based on "what-if": imagining what would happen if some parameter were changed, stories of what the future would be like if such-and-such were changed, like observing a certain social trend and projecting it into the future— "what-if this trend prevails?" And not necessarily in the future: "What would the world be like if such-and-such had happened in history instead of such-and-such?" Or, "What if there was no gravity?" This kind of imagination does not deny reality to produce an "as-if" world, but explores possibilities. Possible worlds are created through altering some factors to see "what-if" and moulding the world into a new fantasy world with its own internal consistency and truth. I have of course oversimplified the problem, speaking of the themes of those stories. Content is not the only criterion: boy meets girl, boy loses girl, boy regains girl are the themes of much great literature. So can be the theme hero beats villain. There is always the question of form, style, depth of character, and all the other features which go into creating not an "as-if" world but a psychologically true world, rooted in inner and outer truths. That applies to science fiction as to all forms of art. The difference between fantasy and imagination is the degree of denial of reality (Lepschy 1986).

In the *Two Principles of Mental Functioning*, Freud speaks of "experimental thought":

> A new function was now allotted to motor discharge which under the dominance of the pleasure principle had served as a means of unburdening the mental apparatus of accretions of stimuli. ... Motor discharge was now employed in the appropriate alteration of reality. It was converted into action.

> Restraint upon motor discharge (upon action) which then became necessary was provided by means of the process of thinking, which developed from the presentation of ideas. ... It is essentially an experimental kind of acting accompanied by displacement of relatively small quantities of cathexis, together with less expenditure (discharge) of them. (Freud 1911: 221)

Thought is a "trial action". Between desire and satisfaction there is a gap. Under the aegis of the pleasure-pain principle this gap is filled by hallucination—the world of "as if". The motor discharge which Freud sees in only energic terms, as a discharge of tension, I would see as a phantasied discharge of beta elements as well—a primitive process of projective identification.

When some reality is experienced I would see this gap as filled with a phantasy not omnipotently adhered to but open to testing. It can be tested in action—"If I cry mother will come to feed me," or "If I defecate my hunger, it doesn't work; I am still hungry." But phantasies are tested not only in action, or by perception of external reality only; they are also tested internally: "If I kill my mother I suffer guilt and loss." Such early phantasies are of a "what-if?", not of an "as-if" kind—they are "experimental" phantasies, preverbal thoughts. They are the basis of rational action. Action is often rightly contrasted with imagination, but to be rational action must be based on imagination: foreseeing "what will happen if I do this rather than that". Play and art both need imagination, but play is primarily a child's activity. It often has a day-dream quality. Play may involve a minimum of imagination, or on the contrary may be very imaginative. It is also of course a beginning of work. It can involve frustration and pain, and necessitate perseverance. But by and large, if it stops being predominantly pleasurable it will be abandoned.

Not so art. Unlike play, artistic creativity involves much pain, and the need to create is compelling. It cannot easily be abandoned. Abandoning an artistic endeavour is felt as a failure, sometimes as a disaster. In creative work itself, whatever the joy of creating, there is also always an important element of pain as well. And it necessitates not only psychic work, which I spoke of in the preceding chapter, but also a vast amount of conscious work coupled with a high degree of self-criticism, often very painful. Artistic creativity has a lot in common with play, but is anything but "child's play".

Also, play is only incidentally a communication, whereas art is not only an internal communication. It is a communication with others. And much of the work consists of creating new means of communication. The little boy's play I describe at the beginning of this chapter was fascinating to an interested observer, but to an interested observer only. The artist's work must change his audience into interested observers. The artist must arouse an interest and make an impact on his audience. Finding new symbolic means of doing so is the essence of his work. Children's drawings, modelling, writing are steps between play and art.

Day-dreaming, dreaming, play, and art are ways of expressing and working through unconscious phantasy and are subject to similar disturbances. But what is the difference between them? The understanding of the night dream is the "royal road" to the unconscious; reality-testing and reality activity are suspended and the working-through occurs in symbolic mental representation only. The day-dream is more defensive. It is rationalized and made acceptable to the waking ego. It is based predominantly on splitting and denial, and belongs mostly to schizoid functioning. But as I have tried to show, in a normal individual day-dreams persist, even when splitting is diminished, and they can evolve and become imagination, which is the basis of both play and art. Play is more than a day-dream. In normal play various aspects of life and its conflicts can be expressed. Unlike a day-dream, it also takes account of the reality of the materials played with, and is thus a process of learning and mastering reality. Art in that way is closer to play than to a dream or a day-dream, but it is more than play alone.

All children, except the illest, and all adults, play; few become artists. Neither dream, day-dream, nor play involve the work, both unconscious and conscious, that art demands. The artist needs a very special capacity to face, and find expression for, the deepest conflicts, to translate dream into reality. He also achieves a lasting reparation in reality as well as in phantasy. The work of art is a lasting gift to the world, one which survives the artist.

References

Freud, S. (1911). Formulations on the two principles of mental functioning. *S.E.*, *12*.

Geissman, C. (1990). L'Enfant aux billes: essais sur la communication chez un enfant autiste. *Journal de Psychanalyse de l'Enfant*, *8*.

Klein, M. (1930). The importance of symbol-formation in the development of the ego. In: Klein (1975).

Klein, M. (1975). *The Writings of Melanie Klein, Volume I: Love, Guilt and Reparation and Other Works 1921–45; Volume II: The Psycho-Analysis of Children; Volume III: Envy and Gratitude and Other Works 1946–63; Volume IV: Narrative of a Child Analysis*. London: Hogarth Press.

Lepschy, G. (1986). Fantasia e immaginazione. *Lettere Italiane*, n. 1, pp. 1–39.

INDEX